Armed Peacekeepers in Bosnia

Robert F. Baumann

George W. Gawrych

Walter E. Kretchik

Cover Photo Credits

Top Photo: Department of the Army
Overlay: Department of the Army

Published by Books Express Publishing
Copyright © Books Express, 2012
ISBN 978-1-78039-676-7

Books Express publications are available from all good retail and online booksellers. For
publishing proposals and direct ordering please contact us at: info@books-express.com

Foreword

By 1990, the Cold War was over and many Americans talked of the "peace dividend" that would befall the country once military spending and commitments could be reduced in what some referred to as the New World Order. Instead, world affairs proved as dangerous and intractable as ever, even more so perhaps than during the period 1945-1990 when the two competing superpowers managed to hold various tribal, ethnic, religious, and political conflicts around the world somewhat in check. Driving home how dangerous the world remained in the 1990s, the US military found itself fighting one major war, Operation Desert Storm, and participating in a variety of other military activities, including three major interventions: Somalia, Haiti, and the Balkans. The Combat Studies Institute has published scholarly accounts of the Gulf War (*Lucky War*), the Somalian venture (*"My Clan Against the World"*), and the involvement in Haiti (*Invasion, Intervention, "Intervasion"*), all of which can be found on the Internet at http://www.cgsc.army.mil/carl/resources/csi/csi.asp. The publication of *Armed Peacekeepers in Bosnia* adds another case study to the Institute's coverage of these post-Cold War US military operations.

With the aid of a generous grant from the US Institute of Peace, Robert Baumann, George Gawrych, and Walter Kretchik were able to access and examine relevant documents, interview numerous participants, and visit US and NATO forces in Bosnia. As a result of their labors, they have provided the reader an analytical narrative that covers the background to the crisis in Bosnia, the largely ineffectual efforts of the UN Protection Force to stop the civil war there between 1992 and 1995, the Dayton Peace Accords of 1995 that produced a framework for ending the civil war and consolidating the peace, the frenetic planning that led to the deployment of US forces as part of the NATO-led multinational force (Operation Joint Endeavor), and the transition of that Implementation Force to the Stabilization Force a year later.

The authors shed light on several of the critical military lessons that have emerged from the US experience in Bosnia—an involvement that continues as of this writing. In general, these cover the cooperation and contention present in virtually any coalition undertaking; the complexity of the local situation and the way in which strictly military tasks have political, social, economic, and cultural ramifications that the military cannot ignore or avoid; the inevitable adjustments peacekeepers have to make to dynamic and precarious situations; and the often unaccommodating role history plays when confronted with concerns about force protection, "mission creep," "end states," and early exits.

In Bosnia, as in countless other operations, a US military force trained and equipped to fight a highly technological, conventional war found itself making adjustments that resulted in performing tasks that many officers considered unconventional and unorthodox. The ability to make these adjustments and to perform these tasks has thus far leant to the success of the US/NATO involvement in Bosnia. Now the United States is engaged in the Global War on Terror and, in the process, has already embarked on stability operations in Afghanistan and Iraq. The case of Bosnia is, of course, unique but the general lessons it provides are relevant to US officers fighting in the current war and should not be overlooked.

THOMAS T. SMITH
LTC, IN
Director, Combat Studies

Preface

The incredibly complex drama of war and edgy peace that unfolded in Bosnia, or Bosnia-Herzegovina, during the 1990s gave birth to a fascinating and instructive series of military operations that constitute the subject of this study. The nature of circumstances and missions in Bosnia poses a variety of challenges to the historian. First, given their recent occurrence, it is remarkably difficult to frame these events in historical perspective. This is in part because many outcomes and consequences reside somewhere in the future. The SFOR mission itself only came to a close late in 2004 as this work was going to press. Equally significant is the fact that vast quantities of relevant documents remain classified. As a result, the chapters that follow necessarily form a preliminary attempt to capture the most important dynamics of the history yet unfolding in this unfortunate country.

An additional hurdle is the chaos that attended the Bosnian Civil War and the nonlinear character of modern post-conflict operations, whether they emphasize peacemaking, peacekeeping or peace enforcement. In contrast to the story of most wars, peace operations in Bosnia did not unfold in a progression of events that yield a seamless narrative. Rather, the course of history in Bosnia was, and remains, a fitful affair. As the final chapter observes, success in peace operations is hard to measure and self-deception is a constant hazard. One critical aspect of this condition was the ceaseless rotation of U.S. and other units through Bosnia. In some respects, the mission began again with the arrival of each new commander, division, brigade, and battalion.

History is most often told from the perspective of commanders, especially in official histories. More recently, interest has grown concerning the viewpoint of individual soldiers. If anything, this work emphasizes the middle ground, the vantage point of field grade officers. This is in part a function of happenstance, since majors and lieutenant colonels constitute a highly accessible population at the US Army Command and General Staff College. Nevertheless, it is the authors' perception that these are most often the individuals best situated to comprehend simultaneously the view from above and below, in other words the whole picture. Regrettably, very senior officers frequently reside within a cocoon of obsequiousness created by military culture and well-meaning staff officers. Thus, all but the most discerning perceive developments through the filtering lenses of operations plans, briefing slides, and third-hand reporting. Conversely, ordinary soldiers, with some notable exceptions, frequently have no grasp of the strategic or operational context in which they carry out their duties. To be sure, no single perspective of modern operations is sufficient by itself. Indeed, if oral history interviews, upon which this study extensively relies, prove anything, it is that every participant has a distinctive experience. Historical truth, then, is at best a thoughtful approximation.

Nevertheless, by virtue of extensive opportunities to interview and confer with participants in peacekeeping and peace enforcement operations in Bosnia, as well as to conduct research in the field, it has been possible discover much. Through the generous cooperation of so many who were directly involved, much information has surfaced that may not be adequately reflected in the complete documentary record whenever it becomes available. In any case, what follows is not a comprehensive or official history of the Bosnian saga, but may offer considerable insight into the business of contemporary conflict and military operations.

Out of respect for the many men and women, soldiers and civilians, living through the episodes described in this book, the authors have not shirked their own responsibility to consider operations in Bosnia in a critical light. The intent is that this work not only analyzes recent history in the Balkans, but also prompts close examination and thoughtful reflection about contemporary approaches to peace operations.

For whatever value this work may hold for its readers, the authors owe a tremendous debt to countless officers from all services and many nations passing through the Command and General Staff College who shared their experiences, journals, notes, maps, and impressions. Equally valuable was the extraordinary assistance rendered by soldiers of many different national contingents serving as members of the Stabilization Force in Bosnia. A special thanks is due the contingents from Britain, Canada, France, and Germany, which went well out of their way to facilitate our research and travel within Bosnia. They freely offered maps, documents, and photographs. In addition, a grant from the US Institute of Peace proved absolutely indispensable to the work of this project.

Finally, a handful of individuals warrant mention for facilitating our research. Dr. Otto Orzech, the SFOR Historian in Sarajevo, assisted with many arrangements as did Dr. Curt King of the Command and General Staff College. Colonel (retired) Jerry D. Morelock, former Director of the Combat Studies Institute, encouraged our pursuit of this project from the beginning. In turn, his successor, Colonel Lawyn (Clay) Edwards, not only extended full support but joined in the research itself and lent the authors crucial assistance in the field in Bosnia. The many other individuals who gave selflessly of their time are too numerous for mention here but their names can be found liberally sprinkled throughout the text and endnotes of this work. Any strengths of this work are a result of their aid; the shortcomings are the responsibility of the authors alone.

Robert F. Baumann, Command and General Staff College
George W. Gawrych, Baylor University
Walter E. Kretchik, Western Illinois University

iv

Table of Contents

Illustrations

Maps

Figures

Photos

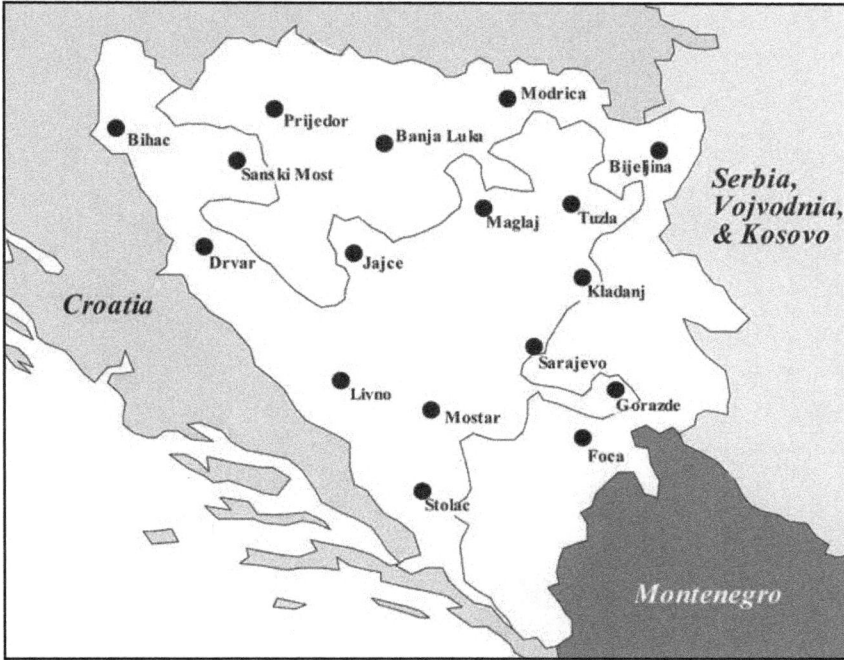

Map 1. Map of Bosnia

Chapter 1

Bosnian Truths

George W. Gawrych

> The first, the supreme, the most far-reaching act of judgment that the statesman and commander have to make is to establish . . . the kind of war on which they are embarking, neither making it for, nor trying to turn it into, something that is alien to its nature. This is the first of all the strategic questions and the most comprehensive.
>
> Carl von Clausewitz[1]

> Being familiar with Balkan history is a significant advantage. Not only does it improve credibility with the locals, it also helps to cut through most of the information they provide. The alternative is to spend the tour being duped by the experts.
>
> Major D. G. Wilson, British Army[2]

Over 150 years ago, Carl von Clausewitz offered sage advice: political and military leaders must understand the conflict into which they send their troops. This wisdom certainly applies to armies embarking on peace support operations. But as pointed out by Major D. G. Wilson, who served in Bosnia with the British army, knowing Balkan history is also important in being an effective peacekeeper. In December 1995, the US Army faced an intellectual challenge as it deployed ground troops with the mission of separating the warring factions in Bosnia and of helping create a secure environment for the conduct of civilian reforms. Understanding the character of Bosnian conflict and negotiating through the region's myths proved no easy task. In fact, much of the US Army entered Bosnia with a general misconception of the conflict.

The Bosnian war was a complex conflict, filled with myths generated in part by the propaganda machines of the participants themselves. The US media tended to portray images of the good and the bad, with Serbs emerging as the villains and Muslims as the innocent victims. Such a dichotomy stemmed, in large measure, from the horrific character of the war in Bosnia. Out of a prewar population of 4.3 million, 2.2 million Bosnians became refugees or displaced persons; between 200,000 and 250,000 were killed. Most of the dead were civilians who fell victim to ethnic cleansing and acts of revenge. Stories of systematic rape and murder in concentration camps added to the brutality of war. The dark side of human nature had raised its ugly head once again in history, and the Serbs appeared to bear responsibility for the phenomenon. How was an American Army to make sense of the Bosnian war as it deployed ground troops for the first time in December 1995, over three and a half years after the outbreak of the hostilities?

One popular explanation for the Bosnian war argues for ancient tribal hatreds whose roots go back centuries, if not over half a millennium. Robert Kaplan popularized the intractable nature of the ethnic and religious conflict in his famous travel book *Balkan Ghosts*.[3] Too many American officers deployed to Bosnia armed with this book as their only professional reading on the region. The Kaplan thesis gained popular currency in the US, leaving most American officers and soldiers with little hope that their brief tour of duty could help build a bright future. Many officers expressed to the authors of this study that they would have benefited from a better and more balanced presentation of the region's history prior to deployment.

Bosnian history, like that of any region of the world, has its bright and dark sides. This chapter examines what the US Army should have understood about the character of the Bosnian war from a historical perspective before deployment. Ethnic cleansing, in fact, had more immediate causes. Moreover, a study of recent Bosnian history shows how the communist leader Jozef Tito was able to bring about some reconciliation among the Bosnian Serbs, Croats, and Muslims despite the trauma of ethnic cleansing in World War II.

Regional Context

Deployment into a theater of operations requires some understanding of the local population and its history. The word Balkan means mountain range in Turkish, an appropriate name for a region noted for the numerous mountains crisscrossing the region in all directions. These mountains have served to fragment the peninsula, encouraging localism and regionalism.

The degree of diversity in the Balkans is staggering, even by the standard of the European continent. Some 70 million people crowd into an area approximately the size of Texas. They speak at least nine different languages—Romanian, Serbo-Croatian, Slovene, Bulgarian, Macedonian, Greek, Albanian, Turkish, and Romany (spoken by many Gypsies)—and identify with three major religions—Roman Catholicism, Eastern Orthodoxy, and Islam. Moreover, before the breakup of the Communist Yugoslav state in 1991, six independent states constituted the Balkans: Yugoslavia, Romania, Albania, Bulgaria, Greece, and Turkey (eastern Thrace). Yugoslavia's demise resulted in the emergence of four new countries: Slovenia, Croatia, Macedonia, and Bosnia-Herzegovina.[4] Even before Yugoslavia's collapse, the Balkans gained a reputation for political fragmentation and internecine strife. In the English language, the verb "balkanize" means "to divide (a region or territory) into small, often hostile, units."

Within the context of all this religious, linguistic, and ethnic diversity, Bosnia has often been called the "microcosm of the Balkans," epitomizing all the peninsula's communal differences.[5] On the religious level, this is quite true. Bosnia is home to the three civilizations of Western Christianity, Eastern Orthodoxy, and Islam, all blending together in a cultural mosaic based on mutual influences. On the linguistic-cultural level, however, Bosnia is unique for the Balkans. Bosnians speak the same language while belonging to three different religions without any one possessing a clear majority. In 2002, for example, estimates placed the population of Bosnia-Herzegovina at approximately 40 percent Muslim, 31 percent Orthodox, 15 percent Catholic, and 14 percent other.

Geography and history help explain the complex character of Bosnian society. The landlocked and mountainous country of Bosnia-Herzegovina today consists of 19,741 square miles or 51,130 square kilometers, roughly the size of West Virginia, with some 4 million inhabitants. Technically, Bosnia refers to the northern, central, and eastern regions, including Sarajevo. Herzegovina encompasses western and south parts centered on the town of Mostar. Hercog comes from the German word Duchy, a term that first appeared in history in the 15th century. This study refers to the entire region as Bosnia, a geographic term first recorded in 958. The name comes from the Bosna River, which begins just outside Sarajevo and flows north to the Sava. Bosnia's historic boundaries since the medieval period have generally been the Sava River in the north, the Drina in the east and southeast, the Dinaric Mountains in the west, and a mountainous border with Montenegro in the south. The mountainous character of the area has confined much of human habitation to the river valleys and mountain passes.

History has consigned to Bosnia the status of a frontier sandwiched between competing civilizations and religious organizations. At first, Bosnia felt the tugs within the Western world. In 395 AD, the Roman Empire split into two parts. The western section remained under Rome's control, while the eastern half became the Byzantine Empire, with its capital of Constantinople, today Istanbul. Bosnia fell between two diverging civilizations represented in the Roman and Byzantine Empires. When Christianity made inroads by the ninth century, Bosnia emerged nestled between the pulls of Roman Catholicism and Greek Orthodoxy. This border status helps explain the sizeable Catholic and Orthodox populations in Bosnia today cited earlier.

The Slavic character of Bosnian society began in the late sixth and early seventh centuries when the Slavs began entering the Balkans as members of a single Slav federation called the Slaveni in medieval texts. The second quarter of the seventh century saw the settlement of two new tribes—the Croats and Serbs—into much of what became 20th-century Yugoslavia. Both tribes possessed an Iranian past, as evidenced from the names of their early tribal leaders. Either the Croats and Serbs were Iranians who absorbed Slavic culture and language while settling the Balkans, or they were Slavs who for a period had fallen under Iranian rule or influence before their migration to the peninsula. Today, close to 99 percent of Bosnians identify themselves as Slavs: Serbs 37, Bosniacs 48, and Croats 13 percent.

The medieval period of Bosnian history eventually saw the establishment of two Slavic kingdoms, Croatia and Serbia. After the Great Schism splitting the Christian Church into two parts, Croatia fell under Rome's influence and practiced Roman Catholicism. Serbia, on the other hand, looked to Byzantine cultural patterns and embraced Greek Orthodoxy. This division has shaped history today. Croats still adhere to the Catholic faith and the Latin alphabet; Serbs, for their part, continue their identification with Orthodox Christianity and use the Cyrillic script.

Bosnia, for its part, had its own heyday. From 1180 to 1463, the region witnessed a period of independence. Her greatest ruler was Tvrtko (1353-91), who briefly ruled as king of Bosnia and Serbia, extending the boundaries of his state to include Croatia and Dalmatia. The inhabitants of Bosnia were referred to as Slavs, as Bosnia remained a geographic term. From approximately 1250 to 1342, Bosnia's rulers sponsored an independent Bosnian Church, Christian in dogma but independent of the pope in Rome or the patriarch in Constantinople. But in 1342, the local ruler permitted the establishment of a Franciscan mission whose activities helped increase the influence of the Catholic Church. For the next century, Christianity in Bosnia suffered from rivalry among the three competing religious organizations, Catholicism, Orthodoxy, and the Bosnian Church. All three faiths lacked sufficient numbers of clergy and churches for the local population to develop strong ties to any faith. The general weak state of Christianity in Bosnia helps explain the conversions to Islam that would gradually come with the Ottoman conquest in the latter half of the 15th century.[6]

Ottoman Rule (1463-1878)

The Ottomans conquered Bosnia in 1463. For the next four centuries, Bosnia experienced Islamic rule, resulting in the Islamization of Bosnian society. Rather than ushering a dark age as depicted in the literature and oral traditions, the Ottoman Empire brought law and order to the Balkan Peninsula, imposing a *Pax Ottomanicum* much like the Romans had imposed order on their subjugated peoples. Ottoman sultans allowed for a high measure of decentralization. Christians and Jews were free to practice their faith according to their religious traditions in such matters as worship, marriage, divorce, inheritance, and death. In addition to institutionalizing a system of religious tolerance, known as the *millet* system, the first sultans lightened taxes and fostered economic development so that, for example, Christian merchants thrived in international trade with Europe.[7]

Ottoman rule changed medieval Bosnia irrevocably.[8] The conquest caused the flight of many Catholics to Dalmatia and Croatia and the influx of numerous Serb Orthodox from Serbia. The Ottoman conquerors brought with them the new Islamic faith and settled relatively small numbers of Muslims in the region. But the major part of Islamization occurred over time with gradual and peaceful conversion of the local Slavic population to Islam over the next century. No major conversions occurred during the actual Ottoman conquest. After 150 years of Ottoman rule, however, government registers record a sizeable Muslim population in Bosnia. The vast majority of Muslims were not new settlers, but rather Slavs who accepted Islam.

Local converts kept their Slavic culture and language, although Ottoman Turkish now functioned as the official tongue in administration. Members from all three religious communities naturally spoke the same language, now Serbo-Croatian. Today, extremists have tried to argue the existence of separate languages: Bosnian, Serbian, and Croatian. But there is only one language, understandable by all Bosnians. To illustrate this point, at the conference in 1995, one translator handled the Serbian, Croatian, and Bosnian language channels.[9] Participants had demanded three separate lines for political, not linguistic reasons.

Officially, the Ottomans recognized religious, not ethnic affiliation. Tax registers identified individuals as Muslim, Orthodox, Catholic, or

Jewish. As regards cultural identity, Bosnian Muslims generally referred to themselves as "Bosniacs," *Bosnaks* in Ottoman Turkish, whereas their Christian neighbors often called them "Turks." Today, Bosniac is interchangeable with Bosnian Muslim, whereas Bosnian generally refers to all three communities.

During the Ottoman period, Muslims were naturally the privileged religious community. Bosnia thus saw the emergence in the towns of a ruling class of Muslim landowners and government officials. Christians and Jews were "second-class" subjects who paid an extra tax in lieu of military service and whose testimony in Islamic courts carried less weight than that of Muslims. But Bosnia was not a land of Muslim oppressors and oppressed non-Muslims. Muslims belonged to the peasantry and often shared the same fate as their Christian counterparts. Moreover, Christians and Jews acquired some status in society as merchants, moneychangers, and physicians.

It is easy either to idealize or to condemn the Ottoman period in Bosnian history. In fact, both the good and the bad of human nature and society blended together into the complex web of Bosnian history. As underscored by the Bosnian writer Ivo Andric in his Nobel Prize-winning novel *The Bridge on the Drina*: "It is true that there had always been concealed enmities and jealousies and religious intolerance, coarseness and cruelty, but there had also been courage and fellowship and a feeling for measure and order, which restrained all these instincts within the limits of the supportable and, in the end, calmed them down and submitted them to the general interest of life in common."[10] Christians and Muslims learned to take from each other "not only women, homes and arms but also songs."[11] A common language helped foster a cultural mosaic among the three religious communities despite periods of oppressive government, foreign wars and internal conflicts, and economic hardship.

Despite the existence of tolerance and harmony, violence also plagued the Balkans under Ottoman rule. The 19th and early 20th centuries were particularly violent. Beginning with the Serb Revolt of 1804, the Balkans witnessed numerous conventional wars, countless rebellions, and periods of sustained guerrilla warfare. These conflicts affected the civilian populations especially harshly. Massacres, destruction of homes, and forced migrations often accompanied armed conflict, touching all communities. Muslims and Christians both had to flee their homes, depending on the conflict. The Serb rebellion of 1804 to 1815, for example, saw the establishment of a small, semiautonomous Serbian state, and the victorious Serbs forced the exodus of all Muslims living

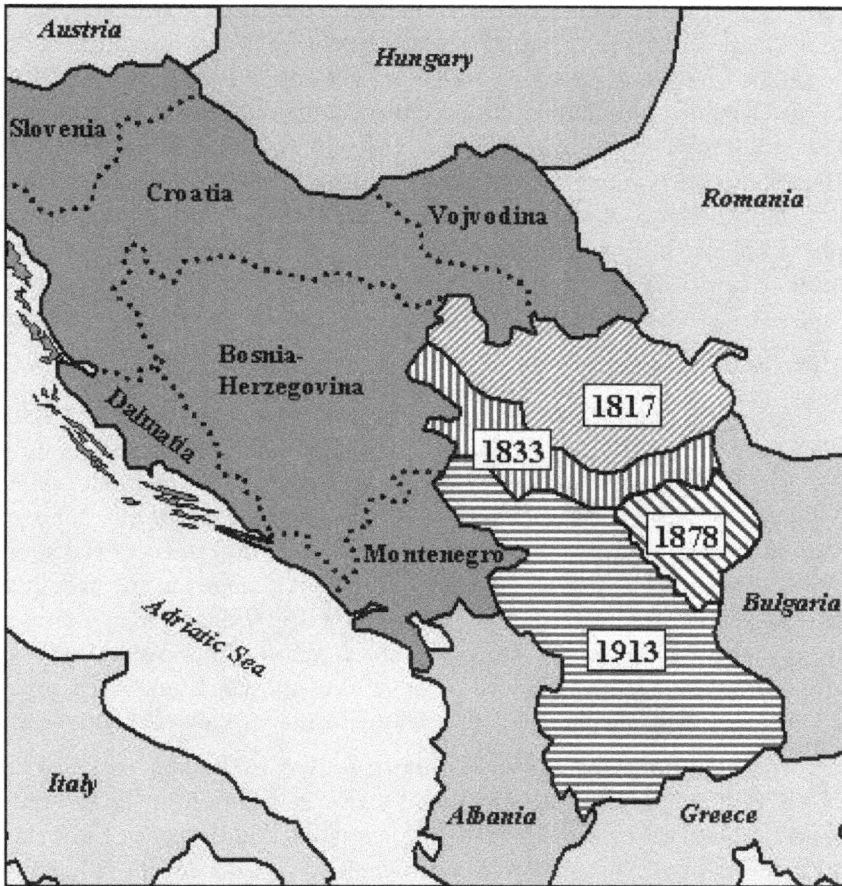

Map 2. The Expansion of Serbia, 1804-1913

in the countryside. Over the next two centuries, Europe has consistently bemoaned the sufferings of the Christians, often to the culpable neglect of the plight of the Muslim populations.

Bosnia had its epochal revolt against Ottoman rule in 1875. The year before saw Bosnia experience a major crop failure. Then in the summer of 1875, Christian peasants in Herzegovina revolted against the imposition of taxes by local tax collectors. The revolt quickly spread to other parts of Bosnia and to Ottoman Bulgaria as well. Muslim peasants in Bosnia joined their Christian counterparts in opposing the local rule of Muslim notables. In Bosnia, the Ottoman government, supported by local Muslim notables, quelled the rebellions. Estimates vary considerably, but some 5,000 peasants were killed and anywhere from 100,000 to 250,000 refugees created in the process. European newspapers naturally emphasized the harsh suppression of the Christian population by Ottoman troops. Reports of the large loss of civilian life and a major refugee problem ignited the fire of public opinion in Europe. Finally, Russia, the self-professed protector of the Orthodox population, declared war against the Ottoman Empire. At the end of the Russo-Turkish War of 1877-78, Austria-Hungary used the Balkan crisis to occupy the Ottoman province of Bosnia with the purpose of establishing order and progress. With the Habsburg occupation, a new phase opened in Bosnian history.[12] Bosnia now entered the political and cultural world of Central Europe, bringing with it a large Muslim population whose roots went as deep and far back as that of its Christian natives.

Habsburg Rule, 1878-1918

After 400 years of Ottoman rule, Bosnia suddenly became a part of the Habsburg Empire in 1878.[13] Though officially under Ottoman suzerainty, in fact, Bosnians found themselves as a veiled protectorate under Vienna's control. Then in 1908, the Habsburg Empire formally annexed Bosnia, thereby cutting any legal ties to Istanbul. Forty years of Habsburg administration (1878-1918) brought significant changes to the province. Bosnia's fate was now directly tied to Central European as opposed to Balkan history. In this strategic reorientation, the Bosnian Muslim community lost its political dominance over the Christians. Moreover, ethnic nationalism changed the way Bosnians viewed themselves.

The Habsburgs occupied Bosnia in an era of Balkan nationalism. In 1878, there were five independent states in addition to the Ottoman Empire: Serbia, Montenegro, Greece, Rumania, and Bulgaria. Each state sported its own nationalism with irredentist designs on its neighbors. Nationalist currents infected Bosnia as well. A national identity now competed with religious and regional loyalties. Tensions between the three Bosnian communities now took on a more nationalist character. Catholics learned to regard themselves as Croats and the Orthodox as Serbs. Bosnian Muslims, for their part, embraced a separate political identity as well.

Habsburg rule gave Bosnia 40 years of central European political culture. The new rulers established a highly centralized bureaucracy by Ottoman standards. In 1878, only 120 Ottoman officials administered the province; by 1910, Bosnia counted 9,533 civil servants. Every adult male, regardless of religious affiliation, had to perform military service in the imperial army, while children attended government schools with Western curricula. All three religious communities participated in the new political freedoms associated with Habsburg parliamentary government.

They founded political parties and elected representatives to serve in the provincial parliament (*Sabor*). To demonstrate fairness, Vienna allotted parliamentary seats according to religious affiliation. In 1910, for example, Muslims received 24 seats, compared with 31 for the Orthodox and 16 for the Catholics.

Demographically and politically, the Muslim community saw a major reversal of position. Muslims constituted close to half the population in 1870; they rapidly dropped to 40 percent in 1879 as many fled the Habsburg occupation.[14] Catholic Croats benefited most from Vienna's rule. Over 200,000 subjects from other parts of the empire, many of them Catholics, settled in the province. The Jesuits joined the Franciscans in pastoral and educational activities. The Catholic population grew from 18.08 percent in 1879 to 22.87 percent by 1910. Muslim proportions declined further, from 38.73 percent to 32.35 percent in the same period. Orthodox Serbs emerged as the largest religious group with over 40 percent. Sarajevo, the provincial capital, saw the portion of the Catholic population increase from 3.3 percent in 1879 to 34.52 percent in 1910.

Despite some favoritism to the Croats, Habsburg rule proved quite tolerant for the Muslim community. Vienna avoided any major land reform. This decision left the Muslim landowning class largely intact, a situation that remained through the outbreak of the Bosnian war in 1991. The Muslim community adjusted to Christian rule and accepted European ways. Forty years of Habsburg rule saw the Europeanization and secularization of the Bosnian Muslim community at the expense of strong ties to the Islamic Middle East. By the end of the Habsburg Empire in 1918, the Muslims had gained the reputation of being a bastion of loyalty to the imperial throne (*Kaisertreue*). In essence, they had tied their fate and future to Europe. For them, Muslim stood more as an ethno-political identity, and faith became more a private matter. This development was in part a direct response to the growing nationalism within the Bosnian Serb and Croat communities. Now, intercommunal relations, whether peaceful or not, took on an ethno-nationalist character.

World War I and the First Yugoslavia (1918-1941)

World War I proved the crucible that led to the creation of the First Yugoslavia.[15] Great Britain and France, as victors, dictated the peace treaties, and both countries wanted to create a large Slavic state to replace the Austro-Hungarian Empire in the Balkans. Serbia presented a very strong claim for the spoils of war. Serbs had not only fought on the winning side, but they had also expended much blood and treasure for

Map 3. The Kingdom of the Serbs, Croats, and Slovenes, 1918-1929

the Allied cause and therefore could negotiate in the postwar period from a position of strength. In fact, they could claim the highest percentage of loss of population of any participant nation in the war. On the other hand, Habsburg Slavs—Croats, Slovenes, and Bosnians—had fought on the losing side and stood dependent upon the good will of the victors.

France and Great Britain pushed for the establishment of a single South Slav state in the Balkans out of the ruins of the Habsburg Empire. Serbia's prewar politicians had wanted a Greater Serbia without Slovenia, but the allies opposed such a move in the hope of creating more stability in the region with a larger state outside of either Austrian or Hungarian control. Therefore, they pushed the Belgrade government to accept a compromise with all the Habsburg Slavs to create the Kingdom of Serbs, Croats, and Slovenes on 1 December 1918. This new European state included prewar Serbia and added Slovenia, Dalmatia, Croatia, Slavonia, Vojvodina, Bosnia, and Montenegro. The kingdom doubled Serbia's prewar population from 6 million to 12 million people. No ethnic group, however, constituted a majority in the new state. Serbs formed approximately 39 percent of the population, with Croats hovering around 23.7 percent, Slovenes 8.5 percent, Bosnian Muslims 6 percent, and Albanians 3.6 percent. Croats, Slovenes, Muslims, and other non-Serbs entered the union expecting equal partnership with the Serbs in a federal state. This expectation was soon dashed.

Despite the rich demographic diversity, the new rulers in Belgrade defined the kingdom as constituting one nation, three peoples. The one nation was Serbo-Croatian, an official category that included all the Slavs: Serbs, Croats, Slovenes, Bosniacs, Macedonians, and Montenegrins. Moreover, Belgrade refused to recognize the Albanians as a separate nationality but identified them as Serbs who had embraced Albanian culture and language. Such a policy left the Albanians as the most disenfranchised and hence most disappointed community in the kingdom.

Serbs from prewar Serbia held a disproportionate amount of political power. The Serbian Karadjordjevic dynasty remained in power, and Alexander returned from exile to assume the throne as king of the new state. He never assumed the mantle of a Yugoslav ruler but instead remained a Serb at heart and in policy. Serbs dominated the Yugoslav government and armed forces. During the period 1920 to 1939, for example, every chief of the army was a Serb, and only one non-Serb served as prime minister. Of 165 generals in the armed forces in 1941, 161 were Serbs, with two each for the Croats and the Slovenes. The disproportionate presence of Serbs in high positions of government and the army created some consternation among the other ethnic communities.[16]

During the interwar period, Croat politicians generally led the opposition to Serb dominance. Bosnia was caught in the midst of the struggles between Serbs and Croats over the nature of the Yugoslav state. Bosnian Muslims formed their own party, the Yugoslav Muslim Organization, headed by Mehmed Spaho. In the 1924 Yugoslav parliament, all the Bosnian Muslim deputies, with one exception, identified themselves as Croats. This identification reflected 40 years of rule by the Catholic Habsburg monarchy. But this was not always a simple choice, nor was it one-dimensional. The Spaho family reflected the problem of ethnic identities. Mehmed insisted on calling himself a Yugoslav; of his two brothers, one referred to himself as a Serb and the other a Croat.[17]

Separated from the Ottoman Empire for more than 40 years, most Muslim political leaders learned the art of compromise from the Habsburg period. Before World War I, they had cooperated with Vienna, deservedly gaining the reputation of *Kaisertrue*. Now Belgrade functioned as the new power broker, and Muslim politicians sought to leverage their weak position with the central government as much as possible. Often, for example, Mehmed Spaho joined the Slovene leadership in an attempt to mediate tensions between the centralist Serbs and federalist Croats.[18] In this, the Bosnian Muslims continued their role of loyalty to the central government.

Non-Serbs experienced a setback in national development when King Alexander established a royal dictatorship in 1929. He also changed the name of the country from the Kingdom of Serbs, Croats, and Slovenes to Yugoslavia, meaning the land of the South Slavs. The change in name represented further institutionalization of a unitary state based on Serb dominance. Alexander, for example, erased the historical boundary of Bosnia and instead divided the region among several *banovinas*, administrative units named after rivers. For the first time in over 400 years, Bosnia disappeared as a name from maps. Bosnian Muslims now found themselves as minorities in several *banovinas* as a result of gerrymandering engineered by Belgrade, all designed to strengthen the power of the monarchy and to enhance the position of Serbs in the country. Bosnian Serbs dominated the local governments of former Bosnia. The king appointed each *ban*, who, in turn, filled positions in the local governments that previously had been elected. Only a global war broke the Serb dominance over Bosnia.

World War II and Ethnic Cleansing (1941-1945)

World War II unleashed an orgy of ethnic cleansing unprecedented in modern Balkan history.[19] Foreign invasion and occupation proved the catalyst for this tragic turn of events. For Yugoslavia, World War II was both a war against foreign aggression and a civil war fought between Yugoslavs. Bosnia suffered the most from the fighting.

In 1938, on the eve of World War II, Belgrade reached a historic agreement with Croatian leaders. Serb politicians agreed to the establishment of an autonomous *banovina* of Croatia that included Bosnia. Belgrade hoped to solidify Croatian support in the event of war. When war did come, the kingdom of Yugoslavia collapsed in rapid fashion. In April 1941, the Axis powers defeated the Yugoslav army in only 11 days. Unlike the one front facing Serbia in 1914, Yugoslavia was attacked from three directions, this time by coalition of German, Italian, and Bulgarian armies. The kingdom disappeared from European maps.

The Axis Powers carved up Yugoslavia into nine different areas. Italy and Germany divided Slovenia into two parts, each gaining its own fiefdom. Italy received Kosovo and incorporated it with Albania. Montenegro theoretically gained its independence, though the country fell under Italian tutelage. Bulgaria gained control of Macedonia and parts of southern Serbia, whereas Hungary grabbed Vojvodina. In addition to the Banat, Germany took Serbia and installed a puppet government under General Milan Nedic. Hitler and Mussolini also created the Independent State of Croatia (NDH), but Germany and Italy each established its own separate zone of influence. The new Croatian state included Croatia, Slavonia, and Bosnia. The Dalmatian coast, however, fell under Italian control.

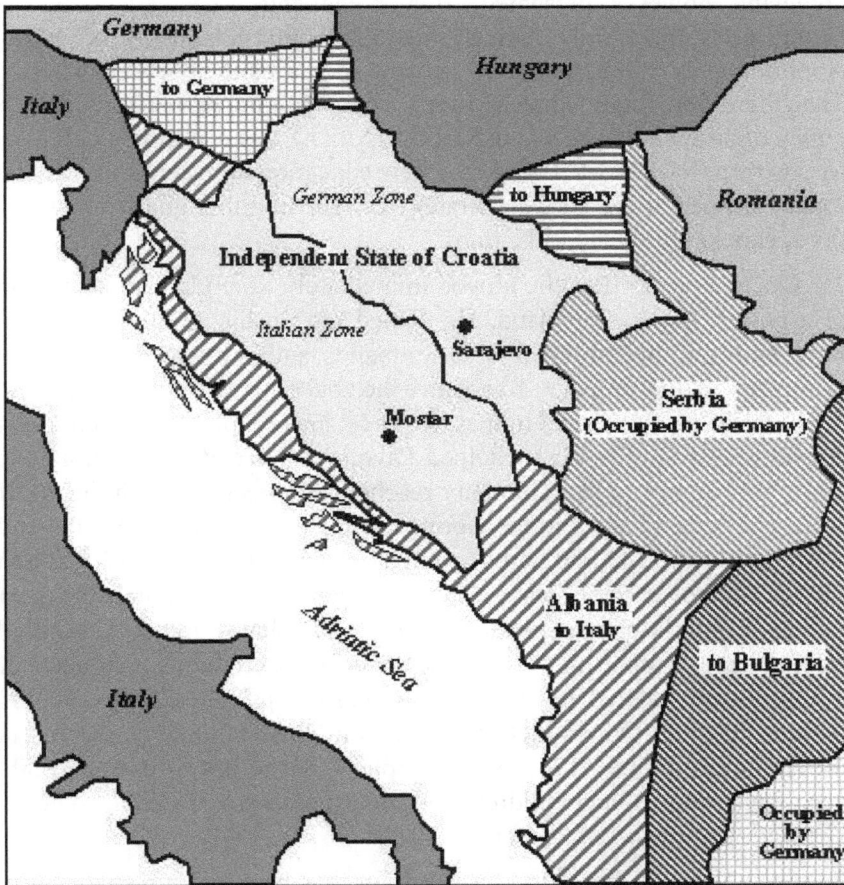

Map 4. Partition of Yugoslavia in World War II

In dividing the spoils of conquest, the Axis powers opened the door for ethnic cleansing. Hitler and Mussolini placed Ante Pavelic, a fascist and racist, as the head of NDH. Born in Herzegovina in 1889, Pavelic drew sustenance from the ethnic and religious divisions in prewar Yugoslavia. In 1926, he founded in Italy a political party, the Ustashe, which on the eve of war numbered at most 12,000 hard-core members in Croatia. The party never gained a grassroots following. But, with Axis support, Pavelic could assume the reins of government without popular backing, and he proceeded to institute a reign of terror and ethnic cleansing.

Pavelic preached a racist theory in line with that of Hitler and Nazi Germany. Croats were not Slavs but belonged to the Aryan race. Serbs, however, were Slavs and hence members of an inferior people. Pavelic wanted to establish a homogeneous state. Creating a pure Croatian homeland, however, presented a major challenge to Pavelic. Catholic Croats constituted only half of the 6,300,000 inhabitants of NDH. Approximately 1,900,000, or 30 percent, identified themselves as Serbs. Then there were the Bosnian Muslims. To create a pure Croatia required a policy of cleansing (*ciscenje* in Serbo-Croatian), that is removing all non-Croats from NDH. Mile Budak, the new education minister, provided the broad outlines of the Ustashe strategy of reaching that goal: "convert a third, expel a third, and kill a third."

Once in power, Pavelic moved immediately to implement his vision of a pure Croatian homeland. He denied citizenship to all Serbs, who were now required to wear blue armbands and were prohibited from using the Cyrillic alphabet. To achieve the goal of an ethnically pure state, the Ustashe regime turned to mass killings, mass deportations, and mass conversions of Serbs. Hitler helped Pavelic in his endeavor. On 4 June 1941, for example, Nazi Germany reached an agreement with the NDH to accept Serb refugees in the German rump state of Serbia. By the end of the war, some 300,000 Serbs had fled or were expelled from Croatia to Serbia. Moreover, the Ustashe established concentration camps, the most famous being Jasenovac, where mainly Serbs, Jews, and Gypsies died from disease, malnutrition, labor accidents, and executions. Estimates of the number murdered in the concentration camps range from 160,000 to over 500,000. Others met their deaths in mass killings conducted in their villages. In July 1941, for example, Ustashe troops executed 500 Serb men, women, and children from the small town of Glina, some 65 kilometers southeast of Zagreb.

Both Nazi Germany and Fascist Italy thus bear much responsibility for the ethnic cleansing that devastated Yugoslavia. First of all, Hitler

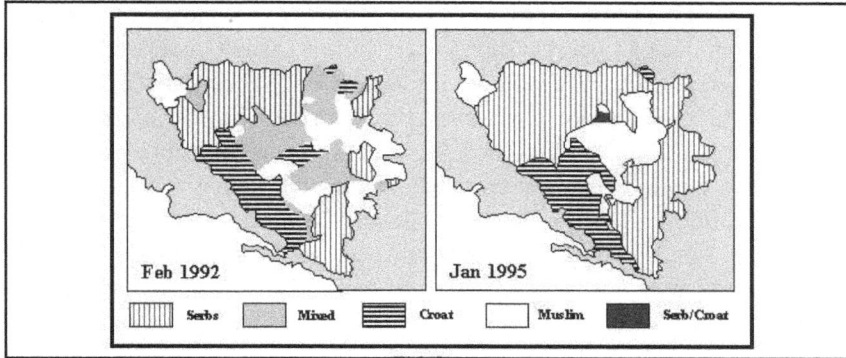

Map 5. Effects of Ethnic Cleansing in the Bosnian War

and Mussolini placed Pavelic in power and then allowed the Ustashe to remain in control until the Axis defeat. Hitler's policy of exterminating the Jews complemented Pavelic's own diabolical intentions toward the Serbs. Moreover, Nazi policies in Yugoslavia encouraged German soldiers to be ruthless and inhumane in putting down any armed resistance from the local population. On 13 October 1941, for example, Hitler ordered the execution of 100 prisoners or hostages for every German soldier killed, and 50 for every wounded German. Rather than resist such an order, the German regular army readily complied with the Führer's wishes. In the worst incident of the war, German troops executed some 7,000 townspeople—including women, children, and old men—from Kragujevac in retaliation for the killing of German troops. Such German atrocities both encouraged the Ustashe to do likewise.

Two resistance movements formed to oppose Germany, Italy, and the NDH. Colonel Draza Mihailovic created the Chetniks, who fought in the name of the Yugoslav monarchy and for Serb nationalism. Jozef Broz Tito (1892-1980), born of a Croatian father and a Slovene mother, founded the Partisan movement based on a Communist ideology. Rather quickly, Partisans and Chetniks turned to fighting each other rather than concentrating on defeating the Germans and Italians. War turned very ugly for all sides in the conflict as innocent civilians found themselves caught in the crossfire. There was little regard for the conventions of war. All sides practiced summary executions. The Chetniks and Partisans often killed German or Ustashe prisoners of war in revenge. Best estimates place the number of Yugoslavs killed in World War II at over 1 million; the majority of these deaths were Yugoslavs killing other Yugoslavs.[20] In other words, Ustashe, Partisans, and Chetniks engaged in a civil war, the Montenegrin Milovan Djilas; the Slovene Eduard Kardelj; the Jew

Moshe Piyade; and the Serb Aleksandar Rankovich. According to Tito, Serbs constituted 44 percent of Partisan troops; many Croats and Bosnian Muslims joined the ranks as well.[22] Tito established many units based on regional compositions, such as the 16th Muslim Brigade, located in Bosnia, and the 10th Zagreb Corps, with its heavy representation of Croats. By the end of the war, the Partisans possessed at least 300,000 soldiers, though official mythology placed the number at 800,000. Most important, Tito, by having the Partisans play a major role in liberating the country, was in an excellent position to create a new Yugoslavia, one not dominated by Serbs.

Tito's accomplishment in World War II was truly amazing and carries some implications for both the Implementation Force (IFOR) and Stabilization Force (SFOR). Despite the horrors of ethnic cleansing of his time, Tito could rally individuals from all the ethnic and religious communities into a single movement opposed to the Axis powers and the Ustashe state. This occurred in the midst of war and ethnic cleansing. In this regard, Tito provided a hope that the new Yugoslavia would bring healing and reconciliation to Yugoslav society. Bosnia, as a microcosm of heterogeneity in the Balkans, would prove a showcase of Tito's experiment.

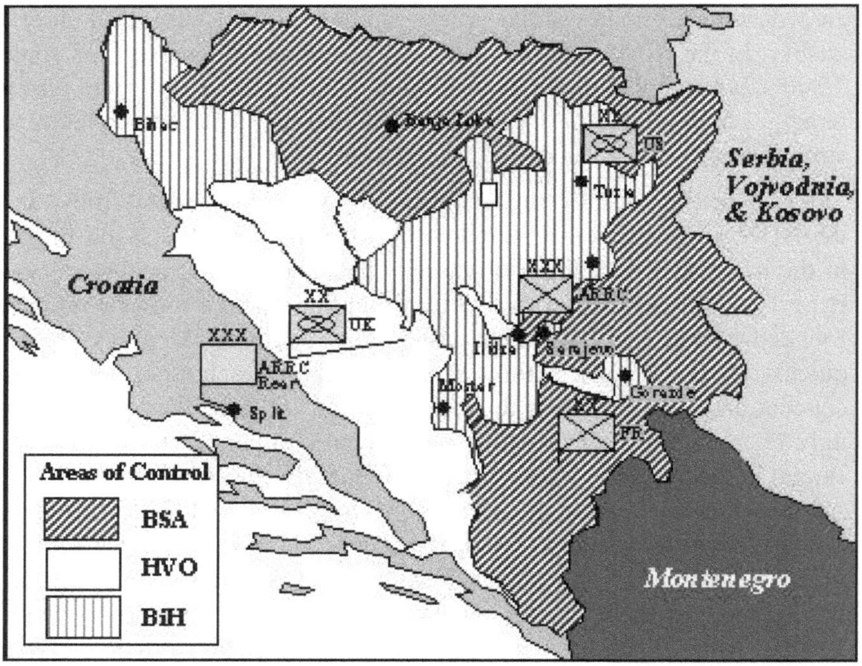

Map 6. IFOR Deployment913

Second Yugoslavia, 1945-1992

Despite the ethnic cleansing of World War II in Yugoslavia, Tito ameliorated communal tensions over a period of 35 years in postwar Yugoslavia.[23] In too many instances, he merely suppressed rather than healed the memories of the ethnic cleansing. But Communist rule, which lasted over two generations, resulted in a modicum of national harmony and reconciliation. Bosnia witnessed the new political and social order based on the slogan of unity and brotherhood.

Upon the conclusion of World War II, Tito's first priority was to secure his own political power. In 1945, his regime killed over 50,000 Ustashe in captivity, in part to ensure firm control over the new state. Tito's new government executed tens of thousands in the years 1946 and 1947 and imprisoned many more. Eventually Tito granted a general amnesty, in part to provide additional labor to an economy desperately short of workers. By 1950, Tito felt secure enough to lighten considerably his reign of terror.

Pragmatism gradually emerged as Tito's approach to the postwar reconstruction of Yugoslav society. Rejecting the Serbian dominance of the interwar kingdom, Tito set out to balance federal power with republic rights. In this regard, Second Yugoslavia fostered cultural and religious diversity, perhaps to a fault. At the beginning, however, Tito kept the reigns of government tightly; he did, however, decentralize more as time went on in his long rule of 35 years.

As promised during the war, Tito divided the postwar Yugoslavia into six federated republics: Serbia, Croatia, Slovenia, Bosnia-Herzegovina, Macedonia, and Montenegro. Serbia, unlike the other five republics, was further subdivided into Serbia proper, the autonomous region (*oblast*) of Vojvodina with approximately a quarter Magyar (Hungarian) population, and the autonomous province of Kosovo with its Albanian majority of 65 to 70 percent. Over time, more and more power devolved to the republics and autonomous regions. Each republic and autonomous region had its own communist party. The League of Yugoslav Communists, formed in 1952, served as the umbrella communist party. A military reorganization in 1969 required each republic and autonomous area to establish its own Territorial Defense Forces. These functioned similar to the National Guard in the US, under some republic control but designed to augment the Yugoslav army in war.

As the republics gained more political power, Tito increasingly assumed the role of final arbitrator who intervened in a timely fashion to settle disputes. To maintain his power, he relied on the secret police, the League of Yugoslav Communists, and the armed forces. All three were imbued with the ideology of Yugoslav ideal, brotherhood and unity of all South Slavs. To help keep the republics in line, Tito also practiced *divide et impera* wherever possible. He applied this principle in ethnically and religiously diverse republics but could not in homogeneous Slovenia. In Croatia and in Kosovo, however, Tito depended on the Serb minorities in each region to fill, in disproportionate numbers, positions in the local communist party and police. In this way, Croatian Serbs and Kosovar Serbs could leverage the majority population of Croats in Croatia and Albanians in Kosovo. In the Croatian capital of Zagreb, for example, in 1971, Serbs made up 56.5 percent of the police force, to 40.8 percent for the Croats, even though the Serb minority constituted only 15 percent of the republic's population.[24]

Tito accomplished much in 35 years of rule. "In a short period after the war, he established a kind of harmony among communities emerging from the bloodiest imaginable civil conflict. He instilled pride in a small country that, even by European standards, had suffered inordinately during the first half of the century. And for the first time in the region's history, a majority of the population enjoyed economic prosperity under his rule."[25] Yugoslavs could travel around the globe, as their passports allowed them to cross more borders without visa than any other passport in the world. Some 800,000 Yugoslavs worked outside the country and sent money back to their families. Tourists from the West flocked to Yugoslavia for vacations, taking advantage of Belgrade's liberal policy toward tourism.

Bosnia gradually emerged as an example of national harmony in Yugoslavia at its best. In the late 1940s, Bosnian Serbs formed 60 percent of the Bosnian Communist Party membership, with Muslims constituting only 20 percent of the total.[26] Initially, Tito expected that the Bosnian Muslims would eventually abandon their religious identity and declare themselves either Croats or Serbs. The first Party Congress after the war stated that "Bosnia cannot be divided between Serbia and Croatia, not only because Serbs and Croats live mixed together on the whole territory, but also because the territory is inhabited by Muslims who have not yet decided on their national identity."[27] Belgrade did encourage the Bosnian political leadership to make a choice between Croat or Serb. In the first Yugoslav *Who's Who*, published in 1956, 62 percent of those with Muslim names identified themselves as Serbs and only 17 percent as Croats. However, the general population was unwilling to reach such an easy accommodation as their politicians. In the 1953 census, for example, over 80 percent of Bosnian Muslims preferred to see themselves as "Yugoslav, nationally undeclared."[28] Most Bosniacs were unwilling to abandon their Muslim identity.

Tito's foreign policy of independence from the Warsaw Pact in the 1950s eventually had its effect on the Muslim nationality issue in Bosnia. Having sacrificed much in World War II, Tito was determined not to fall under Stalin's tutelage. In 1948, he broke with the Soviet Union. Having split with Stalin, Tito wanted to avoid falling under the West's thumb. To help pursue an independent foreign policy based on neither East nor West, Tito joined forces with Nehru in India, Nasser in Egypt, and Sukarno in Indonesia to found the Non-Aligned Movement in 1954.

To win favor among the Muslim states for his nonaligned foreign policy in the Third World, Tito presented Bosnia as a showcase of his regime's religious tolerance. In the late 1950s, the Bosnian Muslims began receiving new rights and privileges. In 1969, Tito granted the Yugoslav Muslim community a separate status, and the 1971 census permitted Bosnians to identify themselves as Muslims rather than as Yugoslavs, Croats, or Serbs. No longer was there the pressure of having to choose a Serb or Croat identity. And the Muslim identity in Bosnia flourished in the 1970s and 1980s. Belgrade allowed increasing numbers of Muslim students to study at Arab universities. In 1977, Sarajevo University established a Faculty of Islamic Theology with Saudi money. All this type of activity helped nurture a Muslim ethnic identity among Bosnian Muslims. The forces for cultural pluralism were certainly strengthened by Tito's policy.

Bosnia appeared to travel a long way down the road of ethnic reconciliation after World War II despite the great diversity of its population. Of the six republics in Communist Yugoslavia, only Bosnia lacked a majority of any community. By the late 1960s, the Muslim population surpassed that of the Serbs for the first time since the eve of the Habsburg occupation of the province in 1878. In 1991, census figures showed a distribution of 43.7 percent Muslims, 31.4 percent Serbs, 17.3 percent Croats, and 5.5 percent Yugoslavs for a population of 4,365,000 inhabitants. These figures are misleading. Approximately 20 to 30 percent of the marriages in Bosnia were mixed. Catholics married Orthodox, Orthodox married Muslims, and Muslims married Catholics. Some families comprised members from all three religious communities. Marriage vows involving individuals from two different religious communities were much more prevalent in towns than villages, the latter tending to be homogeneous rather than mixed in population. Some cities, such as Sarajevo, Mostar, and Tuzla, claimed upwards of 30 to 40 percent mixed marriages.[29] This high percentage of mixed marriages stands as a major achievement of Tito's regime in Bosnia, attesting to some healing in society after the traumas of World War II.

Language and history played a part, no doubt. Bosnians spoke the same language, Serbo-Croatian, readily permitting cross-religious discourse. Moreover, the historical record had created a tradition of religious tolerance and coexistence alongside memories of internecine strife. Most important, however, Tito provided the political incentives and the cultural environment conducive to some reconciliation. The state indoctrinated and rewarded displays of unity and brotherhood while punishing certain nationalist behavior. Public education tried to foster a mind-set and value system of tolerance and coexistence. And Tito had 35 years in which to educate two generations born after World War II.

In some regards, Bosnia represented the test of the Tito experiment to create social harmony while balancing the reality of ethnic, cultural, and religious diversity. Many Yugoslavs in general and Bosnians in particular grew up under Tito with limited and censored information on the ethnic cleansing of World War II. The Tito state only ennobled the Partisan effort and preached unity and brotherhood. Consequently, most Bosnians, especially in the cities and towns, felt at the beginning of 1992 that war would not come to Bosnia. These individuals expressed surprise when the extremists used the media to develop issues centered on the ethnic hatreds of World War II.[30] Perhaps Tito would have done better for future generations if he had squarely addressed the ethnic cleansing in World War II despite the explosiveness of the subject. Burying the issue, however, only left most Yugoslavs naively unprepared to marshal forces to prevent a similar occurrence.

Despite his mistakes, Tito offers a compelling example of the possibility of some reconciliation among members of the three warring factions in the Bosnian war. A pluralistic society needs a fair arbitrator who can punish separatism and reward integration. It takes generations, however, to change attitudes and behavior, but Tito did accomplish much in less than two generations. NATO today has assumed the role of honest arbitrator, and a coherent and impartial strategy has possibilities of some success despite the ethnic cleansing of the Bosnian war.

The Collapse of Communist Yugoslavia

For all his achievements, Tito left Yugoslavia with a number of major problems.[31] The Yugoslav state proved too weak at the federal level to meet the challenges of the post-Tito era. Moreover, the economy began to show signs of fundamental weakness in the last year of Tito's reign. Despite the political and economic problems, Tito's successors kept the state together until the collapse of the Cold War in 1989.

To Yugoslavia's political detriment, Tito had concentrated too much power in his person. He groomed no one to succeed him. More important, Tito unwisely bequeathed a weak central government to his successors. In 1974, he promulgated a new constitution that proved his last political testament. That document accelerated the devolution of power to the republics. It defined the six republics as nation-states endowed with sovereignty but united to Yugoslavia in a confederation. Such language implied that the republics possessed the right to secede on the basis of national self-determination (*narodno samoopredeljenje*). Moreover, the 1974 constitution left power in the hands of an eight-member federal presidency—one representative from each of the six republics and one each from Vojvodina and Kosovo. The president of that body would be rotated annually among the six republics. Such an arrangement seriously weakened power at the center. As noted by one observer of Yugoslavia, "the 1974 Constitution . . . was based on a system of political musical chairs—senior positions would be rotated every year to prevent any single republic or politician from accumulating too much power."[32] This arrangement also hindered the emergence of strong leadership and coherent strategy at the federal level, yet Tito knew fully well that Yugoslavia needed a strong center for unity and brotherhood.

By the end of 1980s, Communist Yugoslavia faced a crisis of gargantuan proportions. The economy had embarked on a downward spiral, beset with a heavy foreign debt, hyperinflation, high unemployment, and a significant decline in the standard of living. A recession in Europe forced many Yugoslav workers to return home, drastically cutting off an important source of foreign exchange. Economic woes on the home front translated into social tensions and national discontent. At one point, inflation hit an unbelievable rate of 1,000 percent. Few societies possess the mettle to withstand such economic pressure without some serious political turmoil. In these troubled times, each republic saw the emergence of local leaders who turned the economic problems into burning national issues. The wealthier republics of Slovenia and Croatia complained of high taxes and waste of government spending on poorer areas such as Bosnia, Macedonia, and Kosovo. International financial aid could have provided critical help, but it was not as forthcoming as in Tito's era. Instead, the West forced Belgrade to implement austerity measures, exacerbating social tensions further. But why the reduced Western aid?

In 1989, Yugoslavia's strategic importance to the West changed dramatically with the Berlin Wall crashing down, signaling the end of the Cold War. Suddenly, the demise of the Warsaw Pact diminished Yugoslavia's strategic value to NATO. As one scholar noted: "What counted for the West was denying Yugoslavia to the Soviet Union . . . once the Berlin Wall fell and the communist regimes in Central and Eastern Europe had collapsed, the purpose was gone. As communism dissolved and East-West cooperation developed, Yugoslavia ceased to be strategically significant."[33] Now the West proved unwilling to bail out Belgrade with easy aid as it had earlier. Problems in Yugoslavia failed to gain the same attention in the West. The US, in particular, was preoccupied with the Gulf War and its aftermath and possessed little energy to focus on what Washington now considered a European matter. The lack of firm will by the US and Europe to maintain Yugoslavia's territorial unity and integrity contributed to the country's disintegration.

The collapse of the Iron Curtain unleashed democratic forces in Eastern Europe and the Balkans. In Yugoslavia, leaders in the republics gained the freedom to compete in parliamentary elections. Extremists turned to nationalism as the best vehicle for addressing political and economic problems. Their demagoguery poisoned the waters in communal relations. One Serb journalist, for example, described the poisonous propaganda in his own community thus: "As Yugoslavs, we had an oppressive communist regime, but we were reasonably tolerant of one another. As Serbs, Milosevic's media have drilled into us how to hate our neighbors. Croats are 'rabbits' when we're chasing them, or 'pigs' when they're chasing us. Muslims are 'dogs' or 'baby killers.' Albanians are just 'filthy rats.'"[34] Information warfare roused people's passions and fears, fueled in large measure by a worsening economy.

Despite all the problems swirling around them, most Bosnians, especially in the Muslim community, supported the maintenance of the Yugoslav state. They had witnessed positive gains under the Tito system and stood to lose in a major political upheaval. Should Slovenia or Croatia gain independence, everything would change in the calculations. In either case, Alija Izetbegovic, who emerged as the head of the Muslim community, threatened to demand independence for Bosnia as well. Should the Muslims embark on this road, Bosnian Serbs threatened to demand union with Serbia, while Bosnian Croats would seek incorporation with Croatia.

Even before the outbreak of the Yugoslav war, Milosevic and Tudjman began plotting to divide Bosnia. In March 1991, both presidents of their respective republics, Serbia and Croatia, met in the former royal retreat of Karadjorjevo, where they agreed in principle to divide Bosnia between Serbia and Croatia. They proved, however, unable to reach any firm agreement on lines of demarcation, and all subsequent meetings of their aides failed to produce a settlement. Bosnia's fate would have to await military events on the ground.

A domino effect began when both Slovenia and Croatia declared their independence on 25 June 1991. The Yugoslav army moved to squash the Slovenian bid for independence, but Slobodan Milosevic, as the president of the Republic of Serbia, blocked the use of military force against the Slovenes. For him, there were too few Serbs in Slovenia to warrant a major military operation. In 1918, it might be recalled, Serbia's politicians had generally opposed the incorporation of Slovenia into the new kingdom for the very same reason. Consequently, the Yugoslav army terminated military operations after only 10 days of fighting in which it suffered 43 killed and 163 wounded. Slovenia, for its part, lost a dozen killed and 144 wounded. The Brioni Agreement of 7 July ended the fighting in the republic, and Slovenia was secure in its newfound independence. Tito's Yugoslavia essentially died with the Yugoslav army's complete withdrawal from Slovenia by 19 July.

War immediately spread from Slovenia to Croatia. There, Franjo Tudjman had embarked on a policy designed to create an independent Croatia. Croatian Serbs feared being second-class citizens. As mentioned earlier, Serbs, who composed 15 percent of Croatia's population, held a disproportionate position in both the police and party. Tudjman moved to redress the imbalance. In response to Tudjman's moves, Croatian Serbs declared autonomy for Krajina and Eastern Slavonia.[35] The stage was set for an armed confrontation between the two communities.

Unlike Slovenia, Milosevic and the senior command of the Yugoslav army were both determined to fight in support of the Serbs living in Krajina and Slavonia. War broke out between Croatia and the Yugoslav state. The Yugoslav army and Serb paramilitary forces cooperated closely in consolidating Belgrade's control over a third of Croatia. Casualties for both military and civilians were high for the period between July and December 1991: over 10,000 killed and 30,000 wounded. Both Serbs and Croats sought to establish homogeneous areas by forcing the flight of people. Meanwhile, Milosevic had consolidated his control over what was left of Communist Yugoslavia: Serbia, Montenegro, Vojvodina, and Kosovo. Bosnia faced the danger of partition between Belgrade and Zagreb.

The international community was finally able to broker a cease-fire in Croatia. The Yugoslav Army withdrew its forces by January 1992. Meanwhile, the UN had authorized the dispatch to Croatia of a United Nations Protection Force, or UNPROFOR, for a period of 12 months. The force came into being on 21 February 1992. Consisting of 15,000 personnel from 26 countries, its primary mission was to help maintain a cease-fire between Croatian and Serbian forces, mainly in Krajina and Eastern Slavonia, while the international community pursued a negotiated settlement to the conflict. In protecting the status quo on the ground, UNPROFOR underscored that violence and ethnic cleansing do pay. The Serb minorities thus gained a modicum of autonomy at the expense of the new state's unity. This example proved attractive for extremists in Bosnia.

The Bosnian War, 1992-1995

The conflict in Croatia spilled over into Bosnia in April 1992.[36] Understanding the character of the Bosnian war and the manner of its conclusion was of vital importance to US ground troops deploying to Bosnia in December 1995. NATO inherited an independent Bosnia whose magnitude of killing, population displacement, and physical destruction dwarfed the other wars in the dissolution of Tito's Yugoslavia.

As Croatia plunged into war in the second half of 1991, Bosnia's politicians jockeyed for power and position. Alija Izetbegovic emerged as the head of the Muslim-dominated Party of Democratic Action (SDA). In December 1991, as president of the Bosnian government, he applied to the European Community (EC) for recognition as an independent state. On 9 January 1992, to undercut Izetbegovic, Radovan Karadzic, the head of the Serbian Democratic Party (SDS), declared the establishment of the Serbian Republic or *Republika Srpska* (RS), with its capital at Pale. Undeterred by this Serb action, on 28 February and 1 March, the Bosnian government held a referendum on the issue of independence. Mate Boban, the head of the Croatian Democratic Alliance (HDZ), supported Izetbegovic on the issue of sovereignty and independence. A vast majority of Bosnian Serbs, encouraged by their nationalist leaders, boycotted the event. Only 66.4 percent of eligible voters, mainly Muslims and Croats, cast their votes, and of these a whopping 99.7 percent favored independence.

The West faced the dilemma of establishing clear goals and a coherent strategy for Bosnia. European countries tended to prefer a division of Bosnia into separate areas, each controlled by one of the three communities. Washington, for reasons that lay outside the scope of this short chapter, opposed any agreement that attempted to divide Bosnia into cantons. In this, the US added to the Bosnian problem by undercutting European efforts in reaching a solution. On 18 March 1992, for example, Izetbegovic, Karadzic, and Boban signed an agreement that created three territorial units within an independent state of Bosnia. Washington, instead of putting its power and prestige behind the deal, expressed its disapproval to Izetbegovic who promptly backed away from the agreement.[37]

On 5 April 1992, Izetbegovic declared the independence of Bosnia. The EC recognized Bosnia as an independent state on 6 April; the US followed suit the next day. Milosevic meanwhile led Serbia, Montenegro, Vojvodina, and Kosovo to declare the Federal Republic of Yugoslavia on 27 April. For its part, the EC, after recognizing Bosnian independence, demanded the Yugoslav People's Army (JNA) withdraw from Bosnia. Between 4 and 10 May 1992, the JNA complied by withdrawing 20,000 troops but left behind 80,000, the vast majority of these being Bosnian Serbs. General Ratko Mladic, himself a Bosnian Serb, took command of most of these officers and soldiers, who now formed the Army of Republika Srpska. Moreover, Serb paramilitary organizations in Serbia joined Karadzic in helping to create a viable Republika Srpska as the first step toward a greater Serbia. The military balance in Bosnia clearly favored the Bosnian Serbs.

Republika Srpska, with the help of the Milosevic government, embarked on an ambitious strategy of uniting all Bosnia Serbs in one state. Some 1.8 million Serbs lived in Croatia and Bosnia. Most were located in the eastern and southeastern parts of Bosnia. A large number resided in the northwestern region, bordering Krajina. Strategically, the Pale leadership set a priority to link up with the Serbs living in Krajina. This goal required establishing control over northern Bosnia stretching from Knin to Serbia through the Posovina Corridor. Muslim-dominated areas Bijejlina, Srebrenica, Tuzla, and Bihac stood in the way; in addition, large numbers of Croats lived in the Posovina Corridor and the town of Brcko. Creating a homogeneous and contiguous Republika Srpska required cleansing these areas of non-Serbs.

The Serbs focused their initial effort on northeastern Bosnia. Several ultra-nationalist paramilitary groups based in Serbia crossed the border to assist Karadzic. At the beginning of April 1992, Serb forces captured Bijeljina. Zeljko Raznjatovic, commonly known by his *nom de guerre* Arkan, and his irregular force called the Tigers massacred over 100

Muslims in town for the expressed purpose of causing a mass exodus of non-Serbs. By September 1992, the Republika Srpska controlled 70 percent of Bosnia. Between 375,000 and 400,000 refugees, mainly Bosniacs, had fled northeastern and eastern Bosnia during this period. Ethnic cleansing had come to Bosnia on a grand scale.

The Serb victories in northeastern Bosnia threatened the Croats and the Muslims, and both communities responded in kind. It is well known that Belgrade and Zagreb had started and helped direct the Bosnian war by providing weapons, training, and salaries to local leaders. But local leaders took their own initiative to implement the ethnic cleansing. Much less known is the role of Muslims in this regard. Izetbegovic, for his part, readily relied on criminals to bolster his forces. In the first weeks of the war, Muslim commanders perpetrated their own atrocities against civilians and forced the flight of many Serbs from their homes. Further, the Muslims rather quickly established their own infamous detention camps, such as Celebici.[38]

On 5 July 1992, Mate Boban, the head of the Croatian Democratic Alliance, proclaimed the Croat Union of Hercog-Bosna with its base at Grude. His Croatian Home Defense managed to seize control of western Herzegovina. The Bosniacs in central Bosnia were thus sandwiched between Serb and Croat states. In January 1993, major fighting broke out between Croats and Muslims in Vitez. Both sides began practicing ethnic cleansing on each other. Though Milosevic and Tudjman bear much responsibility for the Bosnian war, the struggle turned into a civil war, with most deaths caused by Bosnians killing fellow Bosnians.

Even after the outbreak of war in Bosnia, the Sarajevo government managed to reflect the pluralistic character of prewar Bosnian society. As late as February 1993, nearly one year after the outbreak of hostilities, the Bosnian cabinet still comprised nine Muslims, six Serbs, and five Croats. Moreover, Serbs formed fully one-third of the Territorial Defense Forces defending Sarajevo, and a Serb served as the deputy commander. The Croats, for their part, offered their own brigade for the defense of the city during the three years of fighting.[39] Many Sarajevans were still willing to risk their lives for their homes and for a multi-religious, multi-ethnic Bosnia. But such heroism of cross-communal cooperation happened too infrequently in Bosnia as extremists pushed the division of Bosnia into separate and ethnically homogenous territories.

Ethnic cleansing in Yugoslavia differed from the Holocaust of World War II. Nazi Germany sought to eliminate all Jews from Europe. In Yugoslavia, the aim was not to kill every member of a different community in a systematic fashion. Rather, the extremists sought to create homogeneous areas by eliciting mass flight. Select massacres of villages followed by propaganda to cause a major exodus proved a preferred method for achieving that goal. Still, hundreds of thousands perished in camps or were massacred in their towns or villages.

Though representing a minority, ethnic cleansers, with their rabid nationalism, played a dominant role in shaping the character of the Bosnian war. To survive in the lethal crossfire of militant nationalists, individuals and families from all three religious communities confronted difficult choices. Armed units in the countryside or towns became instruments of terror as they occupied new territory. They forced locals from their ethnic group to take up arms for the cause, or they found ready support awaiting them. Neighbors turned against neighbors. Many mixed marriages dissolved in the face of ethnic cleansing. Half of the prewar Bosnian population fled their homes. Those who stayed in the country often turned to their own respective communities for protection and survival and thus had to acquiesce to the demagoguery of their new leaders.[40]

Despite the experience of wars in Slovenia and Croatia, the world community failed to take any solid measures to prevent armed conflict in Bosnia. It was only three months after the commencement of fighting that the UN Security Council extended UNPROFOR's mission from Croatia to Bosnia under a separate command, at first headed by Lieutenant General Lewis MacKenzie, a Canadian. Initially, MacKenzie commanded four battalions with the main responsibility of keeping Sarajevo Airport open for humanitarian relief. In August, French General Philippe Morillon took command of a force that had grown to 7,000 and had bases in Sarajevo, Vitez, Mostar, Bihac, Kiseljak, and Banja Luka. Before its conclusion, UNPROFOR expanded to 38,000 troops from 37 countries. But the force was largely ineffective as the UN peacekeepers possessed very restrictive rules of engagement despite the mushrooming ethnic conflict around them.

The Bosnian war dragged on for three and a half years until December 1995. No side could claim to be the innocent victim, free of guilt. Each warring faction practiced ethnic cleansing to varying degrees and even staged attacks on its own civilian population with the aim of gaining propaganda advantage. Despite culpability on all sides, the Serbs certainly gained the most territory in the war and created the most refugees. They bear responsibility for the majority of ethnic cleansing. The US press, however, portrayed the Muslims as the victims and the Serbs as the guilty party. The Clinton administration, for its part, treated the Serb leadership, whether in Serbia or Bosnia, as the main stumbling block to a political solution. Many American officers, therefore, deployed to Bosnia with images of the Serbs as the "bad guys."

The Dayton Accords

The way the Bosnian war ended helped define the challenges facing US combat troops as they deployed as peacekeepers into Bosnia for the first time in December 1995. During the latter half of 1995, the Clinton administration gradually gained the political will to intervene militarily on the ground. Serious movement in this direction was evident by midsummer. A confluence of different factors helped make intervention a political necessity and militarily feasible.

By May 1995, Europe showed signs of greater resolve. In that month, Britain, France, and the Netherlands had formed the Allied Rapid Reaction Corps (ARRC), a multinational corps staff headquarters that included American officers as well. In particular, the UK committed 5,500 troops of the 24th Airmobile Brigade, France added 4,000 men and women, and the Dutch contributed 180. These were cohesive units, not the potpourri battalions of previous deployments.[41] On 21 July, the day the United Nations War Crimes Tribunal indicted Karadzic and Mladic, the North Atlantic Council authorized an air plan against the Serbs. Four days later, advance elements of heavy artillery of the ARRC deployed on Mount Igman overlooking Sarajevo and quickly engaged in a fire fight with Bosnian Serbs. An aggressive air and artillery operation suppressed Serb shelling of Sarajevo.

Meanwhile, new developments occurred on the ground. Washington had encouraged two of its retired generals, Carl E. Vuono and Crosbie E. Saint, to use their private corporation, Military Professional Resources Incorporated (MPRI), "to train and equip" the Croatian officer corps. This contracting firm helped shift the military balance to Croatia's favor at the expense of the Republika Srpska and ensured an escalation in the armed conflict. On 2 May 1995, the Croatian army launched OPERATION Spark against the small Serb enclave in western Slavonia and captured it in just three days of fighting.

Croatia's military victory sparked Bosnian and Croatian Serbs into action. While the Serbs in Knin moved against the Muslim pocket in Bihac, the Bosnian Serb army led by Mladic mounted an attack on the safe haven of Srebrenica in July. Mladic captured Srebrenica on 11 July 1995 before the watchful eyes of Dutch peacekeepers. His forces then proceeded to massacre 8,000 of the Muslim male population.[42] Buoyed by this victory, Mladic next captured the town of Zepa. Meanwhile,

Bosnian and Croatian Serb forces attacked Bihac in a pincer move from Knin and Banja Luka.

These Serb gains posed a serious threat to Croatia and to the other two warring factions. On 22 July, Tudjman and Izetbegovic signed an agreement to launch a combined military operation against the Serbs. Bosnian Croats and Muslims were also willing to join forces. They had already formed a union, with US pressure, called the Federation of Bosnia and Herzegovina one year earlier, on 1 March 1994.

Croatia commenced OPERATION Storm with 10,000 troops assaulting Knin on 3 August 1995, while the Bosnian Croatian and Muslim armies attacked Serb positions in Bosnia. In three days, the Croatian army captured the Knin region and then proceeded against Bihac in cooperation with Muslim and Croat forces moving from the southwest and center of Bosnia. A NATO air campaign led by the US against the Bosnian Serbs supported ground operations. During the coordinated ground and air campaigns, approximately 150,000 Serbs fled from Knin, Bihac, Drvar, Mrkonjic Grad, and Jajce. This ethnic cleansing perpetrated against the Serbs failed to attract much notice or sympathy in the US. Clinton and the media already had branded the Serbs as the bad guys and Muslims as the victims. Hard facts on the ground would not change that reporting, especially after the horrors in Srebrenica.

Then on 28 August, a mortar round, though some have argued it was a well-placed bomb, hit the Sarajevo market place, killing 37 civilians. The US blamed the Serbs for this atrocity, though some experts have speculated the ordnance was actually a bomb that could have been placed in the marketplace by the Muslims. Washington took this act as a direct affront to its emerging policy in Bosnia.[43] It implemented a month-long bombing campaign that signaled the beginning of new American resolve. NATO launched OPERATION Deliberate Force on 30 August, a day that saw 13 Tomahawk cruise missiles destroy the Bosnian Serb army's command center near Banja Luka. This air campaign lasted three weeks, until 20 September. Eight countries flew 3,515 sorties, with the US contributing two-thirds of the flights. Meanwhile, Croatia and the Muslim-Croat Federation pushed the Serbs out of Bihac and threatened Banja Luka.

In the end, the Bosnian Serb offensives of July 1995 had misfired strategically. Rather than changing the regional balance of power in the Serb favor, they had the opposite effect. The land offensives by the armies of Croatia and the Federation, bolstered by NATO air, had resulted in substantial territorial losses for the Bosnian Serbs. Moreover, the pattern of defeat suggested a major crisis for the Pale leadership: army desertions continued as a major problem, and some units had abandoned positions without a fight. The Republika Srpska now faced the possibility of further reverses if Karadzic did not cut a political deal. Karadzic and Mladic had gravely miscalculated the world's reaction of general condemnation and revulsion to the massacres at Srebrenica. Further isolated from the world community, the Republika Srpska could look only to Milosevic for help.[44]

With his back to the wall, Karadzic expressed a willingness to negotiate a deal that gave the Bosnian Serbs half of Bosnia. Milosevic, for his part, had come to regard Karadzic, Mladic, and the Bosnian Serbs as liabilities. His own priorities were to end the UN embargo on Yugoslavia and to ingratiate himself with the international community. To achieve these two goals, Milosevic saw an opportunity to play the role of a statesman. For its part, Washington was willing to deal with the "bad guy" in Belgrade. Tudjman, for his part, wanted to gain eastern Slavonia and was willing to compromise on Bosnia.

The Clinton administration thus saw a more favorable strategic situation that warranted bringing negotiations to Dayton, Ohio. After

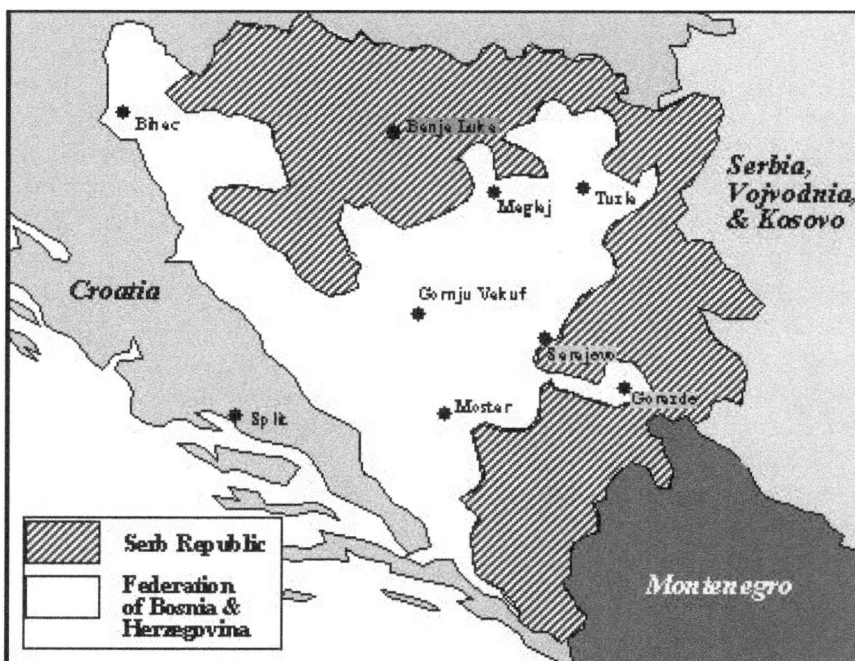

Map 7. Dayton Agreement Map

several weeks of haggling, a historic agreement was finally reached on 20 November. Then, on 14 December all the key players signed the General Framework Agreement for Peace (GFAP). For US ground troops deploying to Bosnia, what was most important was that the Bosnian war had culminated. Militarily, all three warring factions were exhausted with the onset of winter. Little fight was left in the practitioners of ethnic cleansing. Politically, all three warring factions faced diplomatic isolation should they desire to continue their internecine warfare. At Dayton, Tudjman gained eastern Slavonia; Milosevic received the promise of an end to the UN embargo against his country if he coerced the Bosnian Serbs into complying. Croatia and Serbia were ready for an end to hostilities and were willing to pressure their constituencies in Bosnia to cooperate. The Clinton administration and the EC had gained the political will to tackle the Bosnian problem. Most important, Washington had finally decided to commit ground troops. Now, American prestige was at stake with the Dayton Accords.

Conclusion

Bosnia witnessed two periods of major ethnic cleansing in the 20th century, but these two events were aberrations in Bosnian history and not the result of ancient tribal hatreds. In both cases, foreign meddling helped initiate hostilities. World War II saw Nazi Germany and Fascist Italy bring the Ustashe to power; some fifty years later, the Bosnian war witnessed Zagreb and Belgrade arming and directing co-nationals in pursuit of territorial aggrandizement. Each conflict thus degenerated into an ugly civil war in Bosnia as neighbors killed neighbors. To further their aims, militant nationalists on all sides distorted the past to justify ethnic cleansing. They emphasized the worst aspects of history to the point where even people in the Balkans came to believe in communal hatreds as the motive force of Balkan history for centuries. Tragically, many individuals acted on this myth as reality.

Yet, the truth is that despite a history of wars and rebellions as in other parts of Europe, for five centuries, Serbs, Croats, and Bosniacs, or Orthodox, Catholics, and Muslims had learned to coexist in Bosnia. A vast majority of the inhabitants descended from the Slavs who settled the region in the medieval period. Moreover, a single language fostered social dialogue across religious lines. Finally, Habsburg rule integrated Bosnia into the mainstream of Central Europe, helping Westernize and secularize the Muslim population, a process that continued from 1918 to 1992. Despite the ethnic cleansing of World War II, the Communist era of 45 years saw a high percentage of marriages across religious lines. This example alone should offer hope and purpose for American peacekeepers in Bosnia.

As the US Army prepared to cross the Sava River into Bosnia, the strategic situation favored the American deployment. The warring factions were exhausted after three and a half years of fighting and inclined to hibernate for the winter. The Bosnian Croats and Muslims had made territorial gains changing the balance of power in Bosnia, but they lacked the means to continue without foreign backing. The Bosnian Serbs, on the other hand, lacked offensive punch to regain lost ground. More important, both Belgrade and Zagreb were convinced of the need to halt the fighting. Milosevic and Tudjman thus left their Bosnian co-nationals diplomatically isolated and vulnerable to NATO's military wrath. In the community of nations, Dayton legitimized the US Army joining the peacekeeping mission with all the concerned parties. Over 30 nations with close to 38,000 troops were already poised in Bosnia to assist the Americans in implementing the new mandate. In many ways, the US Army was set up for success. But American troops still faced the challenge of taking advantage of this favorable confluence of factors, and they rose to the occasion to fulfill their mission admirably.

Notes

1. Carl von Clausewitz, *On War*, edited and translated by Michael Howard and Peter Paret (Princeton, NJ: Princeton University Press, 1984), 88-89.

2. This statement comes from a British after-action report dated 4 April 1997. I am unable to locate the citation.

3. Robert Kaplan, *Balkan Ghosts: A Journey through History* (New York: St. Martin's Press, 1993). A similar view appears in the now classic by Rebecca West, *Black Lamb and Grey Falcon: A Journey through Yugoslavia* (New York: Viking Press, 1941).

4. Many Slovenes and Croatians today see themselves as part of central Europe and would reject placing their respective countries in the Balkans.

5. The best general history of Bosnia is Noel Malcolm, *Bosnia: A Short History* (New York: New York University Press, 1996). For a better appreciation of Bosnian history, it is important to gain some familiarity with Croatian and Serbian histories as well. See Tim Judah, *The Serbs: History, Myth, and the Destruction of Yugoslavia* (New Haven, CT: Yale University Press, 1997) and Marcus Tanner, *Croatia: A Nation Forged in War* (New Haven, CT: Yale University Press, 1997).

6. John V. A. Fine, *The Bosnian Church: A New Interpretation* (Boulder, CO: Westview Press, 1975); Malcolm, *Bosnia*, 27-42.

7. Charles and Barbara Jelavich, *The Establishment of the Balkan National States, 1804-1920* (Seattle: University of Washington Press, 1977), 3-25.

8. Malcolm, *Bosnia*: 43-136; John V. A. Fine, "The Medieval and Ottoman Roots of Modern Bosnian society," in *The Muslims of Bosnia-Hercegovina*, edited by Mark Pinson (Cambridge, MA: Harvard University Press, 1993), 15-21; Colin Heywood, "Bosnia under Ottoman Rule, 1463-1800," in ibid., 22-53; W. G. Lockwood, "Living Legacy of the Ottoman Empire: The Serbo-Croatian Speaking Moslems of Bosnia-Hercegovina," in *The Mutual Effects of the Islamic and Judeo-Christian Worlds: The East European Pattern*, edited by Abraham Ascher (New York: Brooklyn College Press, 1979), 211-215.

9. Richard Holbrooke, *To End a War* (New York: Random House, 1998), 232.

10. Ivo Andric, *The Bridge on the Drina*, translated by Lovett F. Edwards (Chicago: The University of Chicago, 1977), 283.

11. Andric, *Bridge on the Drina*, 87.

12. Malcolm, *Bosnia*, 132-135.

13. Ibid., 136-155; Jelavich, *Establishment of the Balkan National States*, 141-157; Justin McCarthy, "Ottoman Bosnia, 1800 to 1878," in *Muslims in Bosnia-Hercegovina*, edited by Mark Pinson, 78-82; Mark Pinson, "The Muslims of Bosnia-Hercegovina Under Austro-Hungarian Rule, 1878-1918," in ibid., 84-128; Robert Donia, *Islam Under the Double Eagle: The Muslims of Bosnia and Hercegovina, 1878-1914* (New York: Columbia Press, 1981); and Francine Friedman, *The Bosnian Muslims: Denial of a Nation* (Boulder, CO: Westview Press, 1996), 57-87.

14. McCarthy, "Ottoman Bosnia, 1800 to 1878," 81-82.

15. For a discussion of World War I and Yugoslavia between the two world wars, see Ivo Banac, *The National Question in Yugoslavia: Origins, History and Politics* (Ithaca, NY: Cornell University Press, 1984); Robert Donia and John V.A. Fine, *Bosnia and Hercegovina: A Tradition Betrayed* (New York: Columbia University Press, 1994), 120-135; Joseph Rothschild, *East Central Europe between the Two World Wars* (Seattle: University of Washington Press, 1974), 201-280; Wayne S. Vucinich, "Interwar Yugoslavia," in *Contemporary Yugoslavia*, edited by Wayne S. Vucinich (Berkeley, CA: California University Press, 1969), 3-58.

16. Rothschild, *East Central Europe between the Two World Wars*, 278-79.

17. Malcolm, *Bosnia*, 165-66.

18. Ibid., 168.

19. For material on Yugoslavia in general, and Bosnia in particular, during World War II, see Jozo Tomasevich, *War and Revolution in Yugoslavia: The Chetniks* (Stanford, CA: Stanford University Press, 1975); Walter Roberts, *Tito, Mihailovic, and the Allies* (New Brunswick, NJ: Rutgers University Press, 1973); Milovan Djilas, *Wartime* (New York: Harcourt, 1977); Donia and Fine, *Bosnia and Hercegovina*, 136-56; Malcolm, *Bosnia*, 174-92; Tanner, *Croatia*, 141-67.

20. Malcolm, *Bosnia*, 174.

21. Tanner, *Croatia*, 148-49.

22. Donia and Fine, *Bosnia and Hercegovina*, 152.

23. For the Tito era, see Donia and Fine, *Bosnia and Hercegovina*, 157-93; Malcolm, *Bosnia*, 193-212; Sabrina P. Ramet, *Nationalism and Federalism in Yugoslavia, 1967-1991*, 2nd ed (Bloomington, IN: Indiana University Press, 1992).

24. Misha Glenny, *The Balkans: Nationalism, War and the Great Powers, 1804-1999* (New York: Viking, 1999), 591.

25. Glenny, *The Balkans*, 574.

26. Malcolm, *Bosnia*, 196.

27. Ibid., 197.

28. Ibid., 197-98.

29. Donia and Fine, *Bosnia and Hercegovina*, 6.

30. George W. Gawrych, discussions with officers from Bosnia, Slovenia, Croatia, and Macedonia attending the US Army Command and General Staff College, Fort Leavenworth, KS, 1996-2001; George W. Gawrych, discussions with Bosnians in Bosnia, April 2000 and July 2001.

31. Numerous publications have appeared explaining the disintegration of Yugoslavia: see Susan Woodward, *Balkan Tragedy: Chaos and Dissolution after the Cold War* (Washington, DC: The Brookings Institute, 1995); Leonard J. Cohen, *Broken Bonds: Yugoslavia's Disintegration and Balkan Politics in Transition*, 2nd ed (Boulder, CO: Westview, 1995); Warren Zimmerman, *The Origins of a Catastrophe* (New York: Random House, 1996); Christopher Bennett, *Yugoslavia's Bloody Collapse: Causes, Course and Consequences* (New York: New York University Press, 1995); Laura Silber and Allan Little, *Yugoslavia: Death of a Nation* (New York: Penguin, 1996); Misha Glenny, *The*

Fall of Yugoslavia: The Third Balkan War, 3rd edition (New York: Penguin, 1996): Donia and Fine, *Bosnia and Hercegovina*, 194-219.

32. Glenny, *The Balkans*, 623.

33. James Gow, *Triumph of the Lack of Will* (New York: Columbia University Press, 1997), 26.

34. Zoran Cirjakovic, "What It's Like Being a Serb," *Newsweek*, 19 October 1998, 3.

35. Tanner, *Croatia*, 223 ff.

36. Donia and Fine, *Bosnia and Hercegovina*, 220-80; Carole Rogel, *The Break-up of Yugoslavia and the War in Bosnia* (Westport, CT: Greenwood Press, 1998); Malcolm, *Bosnia*, 213-71.

37. Gow, *Triumph of the Lack of Will*, 85-88.

38. Steven L. Burg and Paul S. Shoup, *The War in Bosnia-Herzegovina: Ethnic Conflict and International Intervention* (Armonk, NY: M. E. Sharpe, 1999), 178-80.

39. Donia and Fine, *Bosnia and Hercegovina*, 9. For excellent firsthand account of Sarajevo's resistance, see Roger Cohen, *Hearts Grown Brutal: Sagas of Sarajevo* (New York: Random House, 1998).

40. For a brief but excellent treatment of the character of this war, see Woodward, *Balkan Tragedy*, 223-72.

41. Gow, *Triumph of the Lack of Will*, 266.

42. For the tragedy of Srebrenica see David Rhode, *Endgame: The Betrayal and Fall of Srebrenica, Europe's Worst Massacre Since World War II* (New York: Farrar, Straus and Giroux, 1997).

43. Richard Holbrooke, *To End a War* (New York: Random House, 1998), 93.

44. Norman Cigar, "Serb War Effort and Termination of the War," in the *War in Croatia and Bosnia-Herzegovina, 1991-1995*, edited by Branka Magas and Ivo Zanic (London: Frank Cass, 2001), 200-235.

Chapter 2

From UNPROFOR to IFOR

Robert F. Baumann

Amid the chaotic and bloody disintegration of Yugoslavia, the UN Protection Force (UNPROFOR) episode was at once both a noble endeavor and a monument to the futility of United Nations peacekeeping in the early 1990s. To Americans, especially as US troops prepared to deploy to Bosnia as part of the Dayton Implementation Force, better known as IFOR, UNPROFOR's principal relevance was that it demonstrated exactly how not to conduct a military intervention in the midst of civil war and humanitarian crisis. Although UNPROFOR strength in Bosnia and Herzegovina reached 38,000 in 1994, it was weaker than even its inadequate numbers implied.[1] Its largest combat elements were battalions, and each of these answered to a different national chain of command. Moreover, UNPROFOR lacked the authority and all too often the firepower to use force in a proactive manner. The lessons that American observers drew from the experience found realization in December 1995 as Task Force *Eagle* crossed the Sava River. Spearheaded by the 1st Armored Division, the US contingent arrived with overwhelming force.

Colonel Greg Fontenot, who commanded the 1st Brigade, 1st Armored Division, later noted, "IFOR was not a peacekeeping force. It was an implementation force that specifically had the authority to compel compliance with the treaty."[2] In short, IFOR brought with it the military strength and an explicit mandate to employ force as necessary to achieve the goals set forth in the General Framework Agreement for Peace (GFAP) achieved at Dayton, Ohio during the preceding month. This conferred on Fontenot and his colleagues an inestimable advantage over their UNPROFOR predecessors—a clear purpose and the means to achieve it.

However unfairly, UNPROFOR by contrast served as the poster child for international vacillation and the failure to match means and methods to political objectives. Although not a formal participant in UNPROFOR, the United States contributed to the climate of indecision that attended UNPROFOR operations and the UN decision-making process. In succession, the George Bush and Bill Clinton administrations loudly condemned the mounting brutality in Bosnia but sought to steer clear of involving the US military. Of the two, Bush was the more skeptical about the wisdom of potential American involvement. Summarizing the president's thinking, former Secretary of State James Baker reflected, "the Bush administration felt comfortable with the EC's [European Community] taking responsibility for the crisis in the Balkans....Most important, unlike in the Persian Gulf, our vital interests were not at stake."[3] Having so recently authored the closing chapter of the Cold War and forged a grand alliance to liberate Kuwait, President Bush simply did not believe that Bosnia was America's problem to solve.

When President Clinton assumed office in January 1993, he carried with him the baggage of the electoral campaign, during which he suggested that the United States could do more. In a strikingly similar fashion, he had issued a public challenge to the distinctly nonactivist Bush policy toward Haiti, where the elected government of Jean Bertrand Aristide had been overthrown. However, in constructing his own policies upon beginning his presidency, Clinton straddled the fence. While publicly committed to a more assertive policy in both cases, he was nonetheless by nature disinclined to employ military force. Ultimately, in both Haiti and Bosnia, the president found that he could not avoid the military option. Meanwhile, Clinton's key advisers were deeply divided as to the proper course of action. Warren Zimmermann, the last US Ambassador to Yugoslavia, described the mixed messages emanating from the White House: "Depending on the degree of American activism desired at the time, Bosnia was variously described as a US strategic concern and a test for the post-cold war world and for American leadership, or else as a civil war, the result of ancient hatreds, and an issue for the Europeans. Everybody, however, could agree with Secretary [Warren] Christopher's characterization of it as a 'problem from hell.'"[4]

To be sure, US politicians received no encouragement from the military to undertake a Balkans mission. Opinion in the US Army reflected minimal enthusiasm, and General Colin Powell, chairman of the Joint Chiefs, urged the president not to commit US forces to a difficult, open-ended mission.[5] Indeed, events gave credence to his assertion. From the outbreak of war in Bosnia in 1992 to the truce negotiated by former president Jimmy Carter in December 1994, not less than 13 cease-fires were agreed upon and broken.[6] Still, in the eyes of Ambassador Warren Zimmermann and others, American policy was paralyzed by a lingering "Vietnam syndrome," which prevented recognition of the essential relevance of Bosnia to the global leadership role of the United States and its position as a moral champion. Among those in agreement was former Secretary of State George Shultz, who asserted "America's most basic interests required the use of force on behalf of the Bosnians."[7]

38

In any event, the European Community and the United Nations proceeded to act in the absence of US leadership or participation. UNPROFOR began as an attempt to curb wanton atrocities during the war between Serbia and Croatia with a headquarters established in still-peaceful Sarajevo. On 21 February 1992, United Nations Security Council Resolution 743 created UNPOROFOR to secure three designated protected areas in Croatia. In short order, the waning war between Serbia and Croatia gave way to an equally brutal struggle over control of ethnically mixed territories in Bosnia. This resulted in an expansion of the UNPROFOR mandate. The cascading events reached a crescendo with a 29 February Referendum on Bosnian independence followed on 7 April by a formal decision of the European Community to recognize the new state of Bosnia-Herzegovina (BiH). The self-proclaimed Assembly of the Serbian Nation of Bosnia-Herzegovina promptly answered by declaring an independent Bosnian Serb Republic, which later became the Republika Srpska or RS (though within different borders).

On 30 April, UNPROFOR moved 40 military observers from Croatia to the Mostar region, where violence soon reached such intensity that they were withdrawn after only two weeks. At about the same time, a majority of UNPROFOR personnel in the Sarajevo headquarters pulled out as well. As was often the case in Bosnia, a well-publicized episode of violence punctuated the steady descent into chaos and focused international resolve to act. A day after Serb shelling of Sarajevo killed dozens of civilians on 27 May, the UN Security Council imposed economic sanctions on what remained of Yugoslavia–Serbia and Montenegro. The UNPROFOR commander in Sarajevo, Canadian Major General Lewis MacKenzie, subsequently succeeded in negotiating a cease-fire that enabled UNPROFOR soldiers to assume control of airport operations there. During the brief lull in the action around the Bosnian capital, other areas of the country burst into flames.

The resultant escalation of violence led in turn to a 14 September UN decision authorizing UNPROFOR to provide security in support of the distribution of humanitarian aid in Bosnia. UNPROFOR subsequently divided BiH into five zones, with a battalion allocated to each. A further step on October 9 was UN Security Council Resolution 776 to ban military flights (other than UNPROFOR) over Bosnia. UNPROFOR's tasks thus included ensuring the safe arrival of aid flights into Sarajevo, monitoring the pullback of heavy weapons from around the Bosnian capital, and preserving freedom of movement for aid convoys sponsored by the international community. On 17 April 1993, UNPROFOR troops assumed yet another task, the demilitarization of the newly proclaimed "safe area" around the beleaguered town of Srebrenica. Similar designation as "safe areas" soon followed for Tuzla, Zepa, Gorazde, Bihac, and Sarajevo. This decision, which signified a major increase in UNPROFOR obligations without commensurate means or resolve, was to prove a source of profound complexity and embarrassment as the mission continued. In this context, even a NATO agreement as of February 1994 to provide air strikes on UNPROFOR's behalf would not have a decisive impact. By 30 November 1994, total UNPROFOR strength reached 38,810, but this figure did not represent concentrated combat potential. Rather, it was a multinational hodgepodge of separate small units, nominally under UN control but in reality answering to different national chains of command. Additional civilian personnel deployed in support of the mission included 727 policemen and 1,870 staffers. UNPROFOR was thus the largest peacekeeping mission in UN history.[8]

Over several years, despite valiant efforts to broker truces and coordinate the free passage of humanitarian aid to besieged areas, UN peacekeepers found that each step forward was greeted by one step backward somewhere else in Bosnia. Because of the fact that none of the three major ethnic groups operated as a political-military united front, negotiations remained endlessly complex, and agreements rarely stood for more than a few months. Often the equivalent of local warlords acted independently. Intrigue, deception, and ever-shifting alliances reflected the agendas of the moment. On one occasion in 1994, following a meeting with the leader of the Serbian extremist SDS party, Radovan Karadzic, Soviet envoy Anatoli Churkin reported to Major General Sir Michael Rose that "he had never been lied to so blatantly as he had been by the Bosnian Serbs."[9] A commerce of death flourished as factions often sold arms to one another. Many self-styled militias, even criminal gangs, participated in the fighting.[10]

The main trouble for UNPROFOR, uncooperative warring factions aside, emanated from the very terms of its mandate. Unfortunately, that mandate enabled UNPROFOR soldiers to deter attacks on civilians but not to employ force except in self-defense. Denied the right to use military force in a proactive manner in support of international objectives, UNPROFOR lacked the leverage to enforce a peace that, in any case, did not exist. Even had it chosen to coerce the factions into compliance, most peacekeeping units would have found themselves outgunned by the warring factions. Consequently, they were subject to innumerable indignities—harassment by snipers, seizure as hostages, and general abuse. According to one internal assessment of the UNPROFOR mission in 1993, in order to enforce or restore a peace, UNPROFOR "must have

Photo 1. The village of Srebrenica became infamous
for the events that occurred nearby in 1995

the means, and authority to use such means, to: 1) credibly demonstrate its resolve; 2) mount a credible show of force; and 3) have the means to effectively protect those it has been tasked to protect against forces equipped with tanks and artillery."[11]

The factions, especially the Bosnian Serbs, routinely obstructed the movement of aid and even the peacekeepers themselves. The brutal and obstinate behavior of Bosnian Serb forces, which had a predominant position on the ground across most of Bosnia, helped fuel a widespread perception outside of Bosnia that they were "the problem." A particularly bitter irony lay in the fact that a majority of UNPROFOR casualties were believed to have been inflicted by Muslims, and secondarily Croatians, the very populations whose protection was initially deemed most urgent.[12] The rationale for such attacks, based on the assumption that blame would fall on the Bosnian Serbs, may have been to galvanize a more forceful and robust UNPROFOR intervention or even involvement by NATO. Evidence also began to accumulate that the Muslim Bosniacs at times fired on their own people in the belief that the foreign media would blame the Serbs.[13]

Occasionally, acts against peacekeepers reflected a clear political motivation. In a particularly troublesome instance, a British Royal Marine working with the United Nations High Commissioner for Refugees (UNHCR) in Sarajevo was killed by Bosnian Muslim police for allegedly resisting arrest.[14] This grim circumstance no doubt contributed significantly to a diminishing tendency among peacekeepers themselves to view the Serbs as the undisputed "bad guys" of the conflict. The Serbs, though openly belligerent, were at least predictable. British Major General Rose, UNPROFOR commander in Bosnia from January 1994 to January 1995, publicly voiced concerns that Bosnian Muslims were manipulating international policymakers.

In general, Rose did his best to champion the UN commitment to neutrality, a position that occasionally put him at odds with the view taken by NATO, to which his own country belonged. As he strained to maintain the lifeline to Sarajevo during the trying summer of 1994, Rose had to deal firmly with both factions. Following a Serb attack on a British convoy on the vital Mount Igman road on 27July, Rose requested air strikes on Serb positions, even if such action required the withdrawal of UN forces to proceed. Conversely, when forces of the Bosnian government used heavy artillery to fire on Serb troops situated within the designated heavy weapons exclusion zone, the British general cautioned that air strikes could be launched against either side. In an attempt to stabilize the situation, Rose offered to place UN peacekeepers between the factions around Sarajevo. In this instance, the BiH government proved reluctant out of fear that such a dividing line might achieve permanence out of political expediency.[15]

The widening gap between appearances and reality in Bosnia led to widespread suspicion, for example, that the Muslim faction would on occasion shell its own people and blame the Serbs so as to retain an edge in the battle for international sympathy. The role of global media, above all CNN, in transmitting powerful images and impressions made them a prime target of faction psychological operations. From the start, Western governments felt acute public pressure to respond to the inhumanity of the Bosnian war. The nature and timing of those responses—from air strikes to new diplomatic initiatives—often reflected outrage over the latest depredations. On several notable occasions, published reports of the scale of Muslim civilian casualties proved quite exaggerated.[16] Not infrequently, the news transmitted from Bosnia reflected a conviction in the press corps that the world had to act to stem the tide of atrocities. Certainly, reports of wholesale executions and ethnic cleansing, normally well founded, contributed mightily to the sense of urgency. For their part, some journalists in Sarajevo grew to believe that UNPROFOR personnel turned a blind eye to the desperate plight of the civilian population there.[17]

Perhaps the ultimate manifestation of the "truth problem" was the controversy that lasts to this day over who actually fired the infamous 28 August 1995 mortar rounds that killed 37 civilians in Sarajevo's Markala market. The incident—generally blamed on the Serbs at the time—played a major role in bringing the United States more fully into the diplomatic process that led directly to the deployment of American troops to Bosnia as part of IFOR for the purpose of shaping international opinion and the diplomatic environment. In any case, of five rounds that detonated in the marketplace, four were clearly determined by subsequent crater analysis to have originated from Serbian positions. The trajectory of the fifth, however, could not be determined to the mutual satisfaction of experts on the scene. This may have been the result of a ricochet off of a building or some other circumstance. According to Canadian Colonel Rick Hatton, who oversaw the crater analysis, the correct and professional assessment was that the Bosnian Serbs were responsible.[18] However, some others, including several British and French officers, suggested that Muslim forces were probably responsible for the final explosion. Hatton believed that there was no evidentiary basis for this conclusion, although he freely acknowledged that Muslim forces had not been beyond resort to such subterfuge on other occasions.[19]

In any case, NATO and the UN soon weighed in officially that the Serbs were in fact responsible. Controversy continued, however, when Russian Colonel Andrei Demurenko, himself an artilleryman serving with UNPROFOR, publicly disputed the finding.[20] His contention was not that the Muslims fired on their own people, but merely that no definitive conclusion was possible. Ultimately, this critical variance of opinion inevitably gave rise to a perception in some circles that the finding itself had been influenced by policy makers seeking to take a firmer hand of the situation.

Overall, given their predicament, UNPROFOR soldiers comported themselves well and laid claim to remarkable achievements as well as tragic failures. The thousands of lives saved in Bosnia by virtue of their efforts came at a severe price to the peacekeepers themselves. Over 200 peacekeepers, the largest share French, were casualties during the war. That they were so often placed in an untenable situation was a source of endless frustration for UNPROFOR veterans. In fairness, according to Colonel Hatton, Canada's director of Peacekeeping Policy from 1996 to 1999, the problem lay not only with the flawed mandate but with the failure of the international community to provide all necessary resources, especially soldiers, to support mission requirements.[21] Indeed, the mission to Bosnia-Herzegovina was funded not by the United Nations but by the eight troop-contributing nations. Predictably, perhaps, each contingent tended to some degree toward a "lassez-faire" approach in which national priorities took precedence over the concerns of UNPROFOR. The failure to establish any semblance of unity of command brought with it assorted negative consequences. The following two cases make the point although there are numerous others. For example, the Canadians were upset in 1993 when French forces unilaterally withdrew soldiers from the town of Pancevo, thereby forcing a major reordering of Canadian logistics plans.[22] Similarly, in the aftermath of the 5 February 1994 shelling of the market square in Sarajevo, a Russian battalion commander flatly declined to redeploy to the Bosnian capital when so ordered by an UNPROFOR general.[23]

No mission requirement posed greater difficulties than the protection of so-called safe areas. Though eventually perceived as a creation of the United Nations, the safe area concept originated (at least in the public arena) with Cornelio Sommaruga, president of the International Committee of the Red Cross headquartered in Geneva, Switzerland. However, he found little support aside from the Dutch government for the notion in 1992, at which time neither the UN nor the major states contributing to UNPROFOR regarded it as practical. At that time, in the view of most observers, the best hope for peace remained the initiative led by Lord Owen and Cyrus Vance, who co-chaired the International Conference on the Former Yugoslavia. Each had deep misgivings about the implications of establishing safe areas. For example, the creation of such areas by definition labeled all remaining territory as unsafe. In addition, if the Muslim population, considered the chief potential beneficiaries of the plan at the time, acted on this perception and migrated in vast numbers to safe areas, the entire scheme would actually facilitate the objective of Serb extremists to establish ethnically pure territories.[24]

Deep into 1993, the picture changed as fighting around Srebrenica captured the international spotlight. As initially conceived in Security Council Resolution 819 of April 16, 1993, the intent was to establish zones "free from armed attacks and from any other hostile acts that would endanger the well-being and the safety of their inhabitants and where the unimpeded delivery of humanitarian assistance to the civilian population." Subsequently, resolution 836 spelled out the UNPROFOR role: "to deter attacks against the areas, to monitor the cease-fire, to promote the withdrawal of military or paramilitary units other than those of the Bosnian Government and to occupy some key points on the ground, in addition to participating in the delivery of humanitarian relief." To facilitate these tasks, the resolution authorized UNPROFOR to take all necessary defensive measures, including the use of force in response to bombardments, armed incursion, or deliberate obstruction of the freedom of movement of UNPROFOR or escorted relief convoys.[25] In addition to Srebrenica, the safe area concept was extended to Sarajevo, Tuzla, Bihac, Gorazde, and Zepa.

Some of those charged with providing security for the UN safe areas harbored grave misgivings from the start. British Colonel P. G. Williams, who commanded the 1st Battalion Coldstream Guards in Bosnia from November 1993 to May 1994 (well before the tragic fall of Srebrenica) contended upon his return to his home base that "the UN has never been in the position to provide inhabitants of its designated Safe Areas with the security the concept appears to imply." Having observed UNPROFOR's great difficulty in finding a willing party to assume control of Srebrenica from the Canadian battalion, Williams was grateful that circumstances had dictated that this particular mission would not fall to a British unit. Indeed, the very selection of units, over which the local factions, the Serbs in this case, had considerable say, betrayed the weakness of the concept. As it turned out, the Bosnian Serbs would not accept any British unit that came with the highly capable Warrior or Scimitar armored fighting vehicles. In other words, they would not give their consent to the presence of any contingent that might effectively contest their control. Lacking sufficient combat power, UNPROFOR units in safe areas could not even ensure their own lines of communication. According to Williams, "[they] were, and remain, under effective control of the BSA [Bosnian Serb Army] where movement in and out, equipment approval and roulement are concerned.

Handing one's men over to become in effect little better than hostages is an unenviable task..."[26]

In a 1 December 1994 report to the United Nations Security Council, the secretary general not only acknowledged widespread difficulties experienced by UNPROFOR in securing the safe areas, but also offered a substantive analysis and tentative conclusions. Foremost among his concerns was the dilemma posed by the Bosnian safe areas of Zepa, Gorazde, and Srebrenica. First of all, the secretary general acknowledged that the safe areas were not in fact "safe." Worse yet, as demonstrated in the case of Gorazde, the presence of many Muslim fighters in the presumed sanctuaries jeopardized the perceived impartiality of UNPROFOR peacekeepers. As noted in the secretary general's report, "After the first use of air power at Gorazde, the Bosnian Serbs regarded UNPROFOR as having intervened on behalf of their opponents." This circumstance resulted in increased obstruction of humanitarian relief convoys by the besieging Serb forces, a form of retaliation that struck at the heart of the UNPROFOR mandate.[27] In addition, it was proof positive of UNPROFOR's lack of leverage with the armed factions. Interruptions of fuel deliveries crippled the peacekeepers' ability to continue patrolling in the vicinities of Zepa, Gorazde, and Srebrenica. During an uneasy cease-fire in a 3-kilometer exclusion zone around Gorazde, UNPROFOR personnel found their movement restricted by both sides (Serbs and Muslims) and were frequently the targets of sniper fire.[28]

A further complication was that not infrequently the predominantly Muslim Army of Bosnia and Herzegovina operated from headquarters located within designated safe areas. Such was the case, for example, in Bihac, which provided a haven for the command of the Fifth Corps. In fact, attacks on Serb positions occasionally launched from within safe areas, thereby conferring on those locations real tactical military significance. Even if inactive, government troops could exploit the safe areas for temporary sanctuary and a chance to maintain their equipment and prepare for future action. Consequently, the United Nations occasionally appeared to be in *de facto* alliance with the BiH government. Under such conditions, it could hardly have been surprising that Bosnian Serb forces saw little reason to exercise restraint. Thus, in November 1993, having withstood an October offensive launched from the Bihac pocket, Krajina Serb forces did not hold back. They shelled the safe area and bombed it from the air. Even the threat of NATO air strikes, bound by the principle of "proportional application of force," had relatively little deterrent effect. Only tactical strikes against positively identified targets known to have violated cease-fire agreements were permissible. The strategic use of air power so as to curb the factions' capabilities or force broad policy change was not authorized. In any case, the full employment of air power faced practical constraints. In particular, the challenging terrain and climate of the Balkans offered abundant cover and concealment.

Sometimes the most useful step taken by UNPROFOR soldiers on the ground was simply to get out of the way. For instance, British Major General Rupert Smith found in 1995 that the withdrawal of military observers from Gorazde paved the way for effective NATO air strikes.[29] In general, peacekeepers were necessary to coordinate the movement of aid, and their presence in communities was regarded as insurance against wholesale acts of slaughter by entity armed forces (most often but not always Serb). Yet, they could be pawns as well in the hands of aggressors. Thus, despite NATO retaliatory air attacks against Serb airfields and missile sites on 18-19 and 21-23 November 1993, the situation actually deteriorated. The Bosnian Serbs immediately curbed UNPROFOR movement in the Sarajevo area, closed checkpoints to UNPROFOR and humanitarian aid traffic, and seized about 250 peacekeepers for use as human shields at selected weapons collection points. Bosnian Serbs proved adept at moving and disguising their heavy weapons, thereby denying pilots the confirmation of targets that their rules of engagement demanded.[30] In similar fashion, following a 25 May 1995 air raid against Serb bunkers at an ammunition storage site near Pale, angry Serb forces seized UN soldiers and chained them as human shields at key weapon sites. The move temporarily paralyzed NATO air power and laid bare the dilemma that the force necessary to compel Serb compliance would inevitably exact a toll on its users that they were not yet politically prepared to pay. This circumstance created tension between the United States and other hawkish elements in NATO on one hand and Rose and other proponents of the UN approach on the other.

In the absence of consensus, restrictive rules of engagement made the timely use of air strikes—which required the approval both of the Yasushi Akashi, the secretary general's special representative to the Former Yugoslavia, and NATO as well—highly problematic. Only rarely could the key actors in such decisions reach an accord. For example, in May 1995 Major General Smith requested air strikes to enforce the heavy weapons exclusion zone but could not gain the support either of his superior, French General Bernard Janvier, or of Akashi based on apprehension that such actions would have an "escalatory" effect.[31]

The inertia of such logic could not be overcome. Summarizing the 1995 failure to use air power effectively to save Srebrenica, author David Rhode stated, "Akashi and Janvier consistently upheld the view that NATO air power was a blunt, dangerous and generally ineffective tool that enraged Bosnian Serbs and put peacekeepers at risk."[32] Consequently, UNPROFOR peacekeepers unfairly bore the brunt of international criticism in instances when they could not effectively protect cities such as Gorazde or Srebrenica. As General Rose put it concerning Gorazde, "I vaguely wondered if Siladzic, Izetbegovic and their supporters in the international press actually believed that the UN, which was doing the most in Bosnia to bring about peace, was responsible for the slaughter. I concluded, sadly, that they probably did."[33]

In reviewing the evolution of the problem, Boutros Ghali's December 1 report returned to refusal of member states to sustain the recommendation put before the Security Council in 1993 that 34,000 peacekeepers would be required to implement the Safe Area regime properly. For its part, the Security Council had seen fit to authorize a force of 7,600. Scattered about the country and often lightly armed, they were considered a credible down payment on the UN commitment to peace in Bosnia. In practice, they were utterly incapable of overawing battle-hardened faction leaders. Remarkably, however, even had the more robust force been in place, it had never been the Secretary General's intention that UNPROFOR peacekeepers would actually defend the Safe Areas. To do so, he concluded, would "prevent UNPROFOR from carrying out its overall mandate in the former Yugoslavia, turn it into a combatant and further destabilize the situation in Bosnia and Herzegovina."[34] Thinking along similar lines, General Bernard Janvier, who commanded UNPROFOR in 1995, suggested that the best solution from a military and political point of view would have been to have the Bosnian Army guard the "safe areas," a task which it also did not want to assume.[35]

To some, such as Warren Zimmermann, the UN view simply did not make sense. "In the hot war in Bosnia," the ambassador contended, "these conditions [restricting the use of force] made the United Nations a symbol of weakness and a candidate for blackmail....The United Nations' weakness reinforces its retreat to the concept that it must act "neutrally", even though in a war of aggression neutrality inevitably favors the aggressor."[36] Put more simply, a force that will not fight possesses little or no deterrent capability. Moreover, a refusal to act to save lives in imminent danger because to do so might jeopardize the free movement of aid convoys whose ostensible purpose was to save those same lives and ease suffering flew in the face of basic logic.

Failure to deter the infamous attack on the safe area in Srebrenica in 1995 became emblematic of the crisis facing UNPROFOR and a principal reason why many critics considered it a failure. While diplomats and generals quarreled over means and ends in Bosnia, the situation on the ground in Srebrenica drifted dangerously. Having already changed hands twice during the ebb and flow of the war between Muslims and Serbs in eastern Bosnia by early 1993, Srebrenica had become the point of temporary settlement of thousands of Muslim refugees. Serb attacks on the city in April 1993 portended a terrible bloodletting that prompted the UNPROFOR commander in Sarajevo, French General Phillippe Morillon, on his own initiative to proclaim the United Nations' interest there. On 18 April, following a flurry of negotiations, a company of lightly armed Canadian peacekeepers—about 170 personnel in all--rolled into the UN camp at nearby Poticari. In theory, the Srebrenica "Safe Area" was demilitarized–that is devoid of assets or formations belonging to any of the armed factions; or at least that is what many perceived the agreement to mean. Sadly, the reality was more complex. UNPROFOR understood the arrangement to signify that demilitarization applied only to the town of Srebrenica itself, and not to the lightly settled surrounding area. In contrast, the Bosnian Serbs recognized no such limitation and would subsequently insist that Muslim militia operating from the surrounding environs violated the agreement. For his part, the Bosnian Muslim commander in the area instructed his forces to turn in only non-servicable weapons or those for which ammunition was scarce. In short, compliance was largely voluntary and Canadian peacekeepers did not conduct intrusive house-to-house searches to verify compliance. In spite of all this, an UNPROFOR Press Release of 21 April declared demilitarization a success.[37]

Although neither the Canadians nor the United Nations possessed the means to verify demilitarization, Kofi Annan, the Under-Secretary General for Peacekeeping Operations, expressed confidence in compliance with the provision.[38] For a time it did not matter and in 1994 the Srebrenica Safe Area was considered a success. Bosnian Government and Serb forces respected a cease-fire along the confrontation line, a fact for which UNPROFOR troops received appropriate credit. However, as was so often the case during the Bosnian civil war, the calm was illusory.

Tragically, as in Bihac, Srebrenica served as a staging area for Muslim raids against Serbian positions. In spring 1995, at which time an undermanned (though larger at about 600 personnel) and outgunned

Dutch battalion had replaced the Canadians, a new and even worse crisis loomed. By July, Serb forces under General Ratko Mladic systematically cornered the Dutch with the threat of superior force as reflected by the presence of tanks and artilery. During the preceding interval, they isolated the peacekeepers and incrementally pealed away their perimeter outposts so as to deny them any clear picture of what was to follow. Directed to deter attacks on the people within the enclave but not to defend the ground on which they resided (a nuance lost on most world observers), the Dutch UNPROFOR soldiers pulled back to avoid an engagement on unfavorable terms. In any case, they had never possessed the combat strength to secure the entire Srebrenica perimeter. The Dutch established eight Observation Posts, each occupied by seven soldiers, along the fifty-kilometer boundary.[39] In the meantime, they had been subject to frequent indignities by the Muslims as well. Dutchbat soldiers were clearly not in control of the enclave. In January 1995, following an attempt to enforce the demilitarization of the safe area, 100 Dutch peacekeepers were detained by Muslim forces.[40] Despite their subsequent release, the weakness of the Dutch position was transparent.

By August, just what the Dutch were doing in Srebrenica at all became increasingly open to question. As of June, Bosniac militiamen openly carried weapons within the Srebrenica enclave.[41] Even if they had possessed the manpower to patrol the enclave actively, the Dutch lacked sufficient fuel. Surrounding Serbs forces prevented more than minimal amounts of fuel from reaching the adjoining village of Poticari, base of the Dutchbat Headuarters, and even restricted the flow of ammunition.[42] Thus lacking mobility, the Dutch added three Observation Posts, which were subsequently used as staging areas for foot patrols.[43]

Again, the puzzling UNPROFOR charter came into play. According to the Secretary-General, "UNPROFOR's protection role is derived from its mere presence: UNPROFOR is neither structured nor equipped for combat and has never had sufficient resources, even with air support, to defend the safe areas against a deliberate attack or to hold ground."[44] The true deterrent effect of presence without capability, or the demonstrated will to use force, would soon be apparent. On June 3, 1995, just a day after the loss of one of the Observation Posts, the Dutch Battalion commander reported, "The Dutchbat is not able to execute any actions nor can it respond to the deteriorating situation." Only three weeks later, he advised his chain of command of the complete isolation of Dutchbat by the BSA, no one having been permitted to enter or leave since April 26.[45]

A combination of factors contributed to the downfall of the enclave and became the source of bitter recriminations later on. First, neither UN personnel nor NATO anticipated either the scale of the attack to come or the murders that would ensue only days later. Despite the predicament in Srebrenica, UNPROFOR assessed the danger of BSA attacks to be greater elsewhere. On July 7, Dutch troops passed a report to Sarajevo asserting that the BSA lacked either the strength or intent to overrun Poticari and Srebrenica. When the assault came soon afterward, the seizure of 55 Dutch prisoners offered the attackers valuable leverage in the tense moments to come. As the situation deteriorated, Lieutenant General Janvier hesitated to call for NATO air attacks both because of confusion throughout the chain of command and the absence of any clear indication that his own personnel in the enclave were in immediate danger. Indeed, some felt that the principal risk to Dutch peacekeepers–particularly those held as hostages–might be aerial bombing itself. This was apparently the view of the Dutch government, which vetoed air attacks on more than one occasion. The Dutch were hardly alone in withholding consent, however. Among the few who actually lobbied hard for air attacks were French President Jacques Chirac and American envoy Richard Holbrooke. Ultimately, two close air support attacks occurred resulting in damage or destruction to two Serb tanks. Whether more extravagant use of air power could have made a difference remains problematic. Certainly, NATO had far greater force available but the highly dispersed Bosnian Serb attacks on the enclave would have offered few lucrative targets.[46]

While many faulted poor intelligence or timidity on the part of the UN command for the disaster, others allocated significant blame to the Bosnian Army command itself. In contrast to Gorazde, for example, the Bosnian Muslims did not make a stand to defend Srebrenica but in fact pulled their troops out of harm's way. Whether this was an act of military pragmatism or political cynicism remains a debated question. Some observers suspected that the Bosnian government was willing to let the enclave fall in order to intensify international opinion against the Serbs and bring direct NATO intervention in the conflict.[47] Others speculated about secret deals involving the Bosnian government, the Serbs, NATO, the UN, Lieutenant General Janvier and others.[48] Meanwhile, the humiliation of Lieutenant Colonel Thom Karreman's Dutch battalion–whose position gradually became untenable--triggered minute scrutiny of the episode in the Netherlands. During the final act of the tragedy, Serb forces compelled the Dutch to open the Safe Area. General Mladic bullied the Dutch and proclaimed Srebrenica a gift to the Serbian people marking an historic reversal of the Turkish conquest of the area.[49] The mass execution of thousands of Muslim men that ensued only days later, served to focus the international spotlight on UNPROFOR's deficiencies and tarnished the entire enterprise. In addition, the endless dickering over the application of even modest NATO air attacks underscored the hesitancy and lack of consensus that characterized the international quest from its inception. On July 11, a ludicrous situation occurred in which Dutchbat peacekeepers hunkered down in bunkers in anticipation of air strikes that never arrived. Meanwhile, officers farther up the chain of UNPROFOR command knew nothing of a specific request for help. In the end, more than seven hours after the initial request, two NATO aircraft dropped two bombs on two BSA vehicles entering the Srebrenica Safe Area.[50] Also, to be sure, American advocates of more forceful application of air power suffered from the apparent anomaly of their own position. Because the United States was not an official participant in UNPROFOR–minus the low profile presence of a few staff officers and advisors–and thus did not have forces on the ground in Bosnia, it did not share in any consequences the more robust air attacks would necessarily have entailed. As the Safe Area disintegrated on July 11, Muslim refugees poured into the Dutchbat compound at Poticari. Dutchbat permitted 4-5,000 refugees to enter but had to close its gates to an additional 15-20,000 remaining outside. All the while, many combat-age males, fearing the worst, decided to try to slip through BSA lines in the direction of Tuzla. A desperate act, it turned out to be the best available option.[51]

Much of the problem, then, boiled down to the paralyzing effect of the two principal tenets of the United Nations approach to ending the conflict in Bosnia: the minimal use of force and the preservation of neutrality. Dedication to minimal force guaranteed insufficient leverage, even had the military presence been larger, to deal effectively with the determined and typically ruthless faction army commanders. In an important respect, the commitment to use only proportional force and no more than absolutely necessary for self-defense reflected the refusal of the international community to understand that it was dealing with a war in Bosnia. Still, the principle of minimal force was an important pillar of neutrality, which was central to the UN methodology. Considered crucial to their role as peacemaker, the commitment to neutrality made UN forces reluctant to apply force in support of humanitarian ends if doing so would contribute to the appearance of taking sides. The problem with neutrality in the eyes of its detractors was that it presumed a certain symmetry in the conflict for which a solution could be brokered by splitting the difference between the objectives of the two sides. If, however, one side was the clear aggressor–as many observers believed the Serbs to be–such an approach tended to condone bad behavior in fact even if it opposed it in theory. It meant in practice that UNPROFOR would not take direct action to prevent ethnic cleansing, a phenomenon it certainly opposed. Years later, in 1998, the UN Secretary General acknowledged the multiple failures attending the collapse of the Srebrenica Safe Area. While roundly condemning the actions of the BSA, the report placed fault most heavily on the reluctance to apply air power: "We were, with hindsight, wrong to declare repeatedly and publicly that we did not want to use air power against the Serbs except as a last resort, and to accept shelling of the safe areas as a daily occurrence." While the report does not fault Dutchbat for its inability to defend Srebrenica, it did question the failure of Dutchbat to report in a timely way the many ominous developments that portended the massacre that ensued. Perhaps surprisingly, the report minimized the significance of the Bosnian Muslim attacks staged from the Safe Areas, asserting that they were inconsequential.[52]

Ultimately, the UN mission suffered from the occasional incompatibility of the two broad and lofty purposes that brought it to Bosnia in the first place: to alleviate human suffering and facilitate an end to the war–both, incidentally, within the context of preserving Bosnia-Herzegovina as a sovereign political entity. At times, it was not possible to fulfill the humanitarian mission without being drawn in some measure into the conflict. In turn, assuming the role of the broker of peace without massive military leverage sometimes left the UN appearing confused and ineffectual in protecting civilian noncombatants desperately seeking sanctuary and a means to survive.

In the end, the use of brute military power played a major role in ending the war. OPERATION Deliberate Force, triggered by outrage over the August 28, 1995 explosion in the Mrkala Market in Sarjevo, hit the Serbs hard and signaled unmistakably that the West had lost all patience with Serb aggression. Of course, the basic shift of military momentum attending Croatia's summer ground offensive (supported by federation attacks) also made clear to the Serb leadership that it was time to seek peace on the most favorable terms possible. Indeed, Serb strategy assumed that 1995 would mark the end of the civil war in any case.[53]

Consequently, the role of allied air power in bringing the Serbs to Dayton is problematic. However, it was instrumental in shaping the behavior of Bosnian Serb forces on the ground. Beginning on August 30, NATO aircraft struck fifty-six approved targets in the areas of Sarajevo and Pale. The bombing paused after two days, but resumed five days later as the Serb forces had as yet failed to comply with an agreement to pull heavy weapons back from Sarajevo was not yet complete. Finally on September 14 General Mladic agreed to abide by NATO demands.[54] For NATO, the outcome justified resort to the use of massive force.

Many NATO observers, who had restively watched the UNPROFOR episode, were determined to set a different tone from the start and the latitude to do so was clearly set forth in the Dayton Agreement. Indeed, Secretary of State Madeleine Albright and the national Security Council had actually come to view the presence of UNPROFOR in Bosnia as a liability, and responsible for thwarting the proper employment of US air power.[55] Accordingly, IFOR would be far more muscular than UNPROFOR and assume a far more assertive posture.

Notes

1. For a full breakdown of UNPROFOR strength and nations of origin of its soldiers, see Annex I, *Report of the Secretary-General Pursuant to Security Council Resolution 947*, 29 March 1995.

2. Colonel Greg Fontenot, interview with Dr. Robert Baumann and Dr. George Gawrych, 2000, Fort Leavenworth, KS.

3. James A. Baker, with Thomas M. deFrank, *The Politics of Diplomacy* (New York: Putnam, 1995), 636.

4. Warren Zimmerman, *Origins of a Catastrophe* (New York: Times Books, 1999), 223.

5. Colin Powell, *My American Journey* (New York: Random House, 1995).

6. Douglas Brinkley, *The Unfinished Presidency* (New York: Penguin, 1998), 451.

7. Zimmermann, *Origins of a Catastrophe*, 217-18.

8. "Former Yugoslavia–UNPROFOR, United Nations Protection Force," compiled by the Department of Public Information, United Nations, September 1996, 41.

9. Sir Michael Rose, *Fighting For Peace: Bosnia 1994* (London: Harvill Press, 1998), 114.

10. Steven Burg and Paul Shoup, *The War in Bosnia-Herzegovina: Ethnic Conflict and International Intervention* (London: M. E. Sharpe, 2000), 136.

11. Major General M. Baril, OMM, CD Military Adviser for the Department of Peacekeeping Operations United Nations Headquarters, New York, "UNPROFOR One Year Later Report," 8 July 1993.

12. Misha Glenny, *The Fall of Yugoslavia: The Third Balkan War* (New York: Penguin, 1996), 201-02.

13. Rose, *Fighting for Peace*, 197.

14. Rose, *Fighting for Peace*, 117.

15. Burg and Shoup, *The War in Bosnia-Herzegovina*, 152.

16. Ibid., 150-51; see also Rose, *Fighting for Peace*, 121..

17. Burg and Shoup, *The War in Bosnia-Herzegovina*, 161.

18. Colonel Rick Hatton, Canadian Army, interview with Dr. Robert Baumann and Colonel Lawyn Edwards, Banja Luka, MND-SW Headquarters, 15 September 2000.

19. Ibid. One alternative theory held that the Muslims either fired the round or that an explosive device was planted in the market. Given the fact of five explosions in total, however, the near simultaneity of the blasts would seem to suggest a common source.

20. Demurenko, incidentally, was a graduate of the US Army Command and General Staff College in Fort Leavenworth, KS, where his opinion was taken seriously by those who knew him.

21. Colonel R. A. Hatton, Canadian Army, interview with Dr. Robert Baumann and Colonel Lawyn Edwards, Banja Luka, MND-SW Headquarters, 15 September 2000.

22. Major General M. Baril, "UNPROFOR One Year Later Report."

23. James Gow, *Triumph of the Lack of Will : International Diplomacy and the Yugoslav War* (London: Hurst and Company, 1997), 147.

24. Jan Willem Honig and Norbert Both, *Srebrenica: Record of a War Crime* (New York: Penguin, 1997), 99-100.

25. Boutros Boutros-Ghali, *Report of the Secretary-General Pursuant to Resolution 844*, 9 May 1994, 1.

26. Colonel P. G. Williams, "Tactical Command in Bosnia: Operation Grapple III - November 1993-May 1994," unpublished paper presented at Camberley on 22 September 1994.

27. Boutros Boutros-Ghali, *Report of the Secretary General Pursuant to Security Council Resolution 959 (1994)*, 1 December 1994, 7, 9.

28. Ibid., 2.

29. David Rhode, *End Game* (New York: Ferrar, Strauss and Giroux, 1997), 366-67.

30. Rose, *Fighting For Peace*, 116; Boutros-Ghali, *Report of the Secretary-General Pursuant to Resolution 947*, 22 March 1995, 7.

31. Honig and Both, *Srebrenica*, 150.

32. Rhode, 365.

33. Rose, *Fighting for Peace*, 113.

34. Boutros-Ghali, *Report of the Secretary General*, 1 December 1994, 7, 16-17; see also "Former Yugoslavia–UNPROFOR, United Nations Protection Force," 13-14. The concept of "light" and "heavy" options for the protection of safe areas first saw the light of day in a tentative proposal drafted by the French government on 10 May 1993.

35. Rhode, *End Game*, 364.

36. Zimmermann, *Origins of a Catastrophe*, 242.

37. Report of the Secretary-General Pursuant to General Assembly Resolution 53/35 (1998), Srebrenica Report, paragraphs 59-62. <http://www.haverford.edu/relg/sells/reports/Unsrebrenicareport.htm> accessed 18 February 2004.

38. Honig and Both, *Srebrenica*, 106.

39. Srebrenica Report, paragraph 226.

40. Honig and Both, *Srebrenica*, 130.

41. Srebrenica Report, paragraph 223.

42. Honig and Both, *Srebrenica*, 128.

43. Srebrenica Report, paragraph 229.

44. Boutros-Ghali, *Report of the Secretary-General Pursuant to Resolution 844*, 4. Honig and Both assert on page 114 that the governments of Britain, France, and Spain insisted on the qualification that the use of force be in self-defense. Their concern was that to do otherwise would drag them into the war.

45. Srebrenica Report, paragraphs 233-35.

46. Tim Ripley, *Operation Deliberate Force: The UN and NATO Campaign in Bosnia 1995* (Lancaster, UK: Center for Defense and International Security Studies, 1999), 142-45; Richard Holbrooke, *To End a War* (New York: The Modern Library, 1999), 68-71.

47. Ripley, *Operation Deliberate Force*, 145-46.

48. Rohde, *End Game*, 357-63.

49. Holbrooke, *To End a War*, 69.

50. Srebrenica Report, paragraphs 297-99.

51. Srebrenica Report, paragraphs 297-305.

52. Srebrenica Report, paragraphs 474, 479.

53. Ivo Daalder, "Decision to Intervene: How the War in Bosnia Ended," *Foreign Service Journal*, December 1998 at <GOTOBUTTON BM_1_ www. afsa.org/fsj/Dec98/Decisiontointervene.html, 2>.

54. Briefing by Lieutenant General Mike Ryan on *Deliberate Force*, Maxwell Air Force Base, Alabama, February 12, 1996, as cited in Michael O. Beale, "Bombs Over Bosnia: The Role of Airpower in Bosnia Herzegovina," unpublished thesis, School of Advanced Airpower Studies, Air University, Maxwell Air Force Base, Alabama, June 1996, 59.l

55. Daalder, "Decision to Intervene," 4.

Chapter 3

Military Planning Before OPERATION Joint Endeavor: An Initial Assessment

Walter E. Kretchik

> The United Nations Security Council is invited to adopt a resolution by which it will authorize Member States or regional organizations and arrangements to establish a multinational military Implementation Force . . ..
>
> General Framework Agreement for Peace[1]

Histories of past military operations tend to avoid the planning phase because fathoming complicated military plans and the methodologies that produced them bedevils researchers. For that reason, negotiating the planning maze that culminated in OPERATION Joint Endeavor is an immense undertaking. Yet, some familiarity with the concepts underlying military operations in Bosnia and Herzegovina is essential for understanding what preceded the alliance-led operation.

This chapter seeks to illuminate the causes and outcomes of military plans by examining headquarters activity through released documents, memoirs, and eyewitness accounts. The assessment is far from complete, for identifying every headquarters and plan over four years of international efforts to end the Balkan war exceeds the scope of this section. Limitations allow for shedding only some light upon certain NATO, US multiservice and US Army headquarters that devised plans to support diplomatic initiatives over the early to mid-1990s. Where appropriate, some judgment will be passed over what happened when selected plans were executed.

Planning Headquarters: An Overview

The numerous military headquarters planning for military coercive power in Bosnia constitute two categories, the first one consisting of multinational entities such as the UN and NATO. Within the UN, strategic planning occurred in a variety of departments to include the Department of Peacekeeping Operations. However, the requisite documents for elucidating the UN planning process remain sparse. It is easier to discern the results of planning as evidenced by the numerous resolutions authorizing the use of military power.

In 1995, NATO represented 16 nations and was the UN's military executor for conditions specified within the General Framework

Agreement for Peace (GFAP).[2] For military action, the North Atlantic Council (NAC) provides strategic planning direction through the Military Committee and the Supreme Allied Commander Europe (SACEUR). When OPERATION Joint Endeavor occurred, US Army General George Joulwan was SACEUR, exercising authority through Allied Command Europe (ACE) and a planning staff within Supreme Headquarters Allied Powers Europe (SHAPE), Casteau, Mons, Belgium. For the Bosnia crisis, operational planning under SHAPE fell primarily to Allied Forces Southern Europe (AFSOUTH), led in 1995 by US Navy Admiral Leighton Smith. The SACEUR also tasked the Allied Command Europe Rapid Reaction Corps or ARRC to develop supporting plans. Founded on *2 October 1992, this operational/tactical headquarters was* essentially British with subordinate multinational combat divisions and brigades. In 1995, British Lieutenant General Sir Michael Walker was the ARRC commander.[3]

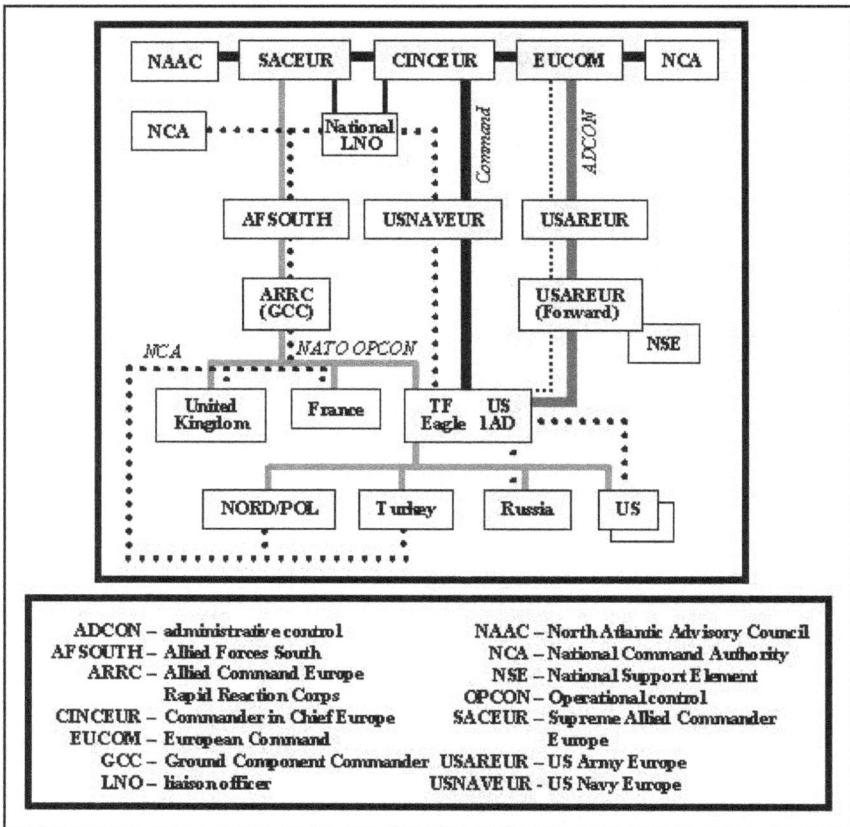

Figure 1. US Forces Command Structure, Operation JOINT ENDEAVOR

Complementing the multinational headquarters was a second organizational grouping, the national military headquarters. At this time, little has emerged as to what planning occurred within most of these entities.[4] For the United States, military headquarters involved with Bosnia planning did so under a national chain of command, not the UN or NATO. Coordination outside of US channels certainly occurred, for a US military liaison cell existed within the UN headquarters in New York City. The US Joint Chiefs of Staff (JCS), a strategic headquarters located in Washington, DC also played a significant role in Bosnia planning, particularly in dealings with the SACEUR.

In addition to his appointment as SACEUR, General Joulwan was also Commander in Chief, US European Command (CINCEUR) in charge of US European Command (EUCOM), a multiservice headquarters located in Stuttgart, Germany. This arrangement required Joulwan to answer directly to the president of the United States and the secretary of defense, with the JCS in an advisory and support capacity. However, the general was usually embroiled in NATO affairs, thus EUCOM's daily operations rested with the deputy commander. Although the SHAPE and EUCOM staffs were not co-located and under separate command channels, the SACEUR/CINCEUR command method offered a nexus for NATO and US military planning in Europe.

While EUCOM contained a number of entities, ground operations planning occurred within US Army Europe (USAREUR), an operational-level, single-service headquarters commanded in 1995 by US Army General William Crouch in Heidelberg, Germany. Under USAREUR were several subordinate US Army headquarters. The 21st Theater Army Area Command (TAACOM), an operational level Army logistics headquarters, was situated in Kaiserslautern, Germany under Major General James Wright. An operational/tactical headquarters, V Corps under Lieutenant General John Abrams was situated in Heidelberg. Vicenza, Italy was the home of the Southern European Task Force (SETAF), a tactical headquarters commanded by Major General Jack Nix. Major General William Nash commanded the 1st Armored Division in Baumholder, Germany, a tactical force under V Corps.[5]

This overview of but a few headquarters gives some appreciation for planning complexity concerning Bosnia. Planning spanned several continents, many headquarters, and numerous chains of command. A particular headquarters might have a strategic, operational, or tactical focus depending upon level of command and mission. In addition, the hundreds of officers involved held different views depending upon

Photo 2. Major General William Nash Commanded
the 1st Armored Division and Task Force *Eagle*

culture, language, education, and experience. With a typical tour for a plans officer being two or three years, personnel turnover was a constant irritant. Officers departed with their knowledge and experience; new arrivals joined in with little, if any, comprehension as to what had transpired previously.[6]

In theory, the various staffs coordinated activities among headquarters through the "nesting of plans" concept where a particular plan supported one published from above. However, peacetime workloads and priorities complicate coordination with a senior headquarters, let alone those below, laterally, and outside the chain of command. As this study argues, chaos ensued when divergent chains of command devised concepts unshared among the greater military planning and execution community.

Bosnia Planning in Context: The Cold War Aftershock

The Soviet Union's demise in December 1991 ended the Cold War and tumbled a bi-polar world order 50 years in the making. Such a tumultuous occurrence prompted numerous security-based organizations and military headquarters to reexamine their charters and missions. The UN viewed the event as freedom to end future conflict through preventive diplomacy and, under the leadership of Secretary General Boutros Boutros Ghali, embarked on an aggressive scheme to do so. NATO also revised long-held views of how the alliance conducted military operations by developing military staffs capable of planning peace operations and out-of-sector deployments.[7] In concert with this procedural housecleaning, the US military in Europe also revamped its planning procedures to prepare for future contingencies.

One crisis that involved both NATO and US military planners was the developing war in the Balkans.[8] Yugoslavia's breakup and rapid plummet into civil war reflected the type of scenario for which military planners in Europe attempted to prepare.[9] However, when the UN passed Security Council Resolution (UNSCR) 713 on 25 September 1991 to enact an arms embargo to quell fighting between the former Yugoslavia and Croatia, NATO and US planners were focused upon OPERATION Provide Comfort in northern Iraq.[10] Further UN efforts produced UNSCR 743 on 21 February 1992 to establish a UN protection force or UNPROFOR in Croatia. That action was followed by UNSCR 749 in April 1992, authorizing a full UNPROFOR in protected areas.[11]

Response With Sea and Air Plans

With the war a threat to NATO security at least through potentially destabilizing surrounding members, NAC members expressed concern in Rome, Italy on 8 November 1991.[12] In July 1992, NATO leaders agreed to use naval force in the Adriatic to monitor UN sanctions imposed upon what remained of Yugoslavia: Serbia and Montenegro. International response also bore fruit later the same month through OPERATION Provide Promise. Under the direction of the UN High Commissioner For Refugees (UNHCR) and UNSCR 761 of 29 June, the US government led an international coalition of 21 nations to assist Bosnia's besieged citizenry by air. The coalition planned its missions through a working group composed of contributing nation brigadier generals and their staffs. Between 2 July 1992 and 9 January 1996, NATO and non-NATO aircraft delivered nearly 200,000 tons of humanitarian aid to Bosnian cities, principally Sarajevo.[13] Later, on 1 February 1993, *AFSOUTH* assumed command of a newly formed headquarters, Joint Task Force Provide Promise. The joint task force oversaw US activities in support of the UN mission from Kelly Barracks near Stuttgart, Germany. Two smaller headquarters detachments located in Naples, Italy and Zagreb, Croatia, also participated. About 1,200 US military reservists from various services were called to active duty, with some individuals serving as plans officers.

These actions characterized the skimpy political will and unclear strategic military guidance that constrained NATO and US headquarters planners.[14] Unwilling to take decisive measures to end the war or provide a clear political end state, UN and NATO policy makers attempted to shape events through sea and air means when using military power. Further, the planning was reactive rather than proactive as the military headquarters slid into the Balkan quagmire through assorted UN resolutions. On 9 October 1992, UNSCR 781 established a no-fly zone over Bosnia and Herzegovina. In response, NATO military planners produced OPERATION Sky Monitor to assist UNPROFOR with detecting unauthorized flights. Later, on 10 November 1992, the UN approved SCR 786, sending 75 military observers to airfields in the war zone. NATO voiced its continued support in December 1992.[15]

Additional UN actions against the belligerents came fast and furious in early 1993. UNSCR 807 extended UNPROFOR's mandate until 31 March 1993, the first of many renewals that culminated with UNSCR 1026 in November 1995. The UN passage of SCR 816 on 31 March 1993 expanded Bosnia and Herzegovina no-fly zone parameters to all fixed- and rotary-wing aircraft flights without UNPROFOR approval. If violations occurred, UN members had authority to take certain measures. In support, the NAC approved a NATO ban on 8 April, with planners contriving OPERATION Deny Flight. The operation commenced on 12 April 1993 under AFSOUTH OPLAN 40101, beginning with 50 fighter and reconnaissance aircraft supplied by France, the Netherlands, and the United States. Later, more than 200 aircraft would operate from Italian air bases and Adriatic-stationed aircraft carriers.

UN sanctions and NATO interdiction operations came under scrutiny in May 1993 as the media saturated the airwaves with appalling scenes of Sarajevo existence. The once charming city that hosted the 1984 Winter Olympic Games was now a charnel house. In response to international pressure, UNSCR 824 of 6 May 1993 declared Sarajevo and five other Muslim enclaves as "safe areas" under UNPROFOR guardianship. The alliance later affirmed its readiness to respond to factional aggression against these locations with UN-approved air strikes. However, the ground combat power necessary to force a settlement remained politically taboo.

With Vance-Owen Peace Plan meetings ongoing since 2 January 1993, peace seemed certain as early as 2 May.[16] However, premature celebrations ended in disappointment when international and primarily US backing failed to materialize. With the war continuing, NATO offered close air support to UN forces if attacked and upon request. NATO military planning also resulted in OPERATION Sharp Guard beginning on 15 June 1993, a maritime interdiction mission in conjunction with the Western European Union that monitored Adriatic ship traffic transiting the

Balkans.[17] To increase pressure upon the warring factions, the UN passed SCR 844 on 18 June allowing for 7,500 troops to deploy to designated safe areas and authorized the use of air power to protect them.

By late fall 1993, the NAC made preparations for stronger air measures against forces surrounding Sarajevo and to interdict troops interfering with humanitarian aid. Such measures not only reacted to SCR resolutions but also again resulted from a general international apathy toward using decisive ground force to cease hostilities. In truth, the war was a potential quagmire for the UN, NATO, European, and US policy makers. With little desire to undertake a lengthy peacekeeping mission, most nations were unwilling to act resolutely. In truth, sea and air power sought to chip away at belligerent will while also helping to quell growing political pressure to take action.

In early 1994, diplomatic initiatives reached an impasse over belligerent territorial issues. NATO officials soon met in Brussels to confirm all previous UN and NAC resolutions and also threaten air strikes to open Tuzla's airport for humanitarian aid. Yet, unsettling events continued that indicated NATO sea and air power alone were ineffective in altering warring faction behavior. In what Christopher Bennett described as a "jolting event" on 5 February 1994, an explosion in Sarajevo's central marketplace killed 68 people, mostly Muslim civilians.[18] In response, NATO warned Bosnian Serb forces to withdraw their heavy weapons or be subject to air strikes. The Serbs chose to comply for the time being but repeatedly violated the Sarajevo safe area later. The attack marked a historical turning point, for killing so many civilians in a single incident magnified global outrage. NATO remained active, for its aircraft shot down four GALEB / JASTREB aircraft violating the Bosnia no-fly zone in late February 1994.

In spring 1994, the United States, Russia, Britain, France, and Germany established a five-nation contact group to settle the armed conflict between the Federation and the Bosnian Serbs. The contact group sought a single-state status for Bosnia with both Federation and Bosnian Serb entities sharing constitutional principles and also a defined relationship with Serbia and Croatia. Later, in July 1994, the contact group proposed a map offering a 51-49 percent territorial compromise between the Federation and Bosnian Serbs. The Bosnian, Croatian, and Serbian governments accepted the overture, but the Bosnian Serbs rebuffed it on 20 July.

Throughout 1994, NATO planners had reacted to tepid international willpower with a policy of punishing belligerents for attacking UN personnel and designated protected areas. On 19 November 1994, UNSCR 958 authorized NATO aircraft to attack Serb nationalist targets in Croatia when fighting erupted between the Bosnian government and antigovernment Muslims in Bihac. Soon thereafter, AFSOUTH plans resulted in aircraft bombing Udbina Airfield in Serb-held Croatia in response to hostile aircraft attacking a UN safe area at Bihac. Later, NATO aircraft destroyed surface-to-air missile sites in Bosnia-Herzegovina that had fired upon alliance airplanes.[19]

With the UN allowing NATO more latitude to attack Bosnian Serb targets via air power, AFSOUTH planners formulated two retaliatory plans. The first was Dead Eye, a concept to disrupt Bosnia's integrated air defense system. NATO aircraft struck the Pale ammunition storage depot on 25-26 May 1995 in response to Bosnian Serb artillery firing into Sarajevo from UN-monitored weapons collection sites. The plan was revamped to meet other situational developments: the seizure of UN peacekeepers, the loss of a NATO F-16 on 2 June, the overrun of Srebrenica on 11 July, and the fall of Zepa on 26 July.[20]

On 25 July and again on 1 August 1995, the NAC specified that further Bosnian Serb offensive action meant continued NATO air power to deter future attacks on safe areas. Military planners responded by developing air attack plans for the defense of each UN safe area by again refining the Dead Eye plan and preparing another air strike plan labeled OPERATION Deliberate Force. OPERATION Deliberate Force was promoted as a peacemaking exercise designed to reduce warring faction military capability for threatening UN forces and safe areas. The plan, however, was not designed to end the war.[21]

The AFSOUTH commander, Admiral Leighton Smith, presented the *Deliberate Force* concept to the NATO secretary general, the Honorable Willie Claes, and the SACEUR on 3 August 1995. Discussions focused on using air power to underpin UN resolutions and NAC decisions.[22] On 10 August 1995, Admiral Smith and Lieutenant General Bernard Janvier, commander of UN Peace Force (UNPF), signed a "dual-key" agreement containing UN-NATO arrangements for implementing air power in the Balkans.[23] Bosnian Serb attacks on Sarajevo on 28 August 1995 caused Admiral Smith and Lieutenant General Janvier to authorize OPERATION Deliberate Force. AFSOUTH planners formulated a series of "strike packages" to first strip away Bosnian Serb air defense systems, then attacked ground targets in the vicinity of Sarajevo from 29 to 31 August. On 1 September, the UN requested a suspension of hostilities to allow negotiation with the Bosnian Serbs. An ultimatum failed to convince the

Bosnian Serbs, so air strikes resumed on 5 September. On 10 September, NATO used Tomahawk Land Attack Missiles to assail additional air defense sites in Bosnia.[24]

Soon after these attacks, Lieutenant General Rupert Smith, the UNPROFOR commander, requested another cease-fire to assess Bosnian Serb intentions. That afternoon, following a Bosnian Serb attack on UN positions near the Tuzla airport, the UN asked for and received NATO close air support. Bosnian Serb command bunkers and an artillery position were subsequently destroyed. Additional NATO air strikes occurred against targets 11-13 September 95. On 14 September, offensive operations were again suspended when warring faction representatives agreed to conditions set out in a UN-brokered peace agreement.[25] By 20 September 1995, UN and NATO decision makers determined that OPERATION Deliberate Force had met its objectives.[26] Air power was one piece of the innumerable diplomatic and military conditions that played out over the summer and fall of 1995 which compelled the warring factions to seeking a peace settlement.[27]

Response With Ground Force Plans

Although NATO sea and air power had played some role early in the Bosnian conflict, a number of ground forces options also arose in the early 1990s. Vacillating political conditions rendered these efforts more a mental exercise than suitable courses of action. In 1992, USAREUR and V Corps tasked the US Army's 1st Armored Division and 3rd Infantry Division to craft several scenarios, the details of which remain classified.[28] It can be surmised, however, that the planning supported AFSOUTH OPLAN 40101, developed in late summer of 1992 to support the proposed Vance-Owen Peace Plan.[29] The OPLAN envisioned replacing UNPROFOR with NATO troops under the ARRC commander but was never executed.

Despite an UNPROFOR in Bosnia by October 1992 under OPERATION Grapple and other mission monikers,[30] the Bosnian civil war threatened to destabilize surrounding countries through refugees and ethnic hatred. To counter this threat, the UN passed UNSCR 795 on 11 December 1992 authorizing an additional UNPROFOR in Macedonia. Labeled as a UN preventive deployment force, a Nordic battalion consisting of Norwegian, Finnish, and Swedish troops arrived in February 1993. In June 1993, American military plans resulted in the first US troops arriving under Task Force *Able Sentry*. The various troop rotations into Macedonia later became a separate mission under UNSCR 983 of 31 March 1995.[31]

As political conditions changed, planners refined OPLAN 40101 but under policy constraint. In 1993 for example, US State Department officials viewed the Balkans situation as a European affair alone, fearing that any US ground force might be drawn into years of peacekeeping duties.[32] Such policy was typical of the international community at large, thus NATO and US military planners found it difficult to develop more decisive military options using ground power.

By early 1993, the Vance-Owen Peace Plan seemed practicable enough for ending the war. As political circumstances sharpened in focus, circumstances demanded a more complete overhaul of OPLAN 40101. In the fall of 1993, 40101 became OPLAN 40103, now reflecting particulars where UNPROFOR would expand in size and necessitate a larger NATO force to replace it. At the time, there was sufficient confidence in the peace process to allow some staff officers a ground reconnaissance to seek possible headquarters locations in the Balkans. The political climate, however, proved too provisory to make Vance-Owen workable, so OPLAN 40103 was put on hold in 1994.

Ground planning tapered off for several months but accelerated in November 1994 when Bosnian Serb military success and NATO sea and air power failed to prevent attacks on UN safe havens and personnel. Senior military officials on both sides of the Atlantic concluded that UNPROFOR was in a desperate situation. Political conditions now changed from considering a UNPROFOR replacement by NATO troops to an extraction of peacekeepers under extreme conditions.[33]

The situation in Bosnia had further deteriorated to such a point by February 1995 that AFSOUTH staff officers underwent a computer-driven exercise to assist in developing the UNPROFOR extraction plan, now designated OPLAN 40104. Under this concept, ground command fell to the ARRC; its staff discerning that the NATO troops required to execute OPLAN 40103 were also necessary for 40104. As contrived, a mobile force of up to nine NATO brigades was to move simultaneously into the Balkans via air, road, and sea means to establish a covering force. In addition to ground forces, NATO naval assets secured the sea line of communications within the Adriatic, while air forces gained air supremacy over the region. Once the NATO forces were in position, AFSOUTH assumed operational control of all UNPROFOR units to direct their out-of-region movement.

Plans are nothing but ideas and require people and resources to execute them. Unfortunately, as with previous ground options, NATO's membership showed little interest in offering up the means to implement them.[34] Some NATO units rehearsed the UNPROFOR extraction mission nonetheless, and the OPLAN underwent several revisions. Eventually, a version made its way to the SACEUR and the NAC for debate and approval.[35] SACEUR OPLAN 40104 "Determined Effort" emerged on 21 July 1995 but without NAC execution approval.

As NATO and US Army personnel devised OPLAN 40104, Bosnia was under a four-month cease-fire brokered by former US President Jimmy Carter in December 1994.[36] When the arrangement expired on 1 May, Bosnian Serb forces soon renewed attacks on Sarajevo and endangered the UN safe area of Srebrenica. These actions now made UNPROFOR extraction a distinct possibility, particularly when Bosnian Serb forces responded to NATO air strikes by taking more than 350 UN peacekeepers hostage.[37]

Although the international community still remained irresolute over ground forces in Bosnia, the UN peacekeeper hostage crisis intensified US Army planning for the UNPROFOR extraction. But the hostage situation and UN peacekeepers scattered about the Balkans meant modifying OPLAN 40104. This variant envisioned using NATO ground troops to remove small groups of peacekeepers near simultaneously. USAREUR's portion of the operation fell to Major General Jack Nix, the commanding general of SETAF, who trained his force for its expected mission.[38]

Several years of UN resolutions, NAC decisions, NATO sea and air power plus US diplomatic push slowly changed international attitudes toward the possibility of committing ground troops. However, it was the UN hostage situation that shocked the international community into action. By taking so many UN soldiers hostage, the Bosnian Serbs directly challenged both UN credibility and NATO's power to protect the peacekeepers via air means alone. On 16 June 1995, the UN passed SCR 998, authorizing 12,500 additional troops as a rapid reaction force to reinforce UNPROFOR.

Representing about a division's worth of combat soldiers, the reaction force authorization was a dramatic shift in what had been UN retaliation policy by sea and air means alone. US spokesmen, however, were careful to state that the French, British, Dutch, and Belgian force would not replace UNPROFOR, although OPLAN 40104 was certainly in the works.[39] With US forces noticeably absent from the UN reaction force, USAREUR forces rehearsed their portion of the UNPROFOR extraction plan during Exercise *Mountain Shield I*. Grafenwöhr, Germany hosted the exercise 7-15 July 1995, bringing together a mixed group of forces.[40]

Apparently undismayed by SCR 998 and what it suggested, Bosnian Serb forces overran Srebrenica and Zepa in July 1995.[41] The Clinton administration soon heightened pressure on the UN and NATO to protect the remaining safe areas by force. Surprisingly, the United States found support within the London Conference of 21 July. With more resolve than previous conferences, the attending members condoned the continued use of NATO air strikes if UN safe areas were threatened.[42] The conference results encouraged US foreign policy makers to step up an all-out diplomatic effort to end the war in Bosnia, although President Clinton was still unable to gather strong congressional support to commit US ground power.[43] NATO now "drew a line in the sand" around Gorazde but lacked the international will to commit ground forces and end the war.

To show US resolve, President Clinton sent National Security Adviser Anthony Lake to Europe, where he presented a US peace initiative to NATO and non-NATO representatives.[44] Peace was possible at the time, due in part to a Croat military offensive to recapture the Krajina region in August 1995. With training support supplied by US government contractors from Military Professional Resources Incorporated, the attack succeeded. Bosnian Serb forces suffered defeat for the first time in four years.[45] The Croat ground offensive demonstrated that the once-dominant Serbs were now in a position where their victory was not certain.

Given this new twist in the ground war, a diplomatic breakthrough seemed likely as the Croat faction consolidated its hold on the Krajina region in mid-August. Then, on 28 August 1995, a Bosnian Serb unit lobbed mortar rounds into the Sarajevo marketplace, killing 38 civilians and wounding at least 85 more. This flagrant disregard for yet another UN safe area and a NATO-designated heavy weapons exclusion zone triggered OPERATION Deliberate Force.

Plans For Closure

During OPERATION Deliberate Force, the Clinton administration further pressured all international parties to bring peace to the Balkans. With belligerents now willing to hold discussions, US policy makers urged European governments to accept that a peaceful removal of UNPROFOR was apropos given the reduced potential for armed conflict with belligerent forces. In light of ongoing peace talks and changing political conditions by early September, the NAC directed the SACEUR to devise a peace-enforcement operation in Bosnia using ground forces. That directive resulted in SHAPE OPLAN 40105 on 15 November 1995, with AFSOUTH subsequently publishing its own 40105 and the ARRC producing OPLAN 60105.

In developing these plans, the military planning process suffered from a lack of firm intelligence, especially concerning how the various combatants might react to a NATO ground presence. Although military planners had transited Bosnia to assess the situation for themselves, commanders and their staffs asked numerous questions that overwhelmed the intelligence community. To fill the information void and deal with changing conditions, the planners devised assumptions. However, even one wrong assumption invalidates the entire plan, thus the rule of thumb is to develop no more than five. As one indicator of the lack of certainty facing planners, AFSOUTH OPLAN 40105 contained 27 assumptions.[46]

In truth, no plan could match Bosnian realties precisely, for political and military conditions changed continually. Although there was international agreement to provide a ground force if a peace treaty was signed, the military plans for doing so were "living documents" modified as additional information came to light. The fluidity of changing roles and missions over the fall of 1995 can be illustrated by one plan that called for training and arming Bosnian Federation forces. Lieutenant Colonel Peter J. Schifferle of V Corps was responsible for the plan. In mid-August 1995, Schifferle was directed to design a contingency operation where the US 3rd Infantry Division would send forces into the Bosnian Federation to arm and train a national army.[47] After many hours of work and briefings to various general officers, his concept found its way to Washington. There the plan was well received initially. Within days, however, the JCS abandoned the plan when the US government showed no support for it.

With the contact group meeting faction foreign ministers and others in Geneva on 8 September 1995, events drove planning for a ground force option. USAREUR had turned its attention to *Mountain Shield II* from 8 to 19 September; the exercise was yet another UNPROFOR extraction rehearsal and also periodic SETAF "normal training."[48] Sometime during the exercise, both General Crouch and Lieutenant General Abrams learned of the NAC's direction to SACEUR to plan for a peace enforcement mission in Bosnia.[49] Lieutenant Colonel Albert Bryant, Jr., the chief of plans for V Corps, was soon ordered to plan not only for a mission that "extended beyond a six-month window" but also one requiring a large sustainment force within the theater of operations.[50] In effect, V Corps developed a plan for its higher USAREUR headquarters. By the end of September, the "USAREUR Campaign Plan" came into being.[51]

The V Corps planners believed that US ground forces might enter Bosnia as early as 1 October. NATO, however, did not release the authority to begin extensive planning for such a force until that date. To save time, US Army plans officers based their ideas upon the existing OPLAN 40104 and its variants. In Bryant's mind, OPLAN 40104 was fairly mature conceptually and rehearsed enough to give commanders confidence in executing a mission in Bosnia. With EUCOM input, USAREUR now contrived a sizeable US force to enter Bosnia from the Adriatic coast. The force would then pass through expected French and German sectors to locate itself near Tuzla.[52]

On 26 September 1995 in New York City, US Assistant Secretary of State Richard Holbrooke met the foreign ministers of Bosnia, Croatia, and Serbia (speaking for the Bosnian Serbs) to agree upon the fundamental principles for a settlement. The offing included a single Bosnian state with territorial division between the Federation and a Bosnian Serb entity using the contact group's formula, plus the drafting of a constitution, free and fair elections, and respect for human rights. In support of the anticipated peace settlement, SHAPE drafted an implementation force or IFOR concept by 6 October.[53] USAREUR and V Corps now prepared the 1st Armored Division for deployment into Bosnia as part of a UN-sanctioned, NATO-led IFOR.[54]

The planning activities ongoing within military channels were every bit as complicated as the political negotiations. NATO force contributions vacillated over size and missions, and non-NATO nations offered up various types of support. Consumed by numerous missions, USAREUR deferred much of the ground force planning to V Corps. To prepare themselves for Bosnia, both the V Corps and the 1st Armored Division participated in Exercise *Mountain Eagle* between 25 September and 15 November 1995.[55] The exercise stressed *probable* IFOR missions, to include stability through treaty enforcement and separating former combatants so the peace process might move forward.

Some critics have attacked the USAREUR staff actions of October and early November 1995 as less than attentive to the potential for ground operations in Bosnia.[56] In evidence to support a critique of USAREUR's lack of expediency, pundits submit that the headquarters failed to establish a staff crisis action cell for Bosnia until December 1995.[57] In its defense, the USAREUR staff was involved with numerous projected and ongoing operations, with Bosnia being but one mission. For that reason, the headquarters had deferred much of the Bosnia planning to V Corps, a capable headquarters but by no means doctrinally organized and experienced to plan for a multinational and multiservice operation without expert augmentation from EUCOM. Regardless, it was V Corps, not USAREUR, that sent 20 planners from within EUCOM to the ARRC for planning coordination.

Meanwhile, Richard Holbrooke and other negotiators meeting with faction representatives in Dayton, Ohio were determined to produce both a permanent peace and consensus for a multiethnic Bosnian state.[58] As the talks progressed under US leadership, some of the ongoing drama percolated downward to NATO and US military officers. Having NATO representatives attend the meetings meant that early preparation for an IFOR deployment was possible given a clearer definition of military tasks, as well as a more unified chain of command.[59] Indeed, NATO military planners had consulted with the contact group negotiators both before and after the Dayton meetings to ensure that assigned military tasks were feasible.

According to Major James Alty, Jr., the Dayton negotiations received a mixed reaction within USAREUR headquarters as late as 1 November. Rumors flew throughout Campbell Barracks in Heidelberg that the talks would indeed result in an IFOR with US force participation. Yet, some officers recalled that USAREUR had experienced such situations before without a ground force deployment due to fuzzy political will and "air strike diplomacy." Moreover, since the alliance was not a formal participant in the talks, many of the military planners believed Dayton to be another false alarm warranting prudence.[60]

Hesitancy soon gave way to pandemonium when the JCS alerted US forces in Europe on 2 November, signifying that a deployment into Bosnia was conceivable. Although US forces had been alerted, as of 4 November, no alliance country but Luxembourg had committed forces— in this case 26 soldiers—to what was now known as OPERATION Joint Endeavor. Probably due to disbelief that a ground force deployment was possible given years of political hesitation, the EUCOM planners had yet to publish a plan for a NATO IFOR. USAREUR, however, was not waiting and by 7 November the V Corps planning cell had a detailed plan to deploy its 300-person headquarters to the theater of operations under the moniker of USAREUR Forward.[61]

The advent of USAREUR Forward remains sketchy, although interviews suggest that both General Crouch and Lieutenant General Abrams had a hand in it. Regardless, USAREUR headquarters officers determined that a US Army command and control headquarters was legally necessary under Title 10 US Code to support US force deployment.[62] Using V Corps headquarters for that purpose also guaranteed that a

US Army maneuver headquarters was in proximity to the theater of operations "in case things went bad." General Crouch had sufficient cause to think that possible.[63] General Joulwan was too buried in NATO affairs to personally command the US force deployment. AFSOUTH was for many Army observers a NATO headquarters built around the US Navy's USNAVEUR and lacked experience in deploying ground forces. As the US Army forces provider, General Crouch argued that USAREUR was in the best position to control the deployment.[64] Doctrinally, V Corps headquarters had the command and control mechanisms and thus became USAREUR Forward.

One may take umbrage with a US corps headquarters overseeing a single reinforced armored division. Indeed, the ARRC protested to AFSOUTH, for SHAPE OPLAN 40105 of 15 November 1995 placed the US 1st Armored Division under ARRC command upon NATO transfer of authority. In response, USAREUR noted that a US headquarters was legally necessary under Title 10 US Code to oversee the force before and after authority transfer, thus providing the legal basis for USAREUR Forward to monitor force protection and provide logistics. That aside, US Army planners also saw USAREUR Forward as keeping a service hand in the NATO operation.[65]

As the Dayton meetings slogged through November, General Crouch directed Major General James Wright, the commander of the 21st TAACOM, to conduct a reconnaissance of selected locations within Bosnia and Croatia. Wright was told to find an intermediate staging base to support the ground operation.[66] Between 15 and 21 November 1995, he and a small group tramped about Croatia, Hungary, and other countries looking for a suitable site. After rejecting several possibilities, USAREUR approved negotiations for the use of the military installation and airfield at Taszar, Hungary.

Selecting the Hungarian air base came from practicality and US military parochialism. Taszar, an insignificant village located just outside the city of Kaposvar, offered a large airfield, barracks, and other facilities—albeit in need of renovation—to support the deployment.[67] Conveniently, the air base was also outside of the NATO area of operations. US Army forces under USAREUR Forward thus avoided answering to NATO command. For example, if the US staging base lay within Croatia, then US Major General William N. Farmen, in command of the NATO rear area, had authority over US Army operations. While Taszar was clearly an ideal location to organize US forces prior to deployment into Bosnia, it also avoided NATO meddling. Farmen was a US Army general but some considered him "much too NATO."[68]

On 14 November, EUCOM issued an alert order for subordinate headquarters to begin execution planning, with USAREUR taking a similar action with V Corps three days later. When the Dayton Accords were initialed on 21 November, USAREUR, V Corps, and the 1st Armored Division were already pressing hard for authority to enter Croatia and Bosnia to establish contracts with the local companies required for logistic support. As a former war zone, much of the Bosnian infrastructure was destroyed, and due to the force cutbacks of the early 1990s, the Army in Europe had insufficient force structure to perform building construction and road repair missions. Moreover, millions of unexploded mines and other ordnance lay about the area of operations, munitions that represented a significant threat to the force. The JCS, however, did not authorize early access to the area because the war continued until peace was formalized in Paris.

The numerous headquarters continued to plan in earnest, and by late November the concept to deploy forces had solidified. Many UNPROFOR units from NATO countries were to remain in Bosnia and exchange their UN regalia for IFOR markings. Non-NATO countries such as Russia also offered up ground forces and were fit in under a NATO command structure. A NATO enabling force of just over 2,600 soldiers materialized to deploy ahead of the main body to establish critical life-support facilities, contract for assistance, provide security, and clear convoy routes. US force size was limited to 20,000 troops in Bosnia and 5,000 in Croatia. The US forces were now obliged to move overland from Germany as the Croatian ports became filled to capacity with other IFOR units.

In mid-November, the US 1st Armored Division formed into Task Force *Eagle*, a multinational headquarters created around the divisional force structure.[69] The planners soon produced OPLAN 95-425 or "Iron Endeavor".[70] This concept called for a national support element to establish itself at Kaposvar and Taszar, Hungary, where US forces gathered and then organized for further movement into Bosnia via road and rail. Then, a line of communication-opening force and an aviation "strike package" moved next up to two weeks ahead of the main body. Headquarters, Task Force *Eagle* (Forward) was then designated to arrive in Tuzla, Bosnia to establish communications and control remaining forces transiting the area of operations. The 1st Brigade and the division's cavalry squadron, 1st Squadron 1st Cavalry, moved next, followed by the 2nd Brigade, the 3rd Squadron 4th Cavalry, and the division main headquarters. The division rear with its logistical base then moved, followed by on-call troops to include the

2nd Battalion 15th Infantry. Ultimately, Task Force *Eagle* would establish a zone of separation between combatants and assist in the movement of opposing troops to garrison areas with much of their equipment.[71]

The USAREUR staff envisioned that most US troops would use rail to keep financial costs to a minimum. Theater airlift was expensive; thus only the 1st Armored Division's advance command post, a security company, and elements of the 3rd Battalion 325th Parachute Infantry Regiment from Vicenza, Italy would use air means. To assist the rail movement during the wintry month of December, the V Corps commander designated Brigadier General Samuel L. Kindred from the Corps Support Command to prepare the intermediate staging base in Hungary. Additional logistics assets prepared a tactical assembly area at Harmon, a temporary camp located on the north side of the Sava River near Zupanja, Croatia. There, Army engineers would live while emplacing pontoon bridges across the Sava River. Other forces could halt there temporarily before crossing, if necessary. Once the bridges were in place, Task Force *Eagle* forces would enter Bosnia and conduct their designated missions.[72]

Chaotic Ground Plans

On 6 December 1995, SACEUR published a final version of OPLAN 40105, "Decisive Endeavor." With the GFAP scheduled for signature in Paris on 14 December, Major General Daniel Petrosky, the USAREUR deputy chief of staff for Operations, briefed the USAREUR campaign plan to Admiral Smith, now designated the IFOR commander, in Naples, Italy. Admiral Smith took umbrage with portions of the plan for several reasons. As IFOR commander, he alone exerted operational command and therefore his headquarters was doctrinally obligated to produce a single campaign plan, not USAREUR. Moreover, USAREUR desired to conduct a tactical (combat-ready) road march across Croatia, a political faux pas since Croatia was a nonbelligerent country. Smith also noted that the SACEUR plan showed US forces falling under NATO command once they crossed the Drava River along Hungary's southern border and entered northern Croatia en route to Bosnia. The USAREUR concept, citing Title 10 issues, designated that NATO transfer of authority occurred once US forces crossed the Sava River along southern Croatia. Moving the transfer of authority line farther south meant that USAREUR controlled US Army forces across Croatia until they crossed the Sava float bridges.[73]

The discord over where NATO transfer of authority occurred reflected the stove-piped planning that preceded the movement of forces into Bosnia. In truth, few planners knew of the Dayton Accords' military aspects until the document was published, thus the IFOR/AFSOUTH concept and the USAREUR campaign plan were not nested concepts. Moreover, the AFSOUTH staff did not grasp the USAREUR campaign plan's tactical nuances, for it was not coordinated with AFSOUTH OPLAN 40105. Consensus came when USAREUR was permitted to carve out a north-south corridor along the eastern side of the NATO rear area in Croatia. Because USAREUR was not under NATO command, the US Army units moving from Hungary to Bosnia had to provide their own security and logistics as they transited Croatia in buses and by convoy.

On 1 December, NATO authorized an enabling force deployment to prepare the way for IFOR, followed the next day by a JCS execute order for US enabling forces to follow suit. SHAPE notified AFSOUTH of those decisions through a force activation order designating C-day; the day initial forces begin movement overseas, as 1 December, with ground deployment, G-day, as 14 December. Later, C-day was reinterpreted as 2 December when G-day slipped to 15 December due to diplomatic delays, causing complications with troop movement schedules and transportation arrangements. Meanwhile, some logisticians dutifully moved IFOR equipment to European ports, then shipped the supplies to the Croatian coast based upon the initial C- and G-day schedules.

In the haste to deploy, military planning became disjointed. Political incertitude, the lack of a single planning headquarters, and people trying to do the right thing created most of the confusion.[74] For example, the lack of centralized planning caused numerous headquarters to devise their own uncoordinated concepts for moving Task Force *Eagle* into Bosnia.[75] Part of this was due to the military adage of "just do something" but also to gain an advantage within the Joint Operations Planning and Execution System (JOPES).[76] To gain leverage in securing limited transportation resources, V Corps headquarters used *Mountain Eagle* exercise data to get the JOPES system moving. Unknown to V Corps, the 1st Armored Division had replaced the *Mountain Eagle* database with new information gleaned from another exercise with the ARRC. Neither V Corps nor 1st Armored Division planners were aware that two different USAREUR logistics headquarters had also devised separate databases for deploying US forces and had also entered that information into JOPES. Chaos ensued when different JOPES databases competed for the limited transportation assets necessary to move one US armored division and its supporting units to Bosnia.

The planning confusion was further compounded by a command decision to discount a directive. On 2 December 1995, the EUCOM staff published USCINCEUR OPLAN 4243 "Balkan Endeavor." Two days later, EUCOM informed its USAREUR counterparts that the imminent deployment of US forces into the Balkans was to be considered a strategic movement, thus involving US Transportation Command (USTRANSCOM) for use of national-level transportation assets such as C-17 aircraft.[77] Under US joint doctrine, EUCOM was tasked to prepare a troop movement list and send it to USTRANSCOM for the creation of Time-Phased Force and Deployment Data. For reasons that remain unclear, the USAREUR staff discounted EUCOM's directive, choosing instead to view the deployment as an operational/tactical move, not strategic. That decision meant that USAREUR could not draw upon US national transportation assets but instead had to depend only upon those in Europe. This decision was allegedly made for two reasons: to keep USTRANSCOM out of the deployment process and thus speed up the movement of forces and also to retain USAREUR control over the deployment of US Army forces.[78]

US Army enabling forces had moved to Kaposvar and Taszar by 8 December 1995. Logistics units under USAREUR command commenced preparations to become a national support element, a headquarters that was supposedly capable of equipping and sustaining all US forces in the theater of operations. In truth, there was little "national" about the national support element, for the USAREUR logisticians were supporting primarily US Army forces. When walking along the freezing tarmac at Taszar, one could see a hodgepodge of US military forces that drew support from their parent services, not the national support element.[79]

In early December 1995, many plans officers worked from NATO and USAREUR documents designed to move the enabling force into position two weeks prior to G-day. Delays in political action and acquiring permissions compressed that timeline to nine days. With some enabling force assets now unable to deploy fast enough to meet the new schedule, main body combat units were reshuffled in movement priority to act as security forces. Thus, the US 1st Armored Division's 1st Squadron 1st Cavalry, which had been scheduled to move after the security forces, was pushed forward faster than anticipated. The deployment change meant that when the squadron arrived in Zupanja, Croatia on 16 December, the unit designated to offload its equipment had not yet arrived. Unable to offload and with no place to sleep in the freezing weather, many troops stayed inside the rail cars without heat.[80]

G-Day coincided with the signing of the GFAP on 14 December, with NATO main body forces then having until 19 December to assume the Bosnia mission. With the peace accord signed on time, the UN Security Council passed Resolution 1031, establishing IFOR. NATO, however, took two days to approve SACEUR OPLAN 10405, thus G-Day slipped from 14 to 16 December. D-day, or mission assumption, then moved to 20 December. Political delays and revisions meant so many changes that military staff officers had difficulty keeping up.

Plans in Motion

On the revised G-day of 16 December, the majority of NATO and US forces commenced movement as about half of the UNPROFOR units prepared to trade their UN trappings for IFOR markings. The ARRC deployed to Sarajevo and assumed command of a multinational three-division force that peaked at 55,000 troops from 35 nations. However, the troop movement now exposed US military planning deficiencies. The slippage in deployment dates clashed with USAREUR's already competing unit databases in the JOPES system. The deployment turned disastrous and the EUCOM staff, which was accountable for moving US forces into Bosnia, worked in a state of continuous upheaval.

Numerous USAREUR planners had expected most trains to take about 24 hours to reach Kaposvar and the intermediate staging base at Taszar by rail from Frankfurt, Germany. Instead, the movement took four days, because military trains had less priority than civilian rail traffic under the privately owned German rail system. With the ongoing Christmas holiday season, military trains were relegated to sidings for hours on end to make room for other rail activity.[81] Moreover, the US military rail deployment crossed a neutral country (Austria) and former Warsaw Pact countries where the trains came under suspicion from border guards. Once at the staging base in Hungary, the forces needed another 10 hours to move to Zupanja, then 2 more hours by road march to reach Tuzla.

Although USAREUR plans called for rail as the primary means of movement for control purposes and to save money, it quickly became apparent that this was a mistake. USAREUR's decision to view the deployment as operational/tactical instead of strategic had limited transportation asset flexibility. With so many changes in force flow due to political wavering, many deploying units arrived at their embarkation railhead sites in Germany to learn that some trains were not there, others were insufficient for the force size, and several had railcars designed to haul different equipment. Most of the required railcars were in France, which at the time was under a national rail strike. Other difficulties arose because many US Army transportation officers had not formulated the USAREUR deployment plans and therefore did not understand them.[82]

The transportation situation worsened when the European rail system proved unable to move 25,000 US troops. USAREUR planners had calculated that Task Force *Eagle* required 20 trains per day, a figure based upon data used during routine training exercises. Upon arrival at their destination in Hungary or Croatia, the trains remained loaded due to the lack of offloading equipment. Civilian rail managers were unable to shift other trains to different lines, and the swelling queue clogged the rail system. Indeed, some trains left Germany in the morning only to return the same night with the passengers and equipment still aboard due to rail congestion farther along the route.

By 24 December, US Army force commanders were in serious trouble as the rail deployment ground to a halt. With possible mission failure looming, the USAREUR staff resorted to moving soldiers via buses, commercial trucks, and aircraft at great financial expense. Circumstances forced USAREUR to request C-17 aircraft as EUCOM had earlier directed. Because nationally controlled aircraft were now involved, Army planners had to use JOPES to notify USTRANSCOM of the requirement. Yet, many USAREUR officers were unfamiliar with such procedures and processing errors occurred. Moreover, at least since 20 December, the force flow and transportation priorities changed an average of 14 times per day, lending further chaos to an already disagreeable situation.[83]

Changing priorities meant that some US Air Force aircraft arrived in Germany to discover that the passengers were not there. To complicate matters further, US Army general officers roamed the airfield flight line and changed Air Force equipment-loading precedence on the fly. As a result, the heavy equipment necessary for offloading trains in Taszar was set aside, which further slowed US Army force deployment. EUCOM interceded on 26 December by ordering USAREUR to cease managing the deployment until things settled down.

With staff officers at numerous headquarters working to the brink of exhaustion, USAREUR requested additional planners from Fort Bragg, North Carolina and Fort Campbell, Kentucky. These officers were graduates of the School of Advanced Military Studies, a one-year course that educated selected mid-grade officers in operational and tactical planning methods. Upon arrival they served as USAREUR troubleshooters, with General Crouch keeping one officer in Heidelberg while another went forward to unravel the confusion in the theater of operations.[84] Circumstances improved by 28 December as the JOPES network stabilized enough for US military aircraft to move a US mechanized infantry company to Belgrade from whence it convoyed to Tuzla. There, the unit met with elements of the 3rd Battalion 325th Parachute Infantry Regiment from Vicenza, Italy.

As order slowly returned, the Balkan winter brought snowfalls and bitter temperatures that threatened the Sava River bridge crossing. Heavy snow caused the river to rise, altering the number of required float bridge sections. The US Army Corps of Engineers facility at Vicksburg, Mississippi had helped in figuring out how many sections were necessary based upon historical flood data.[85] When the water level surpassed initial estimations, USAREUR engineers were forced to take additional bays from European war stocks in Belgium at increased costs.[86]

In addition to Army engineers, US Navy Sea, Air, Land (SEALS) and US Air Force Rapid Engineer Deployable Heavy Operational Repair Squadron Engineer (RED HORSE) units worked long hours along the Sava River in anticipation of the float bridge crossing. However, the bridge sections were delayed in arriving. Too wide to transit Austrian railroad tunnels (as discovered by collisions), the bridge sections had to be hoisted from the railcars and onto wheeled trucks, then hauled to Zupanja. Upon arrival near the Sava, roads choked from snow and ice stymied the bridge-burdened vehicles from gaining access to the river. On 28 December, engineers were constructing a new roadbed to allow the bridge sections to reach the Sava.

That same day, engineer commander Lieutenant Colonel Jack Sterling notified Brigadier General James P. O'Neil from Task Force *Eagle* that the Sava River was near flood level and in danger of overflowing its banks. After much ado, O'Neil gave permission to move the engineers to higher ground on the 29th. Sterling's prediction came true in the early morning hours of 29 December when the Sava burst its banks, flooding the US military camp at Zupanja. USAREUR Forward personnel listened to the unfolding and terrifying events over their radios, fearing that numerous soldiers were drowned. Water rapidly reached 15 feet above ground level, washing away equipment and personal effects in the cataclysm.[87] When dawn broke, however, every soldier was miraculously found alive and without serious injury.

That morning, the relocated engineers resumed the task of emplacing float bridges as the new roadway came into being. But wintry conditions continued to bedevil them, for the floodwaters, mud, and ice prevented offloading the bridge sections. Fortunately, CH-47D helicopter crews

Photo 3. US military personnel narrowly avoided disaster
when the Sava River flooded in December 1995.

Photo 4. Remarkably, the Sava River flood cost US forces
only a brief delay with no loss of life.

from Kaposvar, Hungary had rehearsed the airlifting of bridge sections the previous summer, so they were called forward to drop the sections into the river for assembly. That accomplished, the final bridge piece was locked in place at 1004 on 31 December 1995, and by early evening more than 140 1st Armored Division vehicles had crossed into Bosnia.[88] Task Force *Eagle* now poured into the Multinational Division-North area of responsibility to establish a zone of separation between former combatants.

Plans Assessment

This initial "brush clearing" to make some sense of military preparations for Bosnia confirms that diplomatic vagary directly affected planning. Between 1991 and 1995, political will caused some nations to seek ways to end a horrendous war, while others lacked the interest and resources and remained on the sidelines. In response to UN and NAC decisions, military planners generated a plethora of plans to meet wispy political circumstances. As this chapter illuminated, the plans for employing sea and air power attained mission success through interdiction and physical destruction but failed to coerce the belligerents to any great effect. Sea and air power coercion works when the targeted foe is susceptible to such measures.[89] Ground power, however, is essential to impose will and demonstrate resolve. Lacking political support, most ground options developed over months of work ultimately were shelved or discarded. When political will to bring the war to closure finally gelled in the fall of 1995, a disparate grouping of NATO and US Army plans came to the fore, only to suffer from poor synchronization through a common headquarters. The flaws aside, the deployment phase succeeded more as a testament to the character of the men and women who executed the plans than a triumph of the planning system itself.

It can be said that despite the flap surrounding plan development, military planners helped to bring peace to war-torn Bosnia. Yet, the plans themselves were but one contributor to the overall effort. Indeed, peace came about through a combination of UN resolutions, NAC decisions, US diplomatic efforts, economic sanctions, sea and air power, the eventual threat of a credible ground force, and exhausted warring factions, among other influences. The military plans developed and executed between 1991 and 1995 helped create conditions for the peace process to succeed but were not a panacea by themselves.

This study also shows that UN, NATO and US military planners held little sway over civilian policy decisions. Where military doctrine of the time called for a synchronized planning effort that went up, down, and laterally among headquarters in concert with stated political objectives, the lack of a clear political end state and policy inconstancy turned proactive military planning practice into a reactionary affair. What can be called "backlash planning" meant that diplomatic turbulence had placed the military plans officers in the ignoble position of having to wait for the next round of political machinations to see what had been wrought. Often the outcome of such meetings had little to do with previously developed concepts.

While attaining commitment from civilian leaders remains problematic for military commanders and staffs, part of the Bosnia crisis-planning pitfalls stemmed from stress upon a flawed post-Cold War planning system within Europe, despite what some have said about it.[90] While a successful operation in the long term, NATO and US planning procedures were fraught with glaring deficiencies in coordination that nearly brought disaster. Despite attempts at system overhaul by 1995, the faults can be attributed to entrenched military culture and attitudes. In planning for this operation, officers worked within a new world order where multinational planning had become commonplace not only strategically, but also at the operational and tactical levels. Many officers were trained in the 1980s under Cold War truths where services seldom worked multinational plans at the operational or tactical level. That paradigm no longer fit Bosnian crisis realities. For the post-Cold War military, adjusting from a bipolar world to the post-Cold War disorder was a steep learning curve.

The Bosnia crisis in late 1995 was a time of flux where old military mind-sets clashed with new truths. It took time-constrained duress once the Dayton Accords were agreed to bear this out. While planning under old views resulted in feasible concepts prior to 21 November 1995, the tremendous pressure generated by hourly changes in building an acceptable and suitable IFOR force structure fractured the planning effort after that date. Automation was of little help because the lack of a central headquarters to manage both the NATO and the US military planning effort strategically, operationally, and tactically left many officers to devise their own concepts. Without central control, general officers worked their staffs hard to get the mission accomplished. But constant change to time schedules and published plans baffled people so much that they simply could not keep up. In violation of the centralized planning-decentralized execution rule, the more aggressive headquarters created chaos by taking initiative without weighing the consequences. Localized decisions dramatically affected coalition planning.

As much as this study contributes something toward understanding what went on during years of planning, it can only scratch the surface of some headquarters while ignoring others. Indeed, much more is known about AFSOUTH and efforts within USAREUR at this point than what occurred within the UN, JCS, SHAPE, EUCOM, and contributing nation headquarters. The individuals involved in planning within these entities must come forward to tell their stories so a more complete assessment can be drawn. For their part, the historians working within each headquarters must gain release for the documents from their declassification authorities.

In addition to assessing planning, this chapter argued that two critical events contributed significantly to the end of Bosnia's war. The first was the mortar attack upon Sarajevo's marketplace in February 1994 that heightened global outrage and prompted the Clinton administration to bring US diplomatic pressure to the fray. The second turning point was the Bosnian Serbs taking several hundred UN peacekeepers hostage in May 1995. That vile act so challenged UN and NATO credibility in protecting UN-PROFOR and its interests that a division-size ground reaction force was authorized and planned for. Both events, ironically caused by the belligerents themselves, pushed the history of the conflict in a different direction.

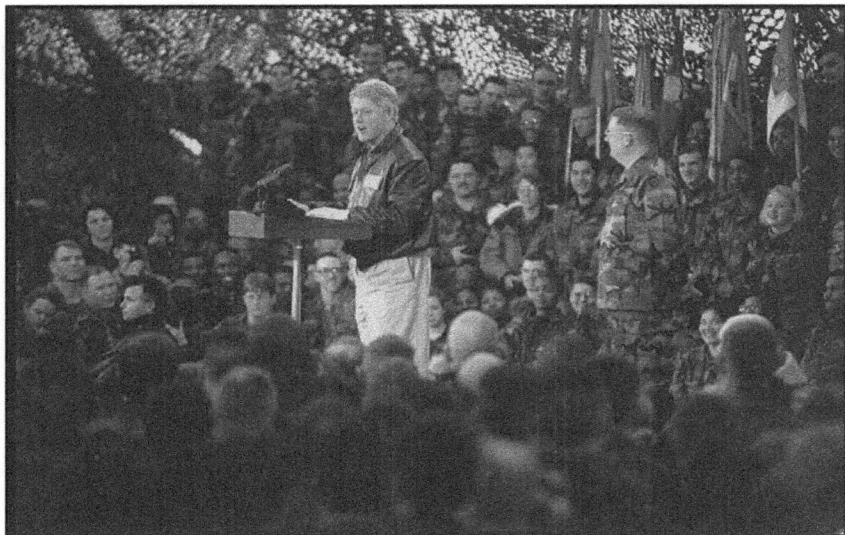

Photo 5. Having made the difficult choice to commit forces in Bosnia,
President Clinton addressed US soldiers.

For all its foibles, the military planning effort that led to OPERATION Joint Endeavor and the deployment of military ground power to Bosnia over the winter of 1995-1996 was a success story. The scope and complexity of the undertaking rivaled OPERATION Desert Shield/OPERATION Desert Storm and thus warrants further scrutiny. If this chapter reveals anything, it is that flexible and persistent people can overcome political friction and planning fog to accomplish the mission at hand.

Notes

1. Dayton Peace Accords, General Framework Agreement for Peace in Bosnia and Herzegovina, 21 November 1995. Available on the Internet at http://www. state.gov/www.current/bosnia/dayframe.html. Accessed 2 February 1997.

2. The General Framework Agreement for Peace was signed in Paris, France on 14 December 1995. Three belligerent representatives—Alija Izetbegovic, Franjo Tudjman, and Slobodan Milosevic—signed the document and approved its entire contents. Representatives of the European Union, France, Germany, the United Kingdom, and the United States witnessed the event but were not signatories.

3. Other headquarters included AFNORTH, which is not discussed here. For a detailed look at NATO organization, see "NATO Handbook," [book online], accessed 18 November 2002; available from http://www.nato.int/docu/handbook/2001/.

4. For example, numerous countries provided forces to IFOR, yet we know nothing about what planning occurred within the military headquarters of Turkey, Sweden, Norway, Russia, Latvia, Lithuania, Poland, and many other countries.

5. See "United States European Command," [document online]; accessed 27 March 2003; available from http://www.eucom.mil/index.htm?http://www. eucom.mil/Standard_tf.htm&0; Internet. Strategic, operational, and tactical levels of war are defined in the Department of Defense *Dictionary of Military Terms* [publication online], accessed 3 April 2003; available from http://www. dtic.mil/doctrine/jel/doddict/; Internet. The US Army-led Task Force *Eagle* alone contained the US 1st Armored Division, brigades from Russia and Turkey, and a Nordic/Polish brigade formed from the soldiers of Norway, Poland, Finland, Sweden, Denmark, Latvia, Estonia, and Lithuania.

6. Personnel turnover and personality nuances are often overlooked when examining planning. Yet they can have dramatic effects upon plans development. It often takes a new planner up to three months to settle in and understand what has happened previously, time not available during crisis. Strong personalities can either support or shut out even the most brilliant of ideas, an especially critical point when senior rank is involved.

7. *Will NATO Go East?: The Debate Over Enlarging the Atlantic Alliance*, David G. Haglund, ed. (Kingston, Ontario: Queen's Copyright in Right, 1996), 18-25.

8. Christopher Bennett, *Yugoslavia's Bloody Collapse: Causes, Course and Consequences*. (New York: New York University Press, 1995), 156-204.

9. Interestingly, citizens of Bosnia and Herzegovina within the federation do not admit that the recent war was a civil war but prefer to explain it as a war of external aggression. One opinion was offered by Radko Mavraic, a noted journalist and the media adviser to the commander, Stabilization Force in Bosnia in 2001. In an interview, Mavraic noted that the war was started from the outside by Serbia. When pressed to explain how he accounted for Bosnians killing Bosnians, Mavraic offered that they were forced to do so by Serb aggression.

Interview with Radko Mavraic by author, Media Center Sarajevo, Bosnia and Herzegovina, 12 July 2001.

10. Gordon W. Rudd, "Operation Provide Comfort: Humanitarian Intervention in northern Iraq, 1991." Ph.D. diss., Duke University, 1993.

11. The most expensive and complex UN peacekeeping mission to date, UNPROFOR consisted of about 38,000 troops from 37 nations, with the largest contingents coming from NATO members such as Britain and France. Approximately 15,000 troops were chartered to provide security for enclave minority groups located within Croatia. The remaining UN forces stationed in Bosnia monitored the peace and assisted in the delivery of humanitarian aide to suffering civilians. NATO force planners considered the consequences and response for NATO (although the soldiers would act under the UN) if one or more of the warring factions decided to attack them. General Sir Michael Rose, *Fighting For Peace, Bosnia 1994* (London: The Harvill Press, 1998), 143. *Lessons From Bosnia: The IFOR Experience*, Larry Wentz, cont. ed. (Washington, DC: Command and Control Research Program, National Defense University Press, 1998), 16.

12. North Atlantic Council, "Rome Declaration on Peace and Cooperation Press Communiqué S-1(91)86, 8 November 1991." [document online]; accessed 19 April 2003, available from http://www.nato.int/docu/comm/49-95/c911108a. htm; Internet.

13. James J. Brooks, *Operation Provide Promise: The JFACC's Role in Humanitarian Assistance in a Non-Permissive Environment.* Newport, RI, Naval War College, 1996. Robert H. King, *NATO's Combined Joint Task Force: Separable but Not Separate.* Newport, RI, Naval War College, May 1995. Tony Capaccio, "Bosnia Airdrop." *Air Force Magazine*, **July 1993, 52-55.**

14. William B. Buchanan, Project leader, *Operation Joint Endeavor-Description and Lessons Learned.* (Washington, DC: Institute For Defense Analysis, 1996), III-2.

15. North Atlantic Council, "Statement on Former Yugoslavia, document M-NAC-2(92)108, 17 December 1992." [document online], accessed 19 April 2003; available from http://www.nato.int/docu/comm/49-95/c921217b.htm; Internet.

16. The Vance-Owen Peace Plan sought to create the idea of multi-ethnicity into the Bosnian political system. The plan meant territorial division and the creation of 10 regions, nine of which had an ethnic majority of one people. One region, Sarajevo, would be mixed. The plan guaranteed ethnic minority representation within each region through a constitutional design fabricated by Finnish diplomat Martti Ahtisaari. In addition to the lack of international and US backing, the Bosnian Serbs rejected the plan. Moreover, various policy makers were reluctant to risk ground forces to overturn Serb military achievement. See David Owen, *Balkan Odyssey* (New York: Harcourt Brace and Company, 1995).

17. "NATO/WEU Operation Sharp Guard," [document online]; accessed 3 April 2003; available from http://www.nato.int/ifor/general/shrp-grd.htm; Internet.

18. Christopher Bennett, *Yugoslavia's Bloody Collapse*, 197-98.

19. AFSOUTH Fact Sheet "Operation Deliberate Force," [report online], accessed 31 March 2003; available from http://www.fas.org/man/dod-101/ops/docs/DeliberateForceFactSheet.htm; Internet.

20. David Rohde, *Endgame: The Betrayal and Fall of Srebrenica, Europe's Worst Massacre Since World War II.* Boulder: Westview Press, 1998.

21. Robert C. Owen, editor, *Deliberate Force: A Case Study in Effective Air Campaigning.* (Maxwell Air Force Base, AL: Air University Press, 2000), xx.

22. Robert C. Owen, *Deliberate Force*, 60.

23. Ibid., 54-60. "Dual-key" imitates the nuclear release requirement for two authorities to give an order of mass destruction.

24. Ibid., 131-75.

25. Richard Holbrooke, *To End a War*, revised edition. (New York: The Modern Library, 1999), 142-52.

26. Steve Hurst, "Bosnian Serbs Escape More Airstrikes," *Cable News Network*, 20 September 1995.

27. Ivo H. Daalder, "Decision to Intervene: How the War in Bosnia Ended," *Foreign Service Journal*, December 1998.

28. Conversations with Major J.D. Johnson and Major Victor Robertson by author between October 1992 and March 1996, Fort Leavenworth, KS and Heidelberg, Germany.

29. David Owen, *Balkan Odyssey*, 31-88.

30. Bob Stewart, *Broken Lives: A Personal View of the Bosnian Conflict* (London: HarperCollins, 1994).

31. "UNPREDEP." [report online], accessed 26 March 2002; available from http://www.un.org/Depts/DPKO/Missions/unpredep.htm.

32. Speech by US Secretary of State Warren Christopher to House Foreign Affairs Committee, 18 May 1993.

33. Wesley K. Clark, *Waging Modern War: Bosnia, Kosovo, and the Future of Combat* (New York: Public Affairs, 2001), 43.

34. Interview with Lieutenant Colonel Al Bryant by Major Richard Thurston, 90th Military History Detachment, February 1996, Heidelberg, Germany. Conversation with Bryant by author, March 1998, Fort Leavenworth, KS.

35. Institute For Defense Analysis, *Operation Joint Endeavor*, III-3.

36. Headquarters, United States Army Europe, *Operation Joint Endeavor USAREUR Headquarters After Action Report*, 2 vols. (Heidelberg, GE: HQ, USAREUR, May 1997), vol. 1, 6. Nicolas Burns, "US Department of State Daily Press Briefing, 12 April 1995." Washington, D.C.: US Department of State, Office of the Spokesman, 12 April 1995.

37. Open Media Research Institute Daily Digest I, II, No. 103, 29 May 1995.

38. Headquarters, United States Army Europe, *Operation Joint Endeavor*, vol. 1, 138.

39. Department of State, "US Department of State Daily Press Briefing, Friday, 6 July 1995." [report online] accessed 17 April 2003; available from http://www.hri.org/docs/statedep/95-07-06.std.html, Internet. Secretary of Defense William J. Perry to Senate Armed Services Committee and House National

Security Committee, 9 June 1995, [document online], accessed 8 April 2003; available from http://www.defenselink.mil/speeches/1995/t19950607-perry. html; Internet.

40. Units included an airborne brigade commanded by Colonel James McDonough, along with the 12th Aviation Brigade, the 11th Aviation Regiment, and the 7th Corps Support Group. Interview with Brigadier General Burwell B. Bell III by author, March 1996, Taszar, Hungary. Linda D. Kozaryn and Casondra Brewster, "Supporting Balkan Peacekeepers," *Soldiers*, August 1995.

41. Tim Ito, "Bosnia and Herzegovina Overview" [document online] (Washington, DC: *The Washington Post*, October 1998, accessed 12 December 2002); available from http://www.washingtonpost.com/wp-srv/inatl/longterm/balkans/overview/bosnia.htm.

42. Department of State, "US Department of State Daily Press Briefing, Friday, 21 July 1995." [report online] accessed 25 April 2002; available from http://www.hri.org/docs/statedep/95-07-21.std.html, Internet.

43. Richard Holbrooke, *To End a War*, 72.

44. "US Envoy Lake Briefs Turkey on Bosnia Plan." *Turkish Daily News*, 15 August 1995.

45. Robert Fox, "Fresh War Clouds Threaten Cease Fire." *Sunday Telegraph*, 15 October 1995. Nelson D. Schwartz, "The Pentagon's Private Army." *Fortune*, 17 March 2003.

46. Headquarters, Allied Forces Southern Europe, OPLAN 40105, 20 December 1995. Archive, Headquarters, NATO Stabilization Force Bosnia, Butmir, Bosnia and Herzegovina, accessed June 2001.

47. Interview with Lieutenant Colonel Peter J. Schifferle by Major Richard Thurston, 90th Military History Detachment, 16 February 1996, Heidelberg, Germany.

48. Heike Hasenaur and Geoff Janes, "On Call For Bosnia," *Soldiers*, December 1995.

49. Schifferle interview.

50. Bryant interview.

51. Ibid.

52. Ibid.

53. Richard Holbrooke, *To End a War*, 185-98.

54. Stanley F. Cherrie, "Task Force *Eagle*." *Military Review*, July-August 1997, 63-72.

55. Headquarters, United States Army Europe, *Peace Enforcement Operations*. Lessons Learned Newsletter 1-95, Mountain Eagle 95, USAREUR. *Operation Joint Endeavor Initial Impressions Report*. Fort Leavenworth, KS: US Army Center for Lessons Learned, July 1996.

56. Institute for Defense Analysis, *Operation Joint Endeavor*, III-23.

57. Ibid., VI-4.

58. Richard Holbrooke, *To End a War*, 232.

59. Interview with former US Political Adviser to SFOR by author, Butmir, Sarajevo, Bosnia and Herzegovina, 14 July 2001. The POLAD, who wished not

to be identified by name, also attended the peace talks where he observed that the Europeans were put on the sidelines.

60. Interview with Major James Alty, Jr., chief of Plans and Operations, deputy dhief of staff for Personnel, USAREUR, by Bryce Benedict, 102nd Military History Detachment, 15 March 1996, Taszar, Hungary.

61. Charles Kirkpatrick, "V Corps in Operation Joint Endeavor" [document online], accessed 31 March 2003; available from http://www.vcorps.army.mil/www/News/2002/june14_endeavor.htm; Internet.

62. For US military commander legal responsibilities, see http://www.access.gpo.gov/uscode/title10/title10.html.

63. Comment by Schifferle. During my time as the USAREUR command historian, I observed conversations between General Crouch and Lieutenant General Abrams that made this point very clear.

64. In actuality, USAREUR and V Corps could have remained in a force provider role. Admiral Smith at AFSOUTH was also in command of US Naval Forces, Europe (NAVEUR). Under joint doctrine of the time, EUCOM could have ordered USAREUR to provide ground forces to USNAVEUR to meet US Title 10 requirements. However, service parochialism was at play here, and Bosnia was, after all, the crisis of the moment.

65. Interview with Lieutenant Colonel Daniel Gilbert, deputy chief of staff For Operations, USAREUR Forward, by author, 19 April 1996, Taszar, Hungary. Interview with Lieutenant Colonel John Baggott, deputy chief of staff For Operations, USAREUR Forward, by Bryce Benedict, 102nd Military History Detachment, 4 March 1996, Taszar, Hungary.

66. Bruce E. Akard, "Strategic Deployment: An Analysis of How The United States Army Europe Deployed VII Corps To Southwest Asia and the 1st Armored Division to Bosnia." Masters Thesis, US Army Command and General Staff College, 1997, 44-45. Interview with Major General James Wright by author, April 1996, Taszar, Hungary. Charles Kirkpatrick, "V Corps in Operation Joint Endeavor."

67. "Taszar Airbase," [document online], accessed 1 April 2003; available at http://www.globalsecurity.org/military/facility/taszar.htm; Internet. The air base was filthy with rats running through the buildings and inadequate facilities for showers, billets, and dining, all of which required upgrading under Brown and Root Corporation.

68. Interviews conducted by the author in 1996 with various members of the US V Corps staff indicate that some US Army general officers were not pleased with General Farmen, whom many thought had forgotten he was a US general. Clearly, various agendas and rivalries were at work here.

69. Task Force *Eagle* contained a Russian brigade of two parachute battalions totaling almost 1,500 soldiers; a Turkish Brigade containing a large Turkish mechanized infantry battalion with its supporting tank company and artillery battery; and a Nordic/Polish Brigade composed of Nordic forces and a Polish parachute battalion. Task Forced *Eagle* totaled about 22,500 soldiers.

70. Stanley F. Cherrie, "Task Force *Eagle*."

71. Headquarters, 1st Armored Division. "OPLAN 95-425 Iron Endeavor," dtd 30 November 1995, Bad Kreuznach, Germany. Center For Army Lessons Learned Archive, Fort Leavenworth, Kansas.

72. See OPLAN 95-425 "Iron Endeavor," Center for Army Lessons Learned Archive.

73. Interview with Major Randall G. Cox, deputy chief, National Coalition Cell, EUCOM, by author, 22 May 1996, Zagreb, Croatia.

74. It is important to note here that official government historians who have voiced the opinion that the planning was much more cohesive contest this point. Most historians, however, have never been planners. Those who worked the various actions continue to hold that trying to cross over between UN, NATO, and US planning channels was often a disjointed affair. See for example Department of the Army, "Bosnia-Herzegovina After Action Review Conference Report, 19-23 May 1996." Carlisle Barracks, PA: Peacekeeping Institute, 1996.

75. Interview with Brigadier General Stanley F. Cherrie, US Army, Retired, by Dr. Robert F. Baumann, February 2001, Fort Leavenworth, KS.

76. JOPES is an automated computerized database that contains unit designations, equipment and personnel readiness status, and locations. Planners use JOPES to determine which units must deploy and in what sequence to deconflict transportation requirements and the use of seaports, air terminals, and rail networks. See Joint Chiefs of Staff, *Users Guide For JOPES*. [document online] (Washington, D.C.: Joint Chiefs of Staff, 1 May 1995, accessed 19 April 2003); available from http://www.dtic.mil/doctrine/jel/other_pubs/jopes.pdf; Internet.

77. The United States Transportation Command was established in 1987 with its headquarters at Scott Air Force Base, Illinois. USTRANSCOM is tasked with coordinating the movement of people and transportation assets to allow the United States to project and sustain forces around the world for as long as necessary. It responds to the needs of the Department of Defense's combatant commanders and is composed of three commands: US Air Force's Air Mobility Command, US Navy's Military Sealift Command, and the US Army's Military Traffic Management Command. The command uses both military and commercial transportation resources. See http://public.transcom.mil/.

78. Institute For Defense Analysis, *Operation Joint Endeavor*, III-23.

79. Personal notes taken as Army component command historian, Operation *Joint Endeavor* by author, Taszar, Hungary, 20 February 1996. My discussions with the Air Force elements there was that they were supplied through Air Force channels, not the NSE. Logistics is a service responsibility but USAREUR Forward was not a joint or multiservice command capable of coordinating service logisitcs.

80. Interview with Major Bruce E. Akard, US Transportation Command by author, April 1997, Fort Leavenworth, Kansas. Akard was sent to Europe to assist USAREUR with transportation planning and to sort out the confusion.

81. The German rail system was operating under holiday conditions at approximately 30-percent staff.

82. Interview with Mr. Heinz Schneider, traffic manager, 39th Transportation Group, 21st TAACOM by Richard Thurston, 90th Military History Detachment, 26 February 1996, Kaiserslautern, Germany.

83. Institute For Defense Analysis, Operation *Joint Endeavor*, IV-11.

84. Bell interview.

85. US Army Corps of Engineers, Vicksburg District, Hydraulics Branch, "Water Control Management," [website online]; accessed 14 April 2003, available from http://www.mvk.usace.army.mil/offices/ed/edh/watercontrol.htm; Internet.

86. See http://www.globalsecurity.org/military/agency/army/srsae.htm.

87. Interview with Chief Warrant Officer 5 Patrick M. Endicott, senior maintenance warrant, 130th Engineer Brigade by author, 28 May 1996, Tuzla, Bosnia.

88. Stanley F. Cherrie, "Task Force *Eagle.*"

89. Robert A. Pape, *Bombing to Win: Air Power and Coercion in War*. (Ithaca, NY: Cornell University Press, 1996), 209.

90. George A. Joulwan, "SHAPE and IFOR: Adapting to the Needs of Tomorrow." *NATO Review,* March 1996, 6-9.

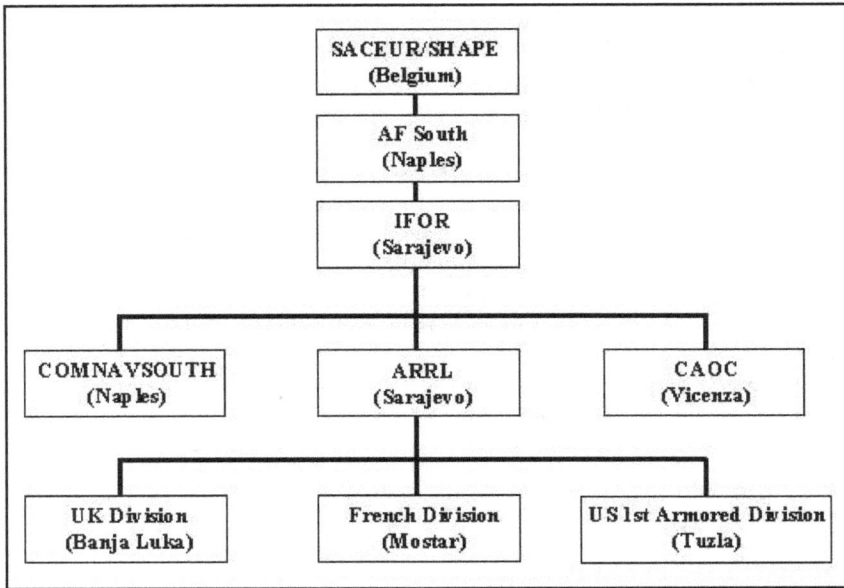

Figure 2. NATO Organization during IFOR

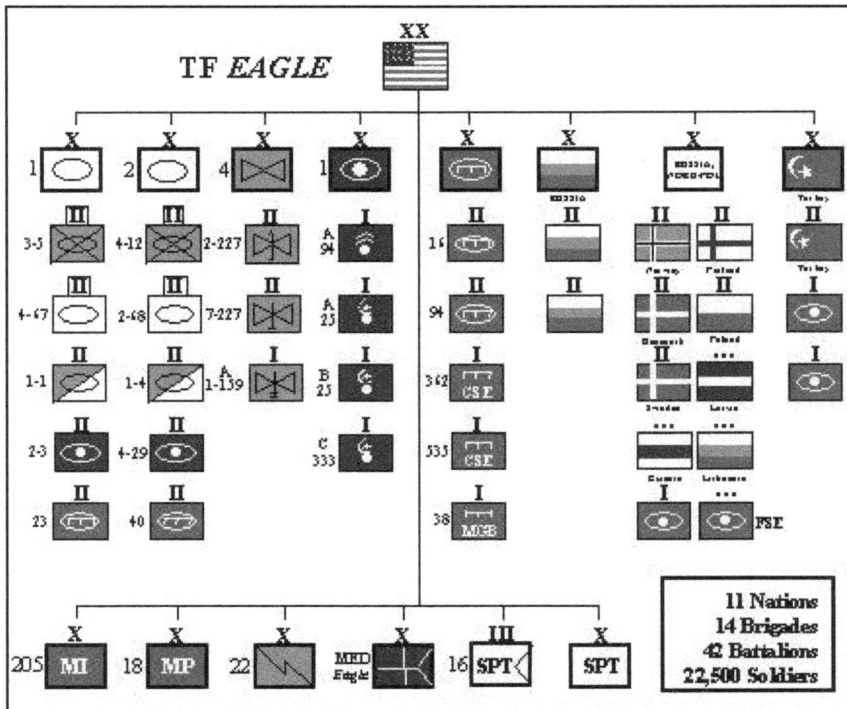

Figure 3. Task Force *Eagle*

Chapter 4

IFOR Redefines the Bosnian Situation

Robert F. Baumann

Two critical factors distinguished the so-called Implementation Force from its predecessor. The first was the presence of American troops. Far more than a token, the 1st Armored Division was a heavy force bristling with combat power. Observers inside and outside of Bosnia regarded American inclusion as proof that the new international force would be more than a symbolic presence. Further proof of this fact was the second distinction between UNPROFOR and IFOR. The Dayton General Framework Agreement for Peace (GFAP) guaranteed that IFOR would not be hamstrung by narrowly written rules of engagement that would effectively blunt its sword and vitiate its authority. Fully empowered to apply force in response to any acts of noncompliance, IFOR quickly commanded the respect of the heretofore uncooperative faction armies.

Colonel Greg Fontenot, who commanded the 1st Armored Division's 1st Brigade as part of Task Force *Eagle*, observed that IFOR's business was "peace enforcement." US forces entered Bosnia in late December 1995 in overwhelming strength and wary of the perils of their surroundings.[1] American personnel crossed friendly Croatia in full battle gear, then proceeded to bridge the Sava River. There, an engineer battalion encamped in a relatively low-lying area, that, though free of mines, posed a serious natural hazard. The Americans paid the price for tempting fate as the waters of the Sava abruptly rose and engulfed tents and equipment. Remarkably, thanks to sound training and the determination of a number of small-unit leaders, no one was lost.[2] Only slightly delayed, US forces pressed ahead with their mission.

Initially, the Americans were uncertain of the attitudes of the so-called Entity Armed Forces—the international euphemism for the organized forces of the three warring factions in Bosnia—and were taking no chances. According to Assistant Division Commander Brigadier General Stan Cherrie, they did not really expect to fight hostile formations, as all early indications were that the locals had lost their taste for battle.[3] Nevertheless, the risk of snipers seemed real enough, and the intermittent percussion of celebratory fire and miscellaneous stray rounds served as a reminder of what conceivably could happen. Moreover, intelligence was limited and trained Army linguists were in short supply.[4] In this climate of

Photo 6. Clearing mines was a crucial task under IFOR

uncertainty, the command established a strict standard of force protection, requiring a minimum of four vehicles for any movement outside of Eagle Base and other US compounds. Patrols went out in strength, and fearsome M1A1 tanks made the intended impression.[5] The first mission task was to clear the agreed zone of separation, or ZOS, between the Entity Armed Forces and establish secure routes of movement. This occurred in phases and without major incidents.

This is not to say, however, that the situation was not complex and did not require an imaginative response by US forces. Clearing the ZOS not only implied the removal of forces and weapons, but also free movement for refugees back to their homes. This process became especially dicey in the vicinity of Brcko, the strategically located town linking the two lobes of the Republika Srpska (RS). To monitor the situation there closely, the United States established an observation post not far from Camp McGovern, which was under the command of Lieutenant Colonel Tony Cuculo. As the first hardy Muslim returnees picked their way carefully through the mines and debris, repairs slowly began. The effort soon picked up momentum in mid-April as construction gangs with all manner of building materials became a conspicuous presence. This evidently alarmed local Serbs, who quickly responded by trying to match Muslim construction efforts. The Serb perception was that the Muslims were trying to establish control on the ground in the ZOS through habitation. Soon the international community had to establish ground rules to determine which refugees were actually entitled to live in the ZOS by virtue of prior residency.[6] However, since most legitimate returnees were Muslims, cooperation from the Serb side was reluctant and slow.

According to the terms of the GFAP, at D+90 the factions were supposed to park all their heavy weapons (tanks, artillery, surface-to-air missiles and so forth) in designated cantonment sites subject to periodic inspection and inventory by IFOR. By D+120 required storage applied further to all weapons over 20 mm in caliber. For practical reasons, the Supreme Allied Commander Europe (SACEUR) extended the deadline to D+180 or 21 June 1996. According to President Clinton's special envoy, Richard Holbrooke, the Pentagon consistently opposed the cantonment and supervision of the entity armed forces' heavy weapons, presumably because it did not want US troops to assume responsibility for implementation of this mission on the ground. However, at Holbrooke's insistence, the military reluctantly agreed to the inclusion of the cantonment plan in Annex 1-B of Dayton. In contrast to annex 1-A, which spelled out IFOR obligations, Annex 1-B established a series of general goals. The difference in nuance gave IFOR a bit of leeway in the event of unforeseen challenges. Once established in Bosnia, however, US commanders proved perfectly willing to impose this requirement on the factions. Because the factions in general were far more pliable and cooperative than was at first feared, this step posed only a moderate risk, and in fact would do much to foster a stable and secure environment in Bosnia. As Holbrooke summarized, "although compliance was never perfect, the cantonment provision proved to be extremely useful."[7]

Within the American sector, Multinational Division-North (MND-N), responsibility for execution of the cantonment regime fell to the S3 Division Artillery of the 1st Armored Division. With only a modest fire-support mission for the artillery in Bosnia, the division artillery drew two additional tasks: mine strike investigations and weapons site inspection. Major Richard Fisher, the assistant S3, played a prominent role in devising the protocol for the mission. The challenge in this instance was that such a mission was entirely new to the US Army, which had no established template for such operations. Therefore, a standard regime was built from scratch based largely on common sense. Fisher's inspection team included two US Army Serbo-Croatian speakers and a weapons expert, an Army captain who had studied Russian in Zagreb. Of 425 sites in MND-N, only about 15 warranted the direct attention of division headquarters. Fisher's team handled division-level inspections, which embraced all storage sites with roughly the battalion equivalent of tanks or artillery. Also of immediate concern to the division headquarters were four declared air defense sites at Zenica (in the Turkish sector), Bijeljina (in the Russian sector), and Oraje and Lipnica (US sector). So that Task Force *Eagle* force protection requirements would not impede Fisher's free movement to conduct his mission, the separate brigades in whose areas given sites were situated assumed responsibility for providing vehicles, security, and explosive ordnance disposal (EOD) personnel. Although IFOR reserved the right to conduct surprise inspections, command guidance was that about 90 percent of all inspections should be coordinated in advance.[8]

From the start, faction compliance was generally good. This was in part because the factions themselves gained a measure of security from the knowledge that their rivals' heavy weapons were being monitored by IFOR. Certain problems arose, however. In the main, these stemmed from questions of weapon identification and consequent discrepancies in inventories. Because the movement of weapons for the purpose of maintenance was permitted, there were on occasion legitimate reasons for discrepancies to occur. Overall, according to Fisher, the Bosnian Muslims were more proficient at accounting and maintenance and therefore encountered fewer difficulties than their counterparts. As for the inspection teams, the Russians had fewer weapons experts among their contingent and thus experienced more frequent discrepancies. Errors were especially common in the identification of weapons that had been improvised from non-matching parts. Moreover, the Bijeljina air defense site in the Russian sector was exceptionally large, thus raising the degree of complexity still further. Meanwhile, the world at large took considerable interest in the inspections, which rapidly became media events.[9]

One important precursor not only to the weapons storage regimen but also the withdrawal of the former warring factions' forces to the lines prescribed at Dayton was the Joint Military Commission (JMC). US Army Colonel Hank Stratman developed the meeting structure as a forum for face-to-face communication among the major players. Brigadier General Stan Cherrie conducted the first JMC meeting on D-2 with representatives of UNPROFOR as well as the factions in attendance. The intent was to establish a common set of rules and expectations with regard to fulfillment of the military annex of Dayton. Within a short time, the meetings also provided a venue for Major General William Nash to issue passing or failing grades to the factions in terms of their compliance. Given a routine channel for communications with all parties, Task Force *Eagle* was able to orchestrate the separation of forces in MND-N and forge a climate of basic confidence. In this respect, the combination of sheer US power and a generally evenhanded approach proved invaluable. Therefore, progress in the implementation of the military annex of Dayton proceeded on schedule. According to Cherrie, "When I left Bosnia on 11 June 1995, we had an accurate count and location of each faction's heavy weapons and were routinely inspecting those sites ourselves, as well as assisting the Organization for Security and Cooperation in Europe in their official inspection efforts."[10]

The most conspicuous case in the American sector in which cooperation was not immediate transpired at Mt. Zep, the location of

Photo 7. General Shalikashvili, US Army Chief of Staff, conferred with Major General Willaim Nash of MND North

Radovan Karadzic's headquarters. When US personnel made their first visit to the compound to conduct an inspection, they were greeted by a defiant, angry mob that spat at IFOR soldiers and tried their patience to the limit. This would prove to be just the first of a number of occasions when American soldiers exhibited admirable restraint and declined to make a bad situation worse. (It also suggested that the Serb extremists knew the Americans were coming and planned a carefully measured response.) Ultimately, American inspectors gained access to the Mt. Zep site only on their third try (to be discussed later in this chapter). They gained entry through a passage in Karadzic's garage that led into the underground storage area. Unfortunately, by this time scarcely any weapons were left at the location, at least in areas reached by inspectors.

Inspections later led to occasional if less spectacular confrontations, and not only with the Serbs. Following the American seizure of weapons from a Bosniac Muslim cantonment site in Celic in early 1997, the US-led removal convoy encountered a hostile crowd at an important intersection. This case, too, suggested that the crowd was part of an organized response. In this instance, Captain Mike Slocum received a request from the ground commander to hover above the crowd in a helicopter and attempt to scatter the demonstrators with the downdraft of his rotor blades.[11] The ploy seemed to help and gradually the convoy resumed movement. Overall, however, defiance concerning weapons inspections remained exceptional in Bosnia.

The Civil-Military Agenda Under IFOR

Whereas compliance with the military annex of the Dayton Accords occurred on schedule and with relatively little recalcitrance on the part of the factions, accomplishment of civil objectives proved tortuously difficult from the start. This was so for several reasons. First, the military objectives specified in the GFAP were on the whole clear, objective, and measurable. Moreover, compliance was directly susceptible to American military pressure. Second, the civil goals generally involved issues of "climate" that depended on the voluntary cooperation of the entire population, which for the most part did not belong to organizations with military chains of command. Third, for the local politicians, armies and weapons had been mere instruments of policy, instruments that could be set aside for the time being without sacrificing true strategic aims. Conversely, civil objectives such as reintegration of the Bosnia's ethnic groups and the nurturing of common institutions threatened to undermine all that the hardened nationalist leaders had fought for. Fourth, noncompliance with Dayton's civil agenda could assume many forms that would prove much more difficult to suppress than overt military resistance.

Among those who embraced the challenge of advancing civil progress in Bosnia under IFOR was Lieutenant Colonel Cuculo, who commanded an infantry battalion designated Task Force 3-5. Self-described as a "quasi-mediator," Cuculo met regularly with local chiefs of police, politicians, and representatives of nongovernmental organizations (NGOs) in search of a modus vivendi that would permit the launching of badly needed social and infrastructure projects. As these meetings evolved into weekly gatherings, Cuculo searched for a common denominator among bitter enemies who on occasion had been former friends. Until he could convince the factions that all sides would benefit, NGOs would have minimal opportunity to begin their work. For example, before housing reconstruction could begin in the ZOS, it was necessary to concede the allocation of raw materials equally among Serb, Croat, and Bosniac civilians. Inevitably, even this Solomon-like solution could not please everyone: "The Serbs relaxed when they saw the first reconstruction target village was not in a contentious area. The Croats sighed in relief, as they were getting more than they expected. But the Bosnia[k]s balked at not receiving a fair share relative to need."[12] Such flawed compromises became familiar fare in Bosnia.

The best basis for deals was common interest, as manifested over such issues as missing persons or grassroots economic exchange. A monument to the latter was the creation of the so-called Arizona Market, an inspiration of Colonel Fontenot, in the US brigade sector near one of TF 3-5's checkpoints. After observing that the locals were attempting to establish informally some sort of trade area—an effort opposed by hard-line separatists who viewed an ethnically mixed marketplace with disdain—Fontenot pressed to give the market official sanction.[13] The transforming effect was remarkable. On this relatively small patch of earth, members of Bosnia's ethnic groups "interacted with each other as though there had never been a war."[14]

IFOR Information Operations

The presentation of IFOR activities to the international public constituted a complex challenge for reasons that sometimes had little to do with the execution of IFOR operations in Bosnia. Initial troubles stemmed from the act of a NATO deployment itself. Perhaps because IFOR was the first major NATO operational deployment, it was to be expected that many practical issues would arise. The first of these related to the organization, manning, and equipping of the public information mission. With IFOR's commencement in December 1995, two skeletal information centers began operations, one in Zagreb and the other in Sarajevo. Functoning well below their authorized strength of 40 individuals for a time, the public information effort had a distinctly ad hoc quality. This condition owed much to the existence of parallel headquarters, AFSOUTH and the ARRC. Guidance was not always consistent. Moreover, approaches differed as AFSOUTH reflected American public information methodologies and the ARRC a predominantly British outlook. Eventually the consolidation of a single headquarters in Sarajevo brought about some reconciliation of the variance within a unified Coalition Press Information Center (CPIC). However, sub-CPICs within the MNDs were not always fully in line with higher headquarters. Still, in addition to the difficulty inherent in combining personnel from a number of NATO and non-NATO countries, the information centers at first lacked a full complement of resources, not to mention soldiers experienced in contracting matters who could resolve existing shortages. Consequently, "In June 1996 IFOR PI had still not all the equipment required in the OPLAN."[15]

Eventually, use of the Internet proved invaluable for the rapid dissemination of information, although not without occasional mishap. For example, sometime following US pilot Sean O'Grady's rescue after being shot down over Bosnia in the fall of 1995, one participant in the mission provided a detailed account over e-mail to his home unit. Unfortunately, the account containing sensitive information found its way far beyond the intended audience. Nevertheless, the advantages of exploiting the internet from an information point of view were considerable. Soon, IFOR operated its own web page including almost daily reports and registered 4,000 queries daily.[16]

Still, most dissonance in the information realm was a result of contrasting national perspectives. British doctrine as outlined in the "green book," published by the Ministry of Defence, for instance, prohibits release of information about current or future operations. Consequently, following an October 1996 incident in MND-SW in which policemen of the Republika Serbska beat a reporter in the ZOS, a British officer refused immediate release of photographic evidence.[17] US doctrine, conversely, advocates maximum transparency within the limits of classification concerns based on the assumption of the public's right to information about governmental activity. Having learned to live under this requirement, US information officers typically regard rapid release of information, consistent with the need to verify accuracy, as a means of support for the operational mission. One direct manifestation of this view was the American faith in the practice of "embedding" journalists with units operating in the field as long as the mission in question does not require an unusual level of confidentiality.[18] Many other armies are uncomfortable with this approach. The logic behind it is that skeptical American (or international) journalists will be more satisfied with their level of access and thus more likely to provide friendly or neutral coverage if able to observe directly the work of armies in the field. Furthermore, as journalists become personally acquainted with ordinary soldiers, they tend better to understand—and thus more effectively to report—the military point of view.

National differences in force protection rules (discussed at length in subsequent chapters) were another focal point of operational friction and clashing perceptions. Whereas rules in MND-SW and MND-SE gave authority to commanders at the lowest levels, the US sector conferred no authority on local commanders to make their own determination. Under guidance from above, the Task Force *Eagle* commander imposed a stringent four-vehicle minimum rule on forces in MND-N (though in reality only US personnel fully complied). In the information realm, rigid force protection in the eyes of many proved a liability. Because of the limited availability of vehicles, this seemingly simple requirement often significantly hampered the timely dissemination of psychological operations (PSYOP) products as did the highly centralized PSYOP approval process. In fact, civil affairs and PSYOP did not receive COMEAGLE approval to operate in two-vehicle elements until 1997.[19] In the interim period, Task Force *Eagle* found it necessary to consolidate small and disparate civil affairs, PSYOP, and counterintelligence elements into company and platoon-size formations. As acknowledged in the 1st Armored Division after-action review, "The external issue associated with extreme Force Protection measures from higher made it impossible for the specialized teams to operate as they had in the past—individually."[20] At times the integrated approach worked well.

Occasionally, of course, it was the subject itself that complicated the public information effort. Few if any issues during IFOR were more contentious among the participating states than the "train and equip" program, which was sponsored by the United States but not by NATO. The intent was to build up the Army of Bosnia and Herzegovina so as to achieve rough parity with the armies of Croatia and Serbia based on the assumption that it would serve as a deterrent to future aggression. This solution conformed to a perception widely held among Americans and many journalists who covered the war that the expansionism of Serbia, and secondarily Croatia, had been the chief cause of war. However, the British and others who had participated in UNPROFOR were not only skeptical of this historical interpretation but feared that the solution itself might encourage the Bosnian Muslims to use their newfound leverage in ways not conducive to regional peace. Given this divergence of viewpoints, it was difficult for IFOR to speak with a single voice. Indeed, for a time public relations guidance on this topic came directly from a spokesman for the secretary general of NATO.[21]

Nevertheless, it would be a mistake to infer from predictable and ever-present points of disagreement among IFOR states that the public information campaign was not, on the whole, well coordinated. Given the formidable mandate to inform not only the public of countries contributing soldiers to IFOR, but also to deal with the contentious host populations of Bosnia and Herzegovina, IFOR enjoyed remarkable successes. Even the reticent American public remained on the whole satisfied with the course of the mission.

IFOR Case Study: The Serial Episodes At Mt. Zep

There were instances when public information had a visible impact at the operational level. The COMARRC (Commander Allied Rapid Reaction Corps), Major General Sir Michael Walker, happened to notice while traveling by helicopter in mid-summer 1996 that there were Serbian tanks on the ground in an unauthorized location near Mladic's bunker at Mt. Zep and the town of Han Pijesak. As noted earlier, according to the Dayton rules, all heavy weapons of any sort were allowed only in designated cantonments. This discovery, incidentally, seemed to contradict reports reaching the ARRC from MND-N that all cantonment sites had been inspected. In fact, the Americans had not yet fully forced the question of inspecting the Mt. Zep site. The trouble was that Mt. Zep was especially sensitive for the Serbs and was under the protection of the 65th Protection Regiment, which had sworn a blood oath to maintain BSA General Ratko Mladic's personal security. Therefore, Serb forces at Mt. Zep showed no inclination to allow an inspection. Indeed, the atmosphere at the Mladic bunker could be described as paranoid.

In fact, the serial crises of July and August followed a steady escalation of tensions around the Mt. Zep weapons storage site. As political pressure to inspect the Mt. Zep site mounted, a potential crisis loomed. An initial attempt to carry out an inspection met with rebuff in February 1996, prompting a show of force by 2nd Brigade. Inspectors gained admission but did not thoroughly examine the area.[22]

Photo 8. Major General Sir Michael Walker,
commander of the Allied Command Group Rapid Reaction Corps,
advised General Shalikashvili of events on the ground in Bosnia

The commander of the 2nd Brigade Combat Team, Colonel John Batiste, whose sector included the nearby village of Han Pijesak, realized the delicacy of enforcing the Dayton rules to the letter. Several weeks before, Batiste in direct negotiations with Lieutenant Colonel Starovic, who commanded 65th Protection Regiment, had granted limited authority to the 65th to patrol a 50-kilometer square area around the Mladic bunker. His intent was to keep the situation calm around a potential flash point between US and Serb forces. Nonetheless, Lieutenant General Walker regarded the American move as an unauthorized infringement of Dayton and directed Major General Nash and Colonel Batiste to inform Starovic that IFOR would not allow such a blatant exception to the governing rules.[23]

One week following Batiste's reversal, Walker made his fateful flight, which was followed by a deliberate photo-reconnaissance mission. With that the makings of a confrontation were present. In light of what was to follow, there is merit in reviewing the actions of Batiste and Walker to this point. Batiste realized the potential volatility of the situation. Furthermore, he realized that the US Task Force *Eagle* command was under considerable pressure from its own national chain of command to avoid a shooting engagement and the casualties that would most probably ensue. The colonel believed that a working arrangement with the 65th Protection Regiment was both a pragmatic option and the best way to preserve the peace. At the tactical level, the decision made some sense. Yet, Walker's assessment that such a deal could undermine Dayton was correct from a strategic point of view. After all, the Mt. Zep site had not yielded to inspection and IFOR had yet to assert the right of unrestricted movement to ensure it. As ever, the importance of precedents loomed large. If the Serbs could create de facto "safe areas" for weapons and persons indicted as war criminals, certainly the other factions could do likewise. Or, the Croatians and Bosniacs might simply conclude that Dayton was toothless and resume the war they had been reluctant to stop in 1995 when the momentum had swung their way.

In any case, the situation at Mt. Zep quickly escalated during 3-5 July. Directed to meet with the commander of the 65th to coordinate reconnaissance flights and inspections, Batiste quickly found himself in a confrontation. The Bosnian Serb lieutenant colonel commanding the 65th threatened to fire on US helicopters. His rash gesture triggered a stern reply from Batiste, who assured him that such an act would be "the worst mistake of your life."[24] Batiste, who was fully prepared to unleash the formidable combat power at his disposal, put his artillery on alert and had his air controller guide a squadron of F-15s to his location, where they circled menacingly. Faced with this display of might, the Bosnian Serbs took no action to interfere with the aerial reconnaissance. Meanwhile, the photographic results on 5 July confirmed what everyone already knew—the presence of not less than eight Serb heavy weapons in protected positions. Batiste informed the Serbs of the evidence in his possession and advised them of his intent to conduct an inspection visit the following day.[25]

During the brief intervening period, US Army Lieutenant Colonel Bill Seymour, who commanded the 40th Engineer Battalion and reported to Batiste, conferred quietly with his Serb counterpart, engineer Major Milenko Avramovic on a separate demining matter at a hotel in Vlasenica and was surprised to get an earful. Avramovic forecast the direst consequences for American forces if they attempted to lay a hand on Mladic. As Seymour summed up the encounter, "I believed that he was being sincere and that his comments were an accurate reflection of his perception."[26]

Avramovic's warnings went right to the crux of the matter from the Serb point of view. US military operations, even including weapons inspections approved by senior Serb political authorities, appeared to pose a direct threat to Mladic. Because the Serbs were well aware of the indictment published by the Hague and the International Criminal Tribunal for Yugoslavia, such an interpretation of events was not illogical. The reality, however, was that the Americans—and probably IFOR as well—wanted little part of the international hunt to punish war criminals and were not in any event required by Dayton to do so in a proactive manner. Moreover, it is surprising that the Serbs had not yet realized this. Perhaps their perceptions were influenced by mounting pressure from the international media and public to bring the architects of mass murder in the Bosnian civil war to justice. Even more likely is the possibility that Mladic and his entourage were jumpy and unsure of their situation.

In the meantime, IFOR Commander Admiral Layton Smith initiated urgent high-level communications with Yugoslav President Slobodan Milosevic so as to secure his leverage in the matter. Although in theory, of course, Milosevic was not in the BSA chain of command, there was little question that the Bosnian Serb leadership looked to him for political and material support. Moreover, it was clear that Milosevic was not likely to cross NATO over the concerns of his junior associates in Bosnia.

This is not to say that the initiative rested wholly with IFOR. Bosnian Serb radio and television outlets broadcast spurious allegations that IFOR had arrested unnamed senior BSA officers. Doubtless intended to incite the local Serbs, the messages also served as a signal to local political

Photo 9. Admiral Smith met the press on a frequent basis

organizers to rally civil resistance against IFOR. Perhaps what the authors of the broadcasts did not realize was that their defiant response only increased the pressure on IFOR to take actions it had thus far avoided. During the 6 July IFOR press briefing held in Sarajevo, Western journalists openly challenged public affairs officers to indicate that IFOR would not back down. One reporter pointedly asked why, if heavy weapons and equipment had been located outside authorized cantonment sites, IFOR had not destroyed or seized them as it was legally entitled to do. The official reply was hedged and equivocal.[27]

In reality, TF *Eagle* was about to cause a major fright. What the US 1st Armored Division was ready to do in a most forcible manner was to compel the Serbs to accede to an inspection. The division and 2nd Brigade Combat Team staffs drafted a plan to break down the door to Mt. Zep. To be sure, OPERATION Gryphon 2 faced several serious military concerns. The Americans lacked crucial information on the presence of mines or other defenses, and they could not be sure that the Serbs were incapable of reinforcing the Mt. Zep site, although aerial reconnaissance could probably enable US troops to intercept any potential late arrival to the party. Thus, with American weapons bristling around the perimeter of the Serb compound, Colonel Batiste entered with a group of 16 soldiers in four armored HMMWVs. Among them was Seymour, who later recalled, "I was acutely aware of the possibility of being held hostage by a bunch of war criminals who were about to find themselves in a very tight box."[28]

At 1400 on July 6, as Batiste's team rolled past the checkpoints and into the compound, they were under aerial surveillance and linked to Major General Nash by FM radio. Unfortunately, the scene that greeted them initially was anticlimactic. The Serbian guards insisted that no one above the rank of NCO was present and that they were not authorized to allow the US inspectors in. In response, Batiste took a firm line, maintaining not only that he would not leave but that he would not relinquish his weapon upon entry into a nondescript, single-story building on the compound. Greeted by a Serb colonel at the entrance, Batiste attempted vainly to assuage concerns that he was on a mission to capture Mladic. He would not back down on his intent to inspect, however, and a tense stalemate followed. The Serb colonel put on a show of bravado with a one-liner straight from the movies: "It's a great day to die."[29] Batiste and Seymour had little choice but to assume that their brash adversary was in earnest.

While Batiste awaited further instructions from Major General Nash, he learned to his surprise that Lieutenant General Walker had sent his

Photo 10. US personnel maintained security checkpoints as needed.

deputy, Brigadier General Charleton Weedy, by helicopter to sort through the situation and defuse the developing crisis. During the wait for Weedy, Serb civilians began streaming to the scene, apparently hailed to the Mt. Zep area by Serb organizers. If IFOR had not yet come to appreciate the remarkable ability of Bosnians of all three major factions to mass in a hurry, this episode certainly made the point. Many of the local civilian demonstrators were in a state of intoxication, and as minutes passed the crowd slowly transformed into a hostile mob, convinced that it was on a mission to rescue General Mladic from arrest.[30] Indeed, before Batiste's crew returned to base, they had been shoved, spat upon, and threatened.

Still, members of the crowd, apparently well coached, knew better than to commit outright violence, although theft of items such as binoculars and cameras was within bounds. The aim was to defeat IFOR and the Americans not by military engagement but in the propaganda war. Had the Serb provocateurs been able to elicit a disproportionate reaction by US soldiers, the implications could have been drastic. Fortunately, the military police who drove the HMMWVs are trained in the nuances of such potentially escalating situations and showed the professional restraint circumstances demanded. As frustrating as the situation was, it could have been far worse. As it was, the eventual pullback led at least one reporter on the scene to conclude that the crowd believed it had succeeded in its purpose. Further, the episode invited comparisons to UNPROFOR that IFOR had intended to avoid.[31]

At about 1800, Weedy had arrived and breezily strolled into the compound. His relaxed air notwithstanding, he was unable to lighten the mood. While the Serb officers who met him did permit a visit to one or more reported tank locations, he was allowed to travel there only while wearing a blindfold. During his separation from the main party, his treatment declined and he was subjected to threats and insults.[32] More to the point, his inspection tour hardly met the Dayton standard. Not only was he restricted at all times, but he never actually saw any heavy weapons. Thus, Weedy, too, failed in his effort to open the Mt. Zep compound. In the subsequent appraisal of Lieutenant Colonel Tom O'Sullivan, at the time a major working as a task force operations officer, "They won that one." Though ready for a tactical fight, "We didn't know how to respond to a loudspeaker," he concluded.[33] Still, if the day ended in a tactical defeat for IFOR, no final verdict had yet been rendered at the operational and strategic levels.

Back at the ARRC, Lieutenant General Walker sized up the situation and decided to play his final cards short of forcible seizure of the Mt. Zep site. The plan that unfolded took careful account of the overall political situation in the Republika Serbska. Recognizing an opportunity both to affirm the credibility of Dayton and influence the balance in RS politics, Walker invoked the support of Serb President Madame Plavsic. As the representative of the more moderate Banja Luka faction of the dominant Serb political party, the SDS, Plavsic also perceived an opportunity to gain leverage against the extremist Pale crowd headed by Karadzic. In a hasty meeting, Walker and Plavsic agreed to join forces. Walker possessed the military might in IFOR that for once could give Plavsic the upper hand against Mladic's forces. In turn, Plavsic, as the elected leader of the RS gave IFOR crucial political leverage among the Bosnian Serb population to help neutralize efforts by Karadzic and Mladic to mobilize a popular aggrievement against IFOR.

On Saturday, 10 August, Walker and President Plavsic visited the site in tandem and were refused access. Once again, the Serbs orchestrated a civil disturbance complete with women and children so as somehow to make a legal IFOR inspection attempt appear menacing to innocent civilians. Having made a final attempt at peaceful resolution, Walker withdrew. The challenge to IFOR authority presented what the ARRC G3, Lieutenant Colonel David Short (UK) later recalled as a "potentially defining moment."[34] At stake was IFOR's credibility as well as that of President Plavsic, who met in Sarajevo with NATO Secretary General Javier Solana. She also received a direct communication from COMIFOR

Admiral Lopez emphasizing the need for full compliance with Dayton. Meanwhile, Walker worked through his options. Though he developed and briefed Major General Nash on a series of graduated responses to the situation that included even air strikes or the seizure of the Mt. Zep site, Walker's winning gambit relied on the subtlety of public information.

Rather than uttering explicit threats, Walker calmly launched OPERATION Fear Naught. Announced at a routine press briefing, the plan entailed an assortment of security measures including an IFOR advisory to members of the international community to evacuate positions in the RS. The UN-sponsored International Police Task Force (IPTF) declared a "code orange" condition, reflecting a state of heightened danger but continued to patrol the RS with IFOR escort on 13 August. As a further precaution, for the time being UN police monitors and most UN staffers either relocated to IFOR compounds in the RS or crossed the Inter-Entity Boundary Line into the federation. Not all agencies viewed developments the same way, however. The UNHCR regarded the elevated tensions less seriously and continued to conduct "business as usual" with the exception of its small staff in Brcko, which temporarily vacated its office. The UNHCR did, however, suspend the operation of buses for returnees between Tuzla and Bijeljina due to the lack of IPTF escort. In reaction, the High Representative, Carl Bildt, took strong exception to OPERATION Fear Naught, terming it "irresponsible." Bildt did not want his people in the RS to relocate to the federation even temporarily out of fear that it might provoke an overreaction by the Serbs, such as the seizure of hostages, or otherwise disrupt the developing relationship with the RS.[35] Ironically, IFOR fully intended that the hard-line Serbs would recognize the extraordinarily serious nature of its actions. Accordingly, IFOR units either withdrew into secure locations or received reinforcements for movement around the RS.[36] If these steps seemed suggestive of imminent military action, that was exactly the point.

Interestingly, the press unintentionally played a part in building Walker's crisis scenario by pounding IFOR press briefers that day with questions about IFOR's resolve. One interrogator explicitly raised the concern over whether IFOR was actually in charge: "After this agreement yesterday, it appears it [IFOR] goes where the Serbs basically say and when they say it can and which escorts they say it can." In response, the IFOR public affairs officer, Canadian Major Brett Boudreau, explained that previous inspection visits in Han Pijesak had deliberately been conducted by small teams to avoid the perception that their ulterior purpose was "to snatch Mladic." The Mt. Zep site, after all, was not an ordinary cantonment but a headquarters. He then added that IFOR was simply relying on a "graduated response" sequence until it would gain complete access. Madame Plavsic's role, he continued, was merely to attend, not participate in the inspection itself. Boudreau's bottom line was that IFOR had not ruled out the forcible seizure option.[37] In sum, the briefing effectively conveyed the sense of urgency about the inspection. Curiously, members of the press in attendance did not seize on the part of the message aimed at Mladic—the removal of international personnel from the RS as part of OPERATION Fear Naught. Rather, they focused on IFOR's apparent reluctance to capture Mladic even when they knew his general whereabouts. In fact, this line of reasoning might have helped soften Mladic's stance.

The unmistakable implication of *Fear Naught* for those who had experienced the bombing campaigns of 1994 and 1995 was that IFOR was clearing the area of potential hostages—or at least getting international assistance workers out of harm's way—so that it would be free to take direct military action. The streetwise Mladic and Karadzic, who, like everyone else, monitored CNN broadcasts, understood the signal and quickly relented without forcing IFOR to take any steps that might have further exacerbated tensions.[38] That same day, after tense hours of delay and a visit by NATO General Secretary Javier Solana, Walker and Plavsic made a seemingly uneventful but critically significant inspection visit to the Mt. Zep site. Dismissing earlier Bosnian Serb refusals of admission as a "small misunderstanding," Plavsic played her role well. The robust presence of forces from 2nd Brigade was an appreciable factor as well.[39] To be sure, crowds did gather but did not attack or impede IFOR inspection.

Even so, Major General Nash kept a Predator observation aircraft aloft above the scene to monitor developments.[40] Indeed, in a pattern characteristic of Bosnian operations, general officers did not hesitate to provide guidance to commanders on the ground. Also typical of IFOR operations, at least in MND-N, was an intensity of focus on the mission that generated a frenetic pace of staff work at all echelons of command. The reality across most of Bosnia, however, was that field operations were extremely decentralized. Thus, the substantive work of patrolling towns and villages, quelling disturbances, arbitrating disputes, and maintaining a muscular but restrained presence fell to battalions, companies, and platoons. Realization of this circumstance proved "enormously frustrating" to many staff officers at the division level whose daily regimen of endlessly writing and rewriting briefings seems a little bit surreal and, at times, nearly irrelevant.[41]

On 14 August, Major General John Sylvester stepped forward to explain to the press that OPERATION Fear Naught "was a deliberate act to ensure that our troops were protected in the event we executed something which we had planned to execute if we weren't able to accomplish what we accomplished in the manner that we did it."[42] This affirmed in the first place that IFOR had not been bluffing and in the second that the Serbs had read Walker's signals correctly. The result was that IFOR overcame a direct challenge to its mandate without resort to force, although it made liberal use of the implicit threat of force. IFOR thus defused the crisis on terms compatible with Dayton.

To be sure, fortune smiled on IFOR during the stalemate. As one journalist at the 14 August IFOR press conference suggested, not all civilian agencies heeded the call of OPERATION Fear Naught and it would still have been possible for the Serbs to seize hostages. That they did not attempt to do so probably indicates that Karadzic and Mladic took Walker's and Lopez's warnings seriously and feared that crossing the line this time might permanently brand them as outlaws in the eyes of IFOR as well as the International Criminal Tribunal. Furthermore, IFOR's military seizure operation against Mt. Zep might well have gone forward in any event. As General Sylvester observed afterward, "...there was thorough coordination with all of those civilian agencies in the first place. They told them that they needed for their own protection to get out of the Republika Srpska based on our warning to them. A number of them chose not to.... There have been a great number of civilian agencies that have chosen to stay in harm's way, and you know, it's kind of you pays you money, you takes you chances."[43]

IFOR Overview

In the end, IFOR succeeded not only because of the skillful use of information, although that was critical. US forces in MND-N amply demonstrated their preparedness to tackle the issue with overwhelming combat power. Major General Nash realized that his credibility was on the line and was ready to execute the plan to seize the Mt. Zep compound. Finally, Lieutenant General Walker's intuitive grasp of how to orchestrate a winning scenario employing threat of force, public information, patience, and diplomacy not only averted a possibly disastrous setback but also strengthened IFOR's hand in the RS and Bosnia as a whole. Still, in point of fact, this inspection was not as complete as needed, a fact to be confirmed by a subsequent, more thorough look a year later.

In light of this and similar experiences, Task Force *Eagle* embraced a coordinated, broad-based and proactive approach to confront the kinds of public disorder that plagued the mission throughout 1996 in the form of a Counter-Demonstration Workgroup chaired by the G3 or division operations. This effort brought together representatives from public affairs, intelligence, and civil affairs, as well as chaplains and the division surgeon to consider the implications of anticipated or scheduled events such as demonstrations or commemorations that could potentially result in riots or confrontations. Task Force *Eagle* could then initiate measures to prevent events from spinning out of control. Especially significant was the dissemination of news about upcoming events. Frequently, high-ranking IFOR commanders lent their voices to television or radio transmissions aimed at calming the public and reminding both citizens and officials or their respective rights and responsibilities under the Dayton agreement. Moreover, civil affairs officers directly contacted local officials and representatives of NGOs to reinforce the message on a personal level.[44]

Meanwhile, IFOR enjoyed great success in implementing the military annex of the GFAP. Within a year, IFOR established at least minimal security and order, improved freedom of movement, established and cleared the ZOS, enforced the cantonment of heavy weapons, conducted inspections, successfully supported elections, maintained a visible presence across the country, and arbitrated disputes among the former warring factions up and down the chain of command. In so doing, IFOR also made important discoveries about areas in which it needed to improve. Less than fully prepared to tackle numerous noncombat scenarios, IFOR planners and trainers sought advice wherever it could be found. One source of information was the recently published US Army Field Manual 100-23-1, *HA Multiservice Procedures for Humanitarian Assistance Operations*, but also invaluable were Nordic and UN manuals that dealt with greater specificity on the kinds of ambiguous, low-level encounters that abounded in Bosnia.[45] To its credit, the Army rapidly adjusted its training to place more emphasis on complex scenarios requiring junior officers to respond immediately and with minimal guidance from above in negotiation, crowd control, and arbitration of disagreements, just to name a few.

Notes

1. Colonel Greg Fontenot, interview with Dr. Robert Baumann and Dr. George Gawrych, Fort Leavenworth, KS, 17 November 2000. Many participants felt that the combat-ready posture demonstrated while crossing Croatia—an ostensible ally—was wholly unnecessary. The intent, however, was to make an indelible impression upon arrival in Bosnia.

2. Major Fred Drummond, interview with Dr. Robert Baumann, Fort Leavenworth, KS, 2000.

3. Brigadier General Stan Cherrie, US Army, Retired, interview with Dr. Robert Baumann and Dr. George Gawrych, Fort Leavenworth, KS, 2000.

4. Task Force *Eagle* After-Action Review, 1328. The Defense Language Institute in Monterrey, CA began full-length courses in Serbo-Croatian only after the deployment began. Prior to that time, any Slavic linguist available received nine weeks of focused training in Serbo-Croatian. According to the Task Force *Eagle* After-Action Review, "The native speaker was worth their weight in gold."

5. Major Simuel Shaw, interview with Dr. Robert Baumann, Fort Leavenworth, KS, February 2000.

6. Randolph Ryan, "On Brcko and Eastern Slavonia," draft chapter for *Rebuilding War-Torn Societies: The Case of Bosnia and Herzegovina* to be published by Harvard University Press, 10-13.

7. Richard Holbrooke, *To End a War* (New York: The Modern Library, 1999), 278.

8. Lieutenant Colonel Richard Fisher, interview with Dr. Robert Baumann, Fort Leavenworth, KS, 27 April 2001.

9. Fisher interview.

10. Brigadier General Stan Cherrie, "Task Force Eagle," *Military Review* (July-August 1997), 70-72.

11. Major Mike Slocum, Interview with Dr. Robert Baumann, November 2, 2001, Fort Leavenworth, KS.

12. Lieutenant Colonel Tony Cucolo, "Grunt Diplomacy: In the Beginning There Were Only Soldiers," *Parameters* (Spring 1999), 118-20.

13. Fontenot interview. As commerce thrived, however, the Arizona Market attracted increasing attention from criminal gangs whose presence in coming years would prove troublesome.

14. Cuculo, "Grunt Diplomacy," 121.

15. IFOR Final Analysis Report, Chapter 2, Public Information Activities, 2 - 2 - 1-15.

16. Ibid., 2 - 2 - 16, 17.

17. Ibid., 2 - 2 - 27; Pascale Siegel, "Information Activities," in *Lessons From Bosnia: The IFOR Experience*, ed. Larry Wentz (Washington, DC: INSS/CCRP, 1997), 182. Evidently, the "green book" was not well known to all British officers. One British lieutenant colonel with whom I spoke had never heard of it.

18. Major Perry Rearick, interview with Dr. Robert Baumann, Fort Leavenworth, KS, 25 April 2001. Of course, this has not always been the US approach. In the aftermath of the Vietnam War, which was characterized by maximum freedom but increasingly critical coverage, the Army withdrew as far as possible from media scrutiny. However, the process of press pooling during OPERATION Desert Storm provoked such a journalistic outcry that the Army revised its position in favor of greater openness.

19. Mark Jacobson, "Tactical PSYOP Support to Task Force Eagle," *Lessons From Bosnia: The IFOR Experience*, ed. Larry Wentz (Washington, DC: INSS/CCRP, 1997), 200-01, 210-12.

20. 1st Armored Division After-Action Review, 341, 343-44. During the spring information offensive of 1996, heavy company teams worked alongside the "information company" to keep the lid on a potentially volatile situation. During this period, Bosnian political and religious leaders elevated customary and authorized visits to gravesites on opposite sides of the Inter-Entity Boundary Line to stage impromptu political theater. Thus combined, US forces headed off trouble before it began.

21. IFOR AAR, Chapter 2, Public Information Activities, 2 - 2 -32 and Lieutenant Colonel David Short, United Kingdom, interview with Dr. Robert Baumann and Dr. George Gawrych, Fort Leavenworth, KS, 8 August 2000.

22. After-Action Review, 450.

23. Lieutenant Colonel Bill Seymour, commander, 40th Engineer Battalion, "Standoff at Mt. Zep: A Confrontation Between 2nd Brigade, 1st Armoreded Division (IFOR) and Bosnian Serb General Mladic's Protection Force," 2, unpublished paper. These are the author's recollection of events concerning Mt. Zep.

24 . Lieutenant Colonel Bill Seymour, "Standoff at Mt. Zep," 2.

25. Ibid., 3.

26. Ibid.

27. IFOR AFSOUTH, Transcript of the Press Briefing, 6 July 1996.

28. Lieutenant Colonel Bill Seymour, "Standoff at Mt. Zep," 4; Lieutenant Colonel Rich Dixon, interview with Dr. Robert Baumann, Fort Leavenworth, KS, 23 May 2003.

29. Lieutenant Colonel Bill Seymour, "Standoff at Mt. Zep," 5-6.

30. IFOR AFSOUTH, Transcript of Press Briefing, 7 July 1996.

31. Ibid.

32. Lieutenant Colonel Bill Seymour, "Standoff at Mt. Zep," 8-9 and Short interview.

33. Tom O'Sullivan, interview with Dr. Robert Baumann, Joint Forces Staff College, Norfolk, VA, 4 November 2003.

34. Short interview.

35. Carl Bildt, *Peace Journey: The Struggle for Peace in Bosnia* (London: Weidenfeld and Nicholson, 1998), 304; Siegel, "Information Operations," 181.

36. IFOR AFSOUTH, Transcript of the Press Briefing, 13 August 1996, 1-2.

37. Ibid., 3-4. It is worth noting that tensions were in a high state in locales other than Han Pijesak on 12 August. Indeed, the 12 August press briefing revealed the shooting of an American State Department Foreign Service officer during the preceding night on the road between Sarajevo and Kiseljak. In addition, reports surfaced of threats in Pale directed at the IPTF should any steps be taken to capture Karadzic. See IFOR AFSOUTH, Transcript of the Press Briefing, 12August 1996. At the 14 August press briefing, British Brigadier Cooke stressed that Solana's meeting with Plavsic had not been to negotiate but to be certain she understood the Dayton terms and IFOR's determination to enforce them. It is probable that she bowed to this reality and made a virtue of necessity by playing her part in the inspection visit with Lieutenant General Walker. See IFOR AFSOUTH, Transcript of Press Briefing, 14 August 1996.

38. Short interview.

39. Daniel Williams, "Bosnia Peacekeepers on Alert After Threat," *The Washington Post*, 13 August 1996.

40. Dixon interview.

41. O'Sullivan interview. The author has spoken with numerous other staff officers whose recollections essentially concur with this view.

42. IFOR AFSOUTH, Transcript of Press Briefing, 14 August 1996.

43. Ibid.

44. *Operation JOINT ENDEAVOR Bosnia-Herzegovina: Task Force Eagle Continuing Operations*, B/H CAAT 3/4 Initial Impressions Report (Fort Leavenworth, KS: March 1997), B-12-13, 32.

45. O'Sullivan interview. Indeed, Americans who were disposed to listen found the advice of those who had served under UNPROFOR to be invaluable.

Chapter 5
Show of Force

George W. Gawrych

I went to Srebrenica to stay with the [American] troops.
Their camp stood on a hilltop above the town. The
soldiers had gone there expecting to rough it a few days,
but no sooner had they arrived than a Brown & Root
convoy had pulled up, and, to their amazement, a crew of
Bosnian civilians had emerged to set up two heated tents
with electric lights and cots, a line of portable toilets,
and a big collection of white-plastic chairs. Rather than
feeling grateful, the soldiers were a little annoyed. In their
disgust many of them chose to sleep outside, crammed
into their vehicles or stretched out in sleeping bags on
the cold ground.

William Langewiesche, 2001[1]

US troops wear helmets and body armor—hence their
nickname, "ninja turtles." They travel in convoys with
guns manned and ready. When they stop, they disperse
to over watch positions, ready to apply defensive force.
At night most retire to fortified camps or outposts as
Romans did on campaigns, cut off from the people they
came to protect.

Lieutenant Colonel Richard R. Caniglia, US Army, 2001[2]

The US Army and other NATO troops successfully achieved the
military tasks of the Dayton Accords within the first year. But the initial
mandate was extended another 18 months and then indefinitely. These
extensions forced the NATO-led peacekeepers to expand their tasks
in support of the civilian implementation of the General Framework
Agreement for Peace (GFAP). In the expansion of its tasks, the US
Army clearly emerged out of step with its allies in how it interpreted and
implemented the Dayton Accords. Ultimately, the manner in which the US
conducted peace support operations said more about American military
culture than about the actual threat to its military forces. Compared with
the British, French, Dutch, Canadians, and Scandinavians, the US Army
appeared more cautious, risk-averse, rigid in its military patrols designed

to establish a secure environment for the civilian reformers. Part of the overall reticent mind-set among Americans stemmed from a general reluctance on the part of the top brass to embrace peacekeeping as an essential mission in the *raison d'etre* for the US armed forces.

An Evolving Mandate

The GFAP was signed in Paris on 14 December 1995. On the next day, United Nations Security Council Resolution 1031 authorized NATO to carry out its military mission under Chapter 7 of the UN Charter for peace enforcement. IFOR's mandate commenced on 20 December 1995 when the UNPROFOR commander, British Lieutenant General Rupert Smith, transferred authority to the IFOR commander, US Admiral Leighton Smith. Annex 1A: *Agreement on the Military Aspects of the Peace Settlement*, provided the NATO-led Implementation Force with clear and concrete tasks attainable during the mandate's one-year duration. The Clinton administration claimed that the US would pull out of Bosnia in a year's time; few believed the attainability of that claim. Over the next five years, the military's mandate would evolve considerably.

The Dayton Accords provided IFOR with the authority to employ force to carry out its tasks. IFOR had the mandate of peace enforcement rather than peacekeeping. Peacekeepers had "complete and unimpeded freedom of movement by air, ground, and water throughout Bosnia and Herzegovina." If anyone resisted, IFOR had the authority for "the use of necessary force to ensure compliance." Robust rules of engagement (ROE) went with peace enforcement so that field commanders could be proactive rather than reactive as had been much the case during UNPROFOR days. GFAP, for example, empowered IFOR with the right to inspect any military installation and use force, if necessary, to carry out its inspection. All three Bosnian armies were required to establish command posts at IFOR brigade, battalion, and other headquarters so that the peacekeepers could control movements within 10 kilometers of the zone of separation (ZOS).

NATO unequivocally backed its written mandate with military muscle. IFOR increased UNPROFOR's troop strength of 38,000 to 60,000. The US deployed Task Force *Eagle*, some 17,500 troops, backed by an impressive lethal arsenal of heavy weapons and all marshaled to provide more effective deterrence than possessed by UNPROFOR. In particular, the 1st Armored Division, under the command of Major General William Nash, formed the main force. The division brought its entire force structure as well as additional echelons above corps assets.

Bosnia was divided into three division-plus sectors: the American-led Multinational Division North or MND-N headquartered at Tuzla; the British-led Multinational Division Southwest (MND-SW) centered in Gronji Vakuf, later transferred to Banja Luka; and the French-led Multinational Division Southeast (MND-SE) with its command located in Mostar. MND-N comprised four sectors: American division at Tuzla; a brigade of Nordic forces and a Polish parachute battalion in Doboj; a large Turkish mechanized infantry battalion with a tank company and artillery battery in Zenica; and two Russian parachute battalions in Ugljevik near Srebrenica. MND-N possessed some 22,500 troops.[3] IFOR located its ground headquarters in the Sarajevo district of Ilidza. SFOR continued operations in Ilidza until moving to the Butmir district of Sarajevo in 2000.

IFOR's year mandate was broken into two phases. Phase I gave the Bosniacs, Serbs, and Croats 30 days (D+30) after the transfer of authority, to 19 January 1996, to withdraw their forces to behind a ZOS on either side of the cease-fire line. The ZOS extended 2 kilometers on either side of the boundary separating the warring factions. The city of Sarajevo, however, required only 1 kilometer. During this first phase, each entity had to "disarm and disband all armed civilian groups, except for authorized police forces." Phase II affected only those areas where the Inter-Entity Boundary Line (IEBL) differed from the agreed cease-fire line. By D+45 (3 February 1996), all combatants would withdraw from areas designated for transfer to another entity. For the remainder of the year, IFOR would patrol the demilitarized ZOS, some 1,400 kilometers in length. All three Bosnian armies had until D+120 to deploy into their barracks and place their heavy equipment in cantonments. American General George Joulwan, the Supreme Allied Commander Europe (SACEUR), later revised the date for cantonment of heavy weapons to D+180. After achieving these tasks, IFOR faced the task of security and logistic support for national and municipal elections.

In addition to clear and attainable military objectives within a reasonable timetable, the GFAP gave IFOR more open-ended tasks. In particular, NATO-led forces were to ensure a cessation of hostilities and to create a peaceful and secure environment for the implementation of nonmilitary reforms. These two tasks involved the holding of free and fair elections, the continuation of humanitarian missions, the protection of refugee returnees, and the supervision of the clearing of minefields and obstacles. One year proved woefully insufficient time for creating a secure and stable environment in Bosnia.

Part of the problem lay with the Dayton agreement itself, the terms of which left room for continuing mischief by faction extremists. The international community recognized the division of the Republic of Bosnia and Herzegovina into two separate entities: the Federation of Bosnia and Herzegovina and the Republika Srpska (RS). Each entity possessed its own regional government, parliament, police force, and army. Moreover, the federation essentially represented the union of Bosniac (Muslim) and Bosnian Croat areas, but even in the federation the Bosniacs and Croats garnished their own separate governmental structures and armies. NATO thus faced an uphill battle in establishing common institutions across the board in Bosnia. Despite the initial acceptance of military facts on the ground, the architects of Dayton provided peacekeepers with several instruments intended for undermining Bosnia's partition and eventually establishing common institutions.

The West viewed elections as a key instrument for rebuilding Bosnia. By prohibiting indicted war criminals such as Karadzic from campaigning for public office, Washington expected to witness the transfer of power to more moderate and compliant political leaders. The electoral process would thus lead to establishing common institutions. More important, Washington and NATO viewed elections as an essential component of an exit strategy.[4] Any delay in holding elections meant the country lacked the political stability necessary to justify NATO's departure. "Elections would demonstrate the degree to which aspects of the Accords, such as inter-entity co-operation, freedom of movement and the right of displaced persons to return to the places of origin" were successful.[5]

Unfortunately, Bosnia was not ready for elections after having just experienced a bloody civil war with ethnic cleansing. But Washington pushed for early elections regardless. Voting at the national level took place on 14 September 1996. IFOR provided support so that officials from the Organization for Security and Cooperation in Europe could secure ballot boxes and certify the conduct of elections as free and fair. The international community prohibited indicted war criminals from seeking office but permitted all three prewar nationalist parties to compete for votes. The results proved very disappointing to NATO.

Although some voter fraud marred the elections, the ethnic parties won by such large margins that any corrections would have had little effect on the final outcome.[6] For the common Presidency of Bosnia-Herzegovina, Alija Izetbegovic (Party of Democratic Action or SDA) won 80 percent of the vote among Bosniac candidates. Momcilo Krajisnik (Serbian Democratic Party or SDS), Karadzic's man, received 67.3

percent of the vote in the Serb community; Mladen Ivanic, an economist, managed a respectable 29.96 percent for his multiethnic coalition. In this regard, the Republika Srpska could claim the most contested election in Bosnia. Among Croatian voters, Kresimir Zubak (Croatian Democratic Alliance or HDZ) carried the vote with a whopping 88.7 percent. For the 42 seats in the common Parliamentary Assembly, SDA won 19 seats, SDS 9, and HDZ 3. The remainder went to smaller parties. Izetbegovic won the vote for the common Presidency with 730,592. Krajisnik came in second with 690,646 and Zubak received 330,377. By gaining the most votes, Izetbegovic became president of the Republic of Bosnia and Herzegovina.

The election results clearly demonstrated that one year was insufficient time for bringing peace and stability to Bosnia. Each nationalist party played on people's fears to garner votes, an appeal that carried some credence given IFOR's one-year mandate. Many voters feared an early NATO pullout would leave them vulnerable to the extremists in other warring factions; their own hard-liners appeared the best bet for security. Bosnian prewar leaders remained in power, some behind the scenes. These individuals were quite willing to continue the struggle for their personal and ethnic interests, although they resorted to means other than the army. Popular wisdom pointed to a high probability of a return to violence should NATO leave with IFOR's expiration date of 20 December 1996.

Shortly after the September national elections, the North Atlantic Council agreed to the inevitable, the extension of NATO's mandate with the replacement of IFOR with the Stabilization Force or SFOR. The command structure for Bosnia changed with SFOR. Both Allied Command Europe Rapid Reaction Corps and the Allied Forces Southern Command disappeared from the theater of operations. The SFOR commander took over the headquarters of the latter in Ilidza, Sarajevo. He wore two hats, commander of SFOR and the US Commander, Europe. This reorganization ensured that all peacekeeping troops came under an American army general, who reported directly to Supreme Allied Commander, Europe, who also was an American general. The US Army wanted control over what was essentially a mission for ground forces. No longer would a US naval admiral command ground forces until 2001.

On 12 December 1996, the UN Security Council Resolution 1088 authorized SFOR as the legal successor to IFOR for conducting peace enforcement under Chapter 7 of the UN Charter. The mandate was set to last for 18 months. SFOR's primary mission was to stabilize the safe and secure environment created by IFOR. Its specific tasks were 1) prevent the resumption of hostilities; 2) promote a climate conducive to pushing the peace process forward; and 3) provide selective support to civilian organizations within its capabilities. This mandate clearly engaged SFOR in nation building. Among the civilian issues requiring military protection were the right of return of all refugees and displaced persons to their prewar homes, the capture of indicted war criminals, and the creation of common institutions.

SFOR assumed control on 20 December 1996 with a mandate of 18 months. Because the first 12 months of IFOR saw no combat deaths of peacekeepers and no major civil upheaval, the North Atlantic Council reduced troop levels from 60,000 to 32,600: 12,400 in MND-N, 9,800 in MND-SE, 7,400 in MND-SW, and 3,000 in Croatia. Each division had four battle groups, essentially reinforced battalions instead of brigades. US troop strength fell from 17,500 to 8,500 with SFOR. On 10 November 1996, the 1st Infantry Division (Mechanized) under Major General Montgomery Meigs replaced the 1st Armored Division in MND-N. In December 1997, NATO decided to extend the mission in Bosnia indefinitely, and Washington once again reduced its contribution, this time from 8,500 to 6,900. By 1999, the number of SFOR troops dropped to 20,000, including 4,000 Americans.

Peace Enforcement in Bosnia

The Bosnian war failed to end the ethnic conflict; the struggle just took on a different form with the entry of NATO. Bosnian political leaders and military commanders from the three warring factions were all naturally disposed to test the resolve of IFOR and its successor, SFOR, always with the intent of gaining some advantage. Generally speaking, Serb hard-liners sought to maintain the status quo, which meant keeping the Republika Srpska as separate an entity as possible. Bosniac nationalists, for their part, wanted to restore prewar Bosnia but with Muslims in charge. Croat radicals, like the Serbs, preferred the status quo and resisted all attempts to dissolve the Croat Republic of Hercog-Bosna as a separate ministate. NATO faced the challenge of helping overcome resistance to the creation of common institutions for all Bosnians without distinction of religion or ethnicity.

NATO deployed to Bosnia with UN authority for peace enforcement rather than peacekeeping. Instead of being encumbered with more *don't*s than *do*s, NATO peacekeepers could be proactive. As a result, commanders had authority at lower levels to employ force if necessary. It was important for IFOR to demonstrate its robust mandate for implementing the Dayton

Accords. While the entry of US ground troops suggested a world very different from that of UNPROFOR, Bosnian political and military leaders still figured to put IFOR resolve to the test. IFOR commanders, for their part, were determined to set the tone for the entire peace operation. Forcing compliance was not always easy, however.

For the execution of peace operations at the operational and tactical levels, GFAP established the Joint Military Commission (JMC) to serve as the central body through which the IFOR commander could fulfill the military tasks of Dayton. JMCs required the senior military commander of each warring faction's army to meet with the IFOR, and later SFOR, commanders. At these regular meetings, held at least once a month, the NATO commander resolved military problems and then demanded compliance where infractions took place. The JMC proved an important instrument for implementing military aspects of the Dayton Accords.

The first JMC meeting took place at Sarajevo Airport on 21 December 1995. In attendance were the High Representative Carl Bildt, IFOR Commander Admiral Leighton Smith, Commander of the Allied Rapid Reaction Corps Lieutenant General Michael Walker, and the Bosniac, Serb, and Croat army commanders. The Bosnian participants formally declared their willingness to comply with the Dayton Accords, while IFOR explained the procedures for conveying military instructions.[7] For IFOR's duration, Admiral Smith delegated routine meetings to Walker. For their part, the MND commanders, as well as their brigade and battalion commanders, used the JMC concept at their command level. Most of the work for the implementation of the Dayton Accords took place at these local JMCs.

In MND-N, Major General Nash, the commander of Task Force *Eagle*, made great use of the JMC. At meetings, he regularly provided each military faction's commander with a report card grading most recent performance. To ensure compliance in its sector, the US Army relied on two American strengths: superiority in firepower and technology. Nash attended meetings with a heavy escort to underscore to his Bosnian counterparts his ability to employ overwhelming force if necessary. When disputes occurred over the veracity of field reports, he readily produced satellite photos demonstrating violations. In such instances, the offending Bosnian commander lost the wind to his sails.[8] Later, Nash noted the effectiveness of information technology: "We don't have arguments. We hand them pictures and they move their tanks."[9] Compliance thus became the order of the day or one faced quick punishment.

MND commanders behaved as conquerors occupying a defeated country. If a faction commander missed a JMC meeting, the IFOR commander could confine that army to barracks; or NATO could cancel a training exercise in an instant with no court of appeal for the injured party. In this sense, GFAP provided NATO commanders in theater with an effective instrument. Still, peace enforcement and peacekeeping present unique challenges to officers mainly schooled for conventional war.

Trained to kill in combat, tactical commanders now had to practice the art of street diplomacy and a graduated escalation in the use of force according to strict rules of engagement. Words became bullets in negotiations, because using weapons was to be a last resort. As Colonel Greg Fontenot, commander of the 1st Armored Brigade of the 1st Armored Division in IFOR, emphasized to his troops, firing a weapon constituted a tactical defeat.[10] Before and during deployment, officers and soldiers learned that killing a civilian would have strategic implications and would certainly create a martyr for the enemy. One Army officer explained the phenomenon as "the Boston Massacre Complex." Shots fired in anger by regular troops could mobilize a people to commit heroic sacrifices for their cause, and the US Army wanted to avoid such an occurrence at all costs.[11] Such indoctrination resulted in amazing restraint by American soldiers when threatened by mob violence (discussed in a later chapter).

Key tasks for tactical commanders included establishing the ZOS, dismantling of police checkpoints to ensure freedom of movement, inspection of weapons sites, support of police operations as needed, and mine clearing. Initially, NATO commanders wanted to avoid having to capture indicted war criminals or to quell civil disturbances. IFOR and SFOR preferred the Bosnian police handle these tasks.

Young company and platoon commanders, usually in their early 30s or mid 20s respectively, faced challenges in executing their missions, especially in the first year. Often, they had to confront potentially explosive situations by judiciously balancing negotiation with intimidation, depending on circumstances. In one case, for example, Captain Fred Drummond, a company commander of the 16th Engineer Battalion, confronted two checkpoints on opposite sides of a bridge, one manned by Bosniacs and the other by Serbs. The respective commanders were both in their 50s, clearly hardened war veterans. In negotiating with them separately, Drummond discovered to his dismay that they threatened to kill the other person if they met face-to-face. The young captain, never seriously trained in the art of negotiations to meet such a challenge, used the Dayton Accords to demonstrate the correctness of his demands. To his relief, both commanders dismantled their checkpoints, and they even shook hands, though somewhat awkwardly.[12]

Setting up checkpoints proved no easy task during politically tense periods. In September 1997, for example, Lieutenant Colonel James Greer, commander of the 1st Battalion, 77th Armor Regiment, was at police headquarters in Brcko when suddenly a group of buses passed by the station headed west. He immediately called Camp McGovern and ordered Lieutenant Greg Sharpe, platoon commander in the 22nd Infantry, to establish a checkpoint on a main road leading to Banja Luka and inspect the convoy of buses for weapons. Unknown to Greer, the buses were en route to Banja Luka to stage a rally or riot against the pro-Dayton government of Biljana Plavsic.[13]

Sharpe established his position at an intersection of two main roads in an open field. Later, he admitted that it would have been better to locate his position on a nearby bridge, where he could maintain a distance between his soldiers and the Serbs. Rather suddenly, some 30 to 40 buses drove up to his checkpoint. All the buses stopped and approximately 1,000 Serbs filed off them and began interspersing among the American troops. Using a radio from Camp McGovern, Lieutenant Colonel Mark Corda, the task force commander, ordered Sharpe to immobilize the buses by shooting their tires, an order rescinded once Sharpe informed them that discharging weapons would most certainly incite the travelers. The young platoon commander also remembered that he did not want to create a martyr for the cause. A Serb camera crew was on hand, ready to film any incident. Having lost control of his unit, Sharpe decided on withdrawing his troops to a safe distance. Only with some difficulty did Sharpe manage to extricate himself and his soldiers. After a brief standoff, headquarters ordered Sharpe to withdraw and establish a second checkpoint. After holding Sharpe there for a couple of hours, headquarters ordered a pullback 5 to 6 miles down the road. There, military police showed up with riot gear that included protective shields. This time, the Serbs began throwing rocks and other objects.[14]

Greer was finally able to stop the buses a couple of kilometers east of Modrica. He decided to gather his vehicles and drive very slowly in front of the buses. Then, the Americans stopped where it was impossible for the caravan to get off the road to bypass. Here, the standoff lasted into the early hours of the next day. By slowing the buses down, the Americans were able to prevent the caravan from reaching Banja Luka in time to participate in a violent demonstration.[15] Other national contingents used the tactics of block, withdraw, and block again to slow down buses en route to the same demonstration in Banja Luka.

Historical Baggage

Peace support missions present challenges to the US Army. Soldiers are trained to be killers in defense of their country's national interests when ordered to wage war by the political leadership. In peace enforcement and peacekeeping, however, an army embraces essentially a police action and therefore must show restraint and use lethal force only as a last resort after having gone through a proper graduated response defined in its ROE. In Bosnia, however, the US Army showed itself much out of step with other Western armies as it practiced peace enforcement and later peacekeeping. The American military establishment brought its own unique mind-set to the theater.

Secretary of Defense William H. Perry ordered the 1st Armored Division to posture itself for mid-intensity conflict.[16] On 19 December 1995, he personally told officers of the division to be "the meanest dog on the block."[17] Put another way, the warring factions needed to know that "there was a new sheriff on the block."[18] This political guidance was prudent for two reasons. First, while indications on the ground suggested that the warring factions had exhausted themselves and were ready for winter hibernation, there still loomed the distinct possibility of combat. Better to be well prepared than found deficient. Second, as a counter to UNPROFOR's weak mandate and general ineffectiveness, IFOR needed to demonstrate to the warring factions that Western resolve had changed dramatically. Rolling into Bosnia fully dressed for combat sent that message.

Other Western armies took a similar approach. UNPROFOR soldiers took off their soft blue caps and put on helmets for patrolling. For the next couple of months, every national contingent maintained a high level of force protection. American soldiers were virtually indistinguishable from fellow soldiers in other armies. Most contingents sooner or later reduced their force protection posture. The US kept it the longest, exhibiting the least inclination to change its combat mind-set toward peace support operations.

Unambiguous intimidation was the order of the day. American displays of firepower were intended to impress war-weary Bosnian fighters on all sides, many of whom looked for a legitimate excuse to cease fighting. In support of his field commanders, Admiral Smith felt it important to underscore his own resolve. On 19 February 1996, he held his first JMC as IFOR commander on board the aircraft carrier *George Washington* in

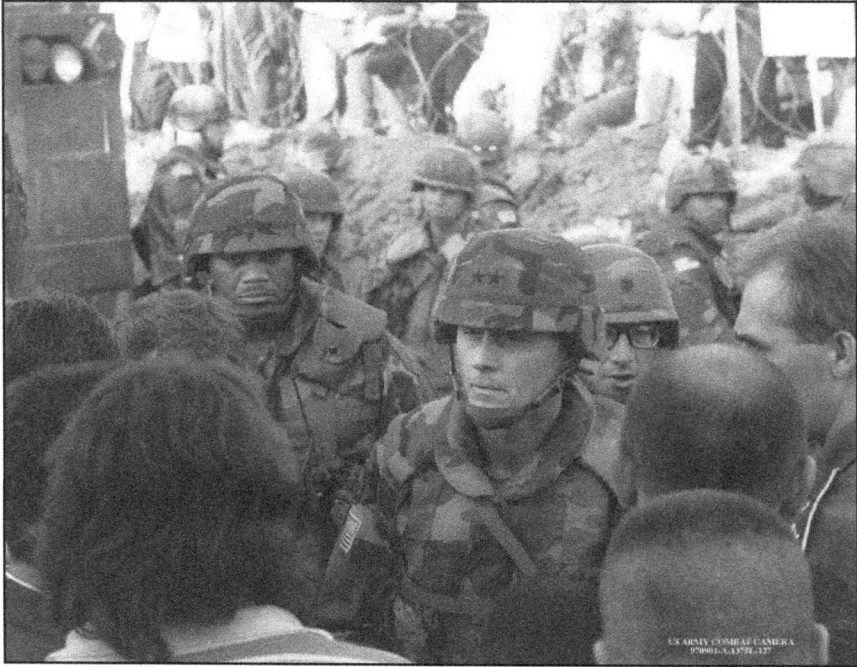

Photo 11. US forces from the rank of private to general officer
maintained a high force protection standard

the Adriatic Sea to display American naval firepower to the commanders
of the three warring factions' militaries. As the theater commander,
Smith was intimidating at the operational level by demonstrating IFOR
capabilities. He expected the Bosnian generals to counsel their political
leaders to comply with the directives of the High Representative.[19] At
the tactical level, NATO armies invited local Bosnian commanders to
view military exercises to demonstrate their own determination and
professionalism.

One can exaggerate the military effectiveness of demonstrations of
overwhelming firepower. It certainly did not work when Nazi Germany
invaded Yugoslavia in World War II. But the situation in 1995 was very
different from that in 1941. In 1995, the leaders of the three warring
factions, as well as the countries of Croatia and Serbia, had signed the
Dayton Accords. Moreover, the Muslim, Croat, and Serb armies were
war weary from fighting, and the cold winter added to the desire of many
soldiers to end three years of fighting, however intermittent. In addition,
the US and Russian entries into Bosnia brought virtually the entire world
into a commitment to peacekeeping. For one warring faction to take on

such a global coalition without a strong ally would have smacked of sheer folly. Finally, the Dayton Accords represented a partial victory for the ethnic cleansers because they gained, at least for the immediate future, safe havens under their control or influence. A more relaxed posture appeared most appropriate.

Despite a pattern of general compliance on the part of Bosnian militaries, American senior commanders held firm to maintaining combat dress and behavior as signs of professionalism throughout the deployment. For Americans, a statement by one Bosniac corps commander underscored the correctness of this attitude: "All of my men out there are fighters, not yet soldiers. You Americans are soldiers. You all dress alike, you all have discipline, you have clean weapons at the ready, you always travel in four vehicle convoys, even your helicopters fly in formation. Soldiers do that and we notice it."[20] As one American junior officer noted rather sarcastically, "the Kevlar helmet became the dome of discipline."

American politics helped drive this military mind-set. The Clinton administration committed ground troops to Bosnia reluctantly, and the political leadership in Washington wanted matters to go as smoothly as possible to avoid any negative reactions from the American public. Perry underscored this concern to General George Joulwan, the Supreme Allied Commander, Europe, and other senior American officers when he stated in a meeting with them that Washington wanted no casualties.[21] Commanders in attendance understood that success of the operation depended on keeping casualties to a minimum, and they communicated this aim down the chain of command by a heavy emphasis on force protection. American ground troops deployed into Bosnia with a clear mission statement: "On order, Task Force *Eagle* deploys to SECTOR TUZLA, Bosnia-Herzegovina, and conducts peace enforcement operations to compel compliance with the peace accord; ensures force protection."[22] Defining force protection as an essential task represented a recent development in American military culture.

Force protection emerged as a hot topic in the US military by the early 1990s. Before then, the mission came first, but inherent in any military operation was a concern for casualties. Force protection, however, reflected an increased concern for loss of life, more for political reasons, placing it in potential conflict with mission accomplishment. The Gulf War had already provided clear indications of this development. In his semiofficial study, retired Army Colonel Richard Swain, Third Army's historian in this conflict, argued that plans for *Desert Storm* placed the highest priority on minimizing allied and civilian casualties. This goal had become ingrained from the Vietnam era when Walter Cronkite weekly updated American casualties for his viewing audience. In the Gulf War, the Army avoided night operations to limit friendly fire and methodically advanced with three divisions in VII Corps in mass rather than exploit success with a rapier-like thrust. Consequently, the US Army approached the Gulf War with a growing desire for a tidy battlefield, reflecting a primary concern over casualties.[23]

The tragedies of Mogadishu in Somalia and Khobar Towers in Saudi Arabia helped transform a general concern for casualties into the concept of force protection. Somalia created a myth that public will in the US was a fragile commodity that would easily turn against military operations once American soldiers were killed in action, especially when disturbing images appeared on television. This reasoning became known as the "Somalia Syndrome," the false view that the American public has little tolerance for casualties. The bombing of Khobar Towers in Saudi Arabia, for its part, ended the career of the Air Force general in charge of the base. This incident underscored for commanding officers the imperative for maintaining a high vigil of force protection. As one syndicated writer heard from a senior officer in Bosnia, "But I'll tell you what: if you as a commander take casualties for *any* reason, the *first* question that gets asked is 'What level of force protection did you take?'"[24] Both soldiers and officers readily admit to the underlying principle for commanders in never letting down one's defenses: "CYA. Cover your ass."

By making force protection part of the mission statement for deployment into Bosnia, the US Army created an aim that competed with the ostensible purpose of the mission. Stationed in Bosnia in 2000, Colonel Chris Baggott, commander of the 3rd Armored Cavalry Regiment, underscored the inherent problem of force protection as part of the mission. As he observed, successful command has come to mean, in large part, returning home with no casualties. Commanders are pressured, unconsciously or consciously, into taking a short-range approach to their assignment and therefore are reluctant to take risks. Exit strategy becomes personalized— don't get anyone killed.[25] American political advisers (POLADs), senior State Department officials assigned to advise the SFOR and MND-N commanders on political matters, observed this tension.[26] Force protection can become a way of soothing a commander's conscience and the concern of his superiors.

The political culture back in the US reinforced this military mind-set. The Clinton administration sought a quick exit and thus wanted minimal commitments and short-range perspectives. They were, furthermore, leery of casualties. All this was not lost on commanders in the field.[27] But the roots of the problem went deeper than just the current administration or political traditions to overseas deployments.

From a historical perspective, the Vietnam War had left a scar on the military psyche. The US Army developed an aversion to unconventional missions. In particular, the military establishment resisted embracing peacekeeping as part of its *raison d'etre*. Consequently, the Army top brass went into Bosnia determined to interpret its military mission in a narrow sense. Getting involved on the civilian side smacked of nation building, and Vietnam veterans remembered how that mission complicated the combat effort in Indochina. Subsequently, a foremost "lesson learned" from Somalia held that nation building leads to mission creep, and expansion of a military's role into civilian affairs has deleterious effects. Therefore, the US interpreted the military clauses of the Dayton Accords narrowly and, like the Clinton administration, wanted to get out as quickly as possible. High Representative Carl Bildt discerned two different approaches toward Bosnia, observing that "a pattern was established right from the onset: the US would focus on military matters and limit its involvement in the civilian arena, while the Europeans were wary of a peace effort that was too military in a narrow sense, and too limited in terms of the time element."[28] General Wesley Clark, who became Supreme Allied Commander, Europe, in July 1997, concurred with part of Bildt's evaluation. "The Pentagon wanted success, too, but sought to keep the mission as limited and as risk-free as possible."[29]

One area outside the military's purview was pursuing persons indicted for war crimes, commonly referred to as PIFWCs. The US Army's senior leadership considered this task as counter to the peace enforcement or peacekeeping mission. Pentagon officials argued that this was a matter for the Bosnian police. General John Shalikashvili, chairman of the Joint Chiefs of Staff from 1993 to 1997, underscored his guidance to American troops in Bosnia: "I made it clear that I would not support using the military to hunt down war criminals. We weren't going to take them unless we stumbled upon them. I felt that the military had a horrible track record in chasing these kinds of criminals. Look at Mogadishu."[30] American soldiers would arrest individuals only if encountered on patrols. Or the Bosnian police would conduct the operation, with IFOR or SFOR providing support by sealing off the surrounding area. Such a dynamic brought a political benefit. Local police chiefs could excuse their participation to their political heads by blaming coercive pressure from NATO.

During 1996 and the first half of 1997, NATO failed, for the most part, to detain any indicted war criminals. Then from 10 July 1997 to 2 October 1998, SFOR captured nine, though others were seized by Americans.[31] But the Americans could not escape the fallout of actions in other MNDs. On 10 July 1997, when the British captured one Serb indicted war criminal and killed a second, MND-N expected to feel Serb wrath. And it did. On 12 July, a bomb exploded in Zvornik before several international offices. Nearly two weeks later, an antitank rocket struck a parked IPTF vehicle. No one was hurt in either incident. American patrols, for their part, suddenly experienced several incidents of bottle throwing, spitting, and obscene hand gestures.[32]

In summary, the US Army embarked on peacekeeping in Bosnia with some reticence. Based on the experiences of Vietnam and Somalia, the senior leadership wanted to avoid nation building at all cost, lest Bosnia turn into a quagmire. American commanders needed prodding from the highest levels of command to broaden their actions in support of the mission. Moreover, force protection carried a major importance within the context of the overall mission of securing a peaceful environment. This general mind-set made for some controversial and questionable practices and behavior by the US Army.

Soldiering Without War

At the small-unit level, the Americans took extraordinary precautions to ensure the safety of American soldiers as required by the mission statement cited earlier. In fact, compared with the other national contingents, the US Army has adopted the most extreme approach to force protection in Bosnia. Much debate has occurred over the wisdom of its practices.

During IFOR, American commanders regarded patrolling as a combat mission. This made sense given the initial uncertainties. Policy required American soldiers to wear Kevlar helmets and flak jackets at all times. Machine guns on vehicles were in a position ready to fire. Foot patrols had soldiers sporting rifles in their hands. Any movement or patrol off the camp required a minimum of four vehicles. This ensured a "buddy system." If one vehicle broke down, two could go for help while one remained with the disabled vehicle.[33] All this was intended to protect soldiers and intimidate the locals. The rationale for such an approach, especially during IFOR, was not hard to grasp.

Practices on base were rather extreme, however. American soldiers had to wear "full battle rattle" at all times, including a Kevlar helmet and flak vest. They carried their rifles on their shoulders while outdoors. Soldiers brought their weapons to the mess hall. The three authors of this study ate on Eagle Base in Tuzla in September 2000 and saw rifles parked in holders at the end of tables while soldiers ate. Other armies prohibited weapons in dining facilities.

Force protection during IFOR carried some contradictions. Officially, a soldier could jog on base in running gear but a guard with full body armor had to be in an overwatch position on the route. Requiring full battle rattle in camp struck many as odd, especially since initially the soldiers slept without their gear in tents that offered no protection from mortar or sniper fire.[34] Meanwhile, American special forces working in local communities kept a low force protection posture so as not to create unnecessary barriers between themselves and the people. Rather comically, they had to put on the full body armor to enter American bases, which were obviously more secure than their own neighborhoods in town.

A great disparity in practice existed between American soldiers serving in Sarajevo and those in MND-N. In Sarajevo, the Americans, with a rare exception, fell under NATO regulations with a very different force protection policy. Here, Americans wore soft caps and could visit the city and eat in restaurants. Moreover, Americans did not wear the SFOR patch but the conspicuous US flag on their uniforms. This practice contradicted the argument for high force protection because it made Americans very easily identifiable for any terrorist bent on killing an American soldier. Here it seemed excessive American patriotism outweighed concern for safety of troops.

One story brings out the sharp contrast in peacekeeping styles in evidence during IFOR. An American base at Lukavac just west of Tuzla had a small contingent of approximately 20 British soldiers. The base commander required that the British drink their beer behind an 8-foot covered fence so that American soldiers, dressed in full body armor both outside and inside buildings and sporting weapons, could not observe the regular festivities. But the fence could not hide the alcohol smell or the presence of empty beer cans in the trash the next day. The British could also receive permission to eat in town, while the Americans were confined to base unless on patrols or special assignments, all requiring four vehicles. The American soldiers were a bit demoralized by the restrictions. One American officer later joked about this arrangement: "our [American] stiffness entertained them [the British] to some extent."[35]

Photo 12. US soldiers in body armor and helmets
mingled on the streets of Bosnia

Photo 13. Canadian soldier on patrol with translator

Photo 14. A British soldier helps keep order on MND SW

Gradually, the Army softened its policy, but it took years for changes to occur. In June or July 1997, for example, General William Crouch, then SFOR commander, visited Camp McGovern and heard complaints from soldiers about having to wear a helmet while on base (the requirement to wear a flak jacket had been removed). That evening, MND-N changed its force protection policy. On base, soldiers could wear soft caps instead of Kevlar helmets. Morale went up on the bases as a result. Apparently, there had been some discussion about relaxing force protection on bases, but the general's intervention ensured an earlier implementation of the change. Full battle rattle attire remained operative for outside the base, however.[36] Eventually, a two-vehicle requirement replaced the four-vehicle convoy.

Some senior commanders advocated change but found it difficult to implement because of an ingrained mind-set. General Meigs, SFOR commander from October 1998 to October 1999, encouraged his American division commanders to permit their troops on patrols to use soft caps and keep their flak jackets and Kevlar helmets in their vehicle when the threat was very low. Meigs felt a lower force protection posture, such as soft caps and no flak jackets while on foot patrols, provided flexibility and enhanced a sense of normalcy. A shift from soft caps to helmets on foot patrols, for example, sent a clear signal to the local population of increased seriousness. But his generals resisted the suggestion. According to Meigs,

Major General Kevin Byrnes, commander of the 1st Cavalry Division, contended that it was "too late in his tour" for such a major change. His replacement, Major General James Campbell of the 10th Mountain Division, expressed no desire "to break tradition."[37] Interestingly, Meigs had failed to take such a step earlier when he had commanded the 3rd Infantry Division in 1997.

Later, Campbell admitted to receiving pressure from senior officers to change his force protection policy. "They thought I was too far in the past." He was clearly aware that "in some cases, they [allies] laughed at us." In his defense, Campbell argued that it was far better to adhere to a stricter policy than have to inform parents of the death of a loved one. But he did modify the policy a little. On patrol, the battalion commander could allow his soldiers to leave their flak vests in their vehicle but keep them "within arm's reach." Some officers took advantage of this new policy; others did not. Later, Campbell admitted a little disappointment when he discovered that some commanders rigidly adhered to the former policy requiring soldiers on patrol to wear flak jackets at all times.[38]

After Campbell's departure in March 2000, Major General Robert Halverson, commander of the 49th National Guard (Texas) Armored Division, replaced him. The 49th staffed the headquarters while a regular Army unit, the 3rd Cavalry Regiment, conducted field operations. Despite a reduced force structure from 5,400 to 3,900, Halverson implemented the use of soft caps in certain safer areas. Again, it was the local commander's call, and some commanders took advantage of this new flexibility. From Halverson's vantage point, soldiers appeared to embrace and like the change where it was applied. Halverson believed that soft caps projected an image of a kinder and more caring soldier than did full combat attire. He also understood that, irrespective of force-protection levels, killing an American soldier was not a difficult task for a determined adversary. In any case, the threat was insufficient to warrant a high level of force protection.[39] One National Guard officer noted, perhaps with a bit of exaggeration, that the police blotter in Houston had more incidents in a day than all of Bosnia in a month. The year was 2000, five years after the initial American deployment, a period that witnessed no combat casualties.

Although the former warring factions seemed determined to avoid inflicting fatal casualties, to some degree, IFOR and SFOR were lucky that no soldiers fell in combat or in armed attacks. In July 1997, for example, Serb extremists launched a series of bombings and rocket launchings to protest the capture of the first indicted war criminal and the killing of a second by British forces. Despite the increase in violent incidents, one unit history noted that "We . . . felt an attack directed at SFOR personnel and installations would be highly unlikely. . . . It became clear that the individuals or groups responsible were very careful to ensure no one would be injured by their terrorist attacks and may have launched a campaign of terror [only] to intimidate SFOR and the International organizations in the RS."[40]

The concern for casualties affected all aspects of the deployment. Commanders naturally fell into restricting the social life of their troops as much as possible. For the first five years, General Order #1 prohibited officers and soldiers from drinking alcohol except under very restrictive circumstances. A reporter described life on Eagle Base during the 2000-2001 tour of the 3rd Infantry Division (Mechanized) thus: "The soldiers live in surprising isolation. Those who go out on patrol are generally forbidden to sit in cafes, to shop in the local markets, or to socialize with the Bosnians. Two thirds of the soldiers never even go out on patrols, and live almost entirely restricted to the base, where they serve in 'support' roles as guards and office workers, and seem to spend most of their leisure time eating and then trying to lose weight. . . But when soldiers talk about tough duty in Bosnia, they usually mean General Order #1—a nearly total prohibition on alcohol for American troops."[41] MND-N finally relaxed the restrictions on drinking by 2001, permitting one or two beers on a more frequent basis.

To address boredom on base, MND-N began to permit escorted trips to Tuzla and Sarajevo. In May 1997, morale, welfare, and recreation specialist Michaela Vance had to work three entire months to arrange an outing to Sarajevo from Eagle Base. Her achievement was so noteworthy that *The Stars and Stripes* published an article on the experience titled "Seeing the Sights of Sarajevo: M[orale] W[elfare] R[ecreation] tour gets SFOR troops off base and to somewhere new." Vance found, much to her dismay, that "there was no prior history of how to get it arranged."[42] When her small group finally arrived in the Bosnian capital, the troops could shed their bulky flak jackets and leave them behind. Unlike their American counterparts stationed in Sarajevo, the "tourists" from Tuzla had to take their rifles with them, locked but not loaded. Sergeant Thomas White found the excursion invigorating: "It feels good just to mingle with the people, to get out with the country. That seems what the Bosnians wanted to see. I guess they can't understand why we're in the camps and not out doing a lot of things like going out to eat like we did today, helping the economy a little bit."[43]

Some division commanders permitted a limited number of such excursions. Under his watch, Halverson encouraged his troops to do such visits. He felt it helped morale and gave the soldiers a sense of mission.[44] Major General Walter Sharp, commander of the 3rd Infantry Division, permitted this policy, but "not many" soldiers seemed to take advantage of this opportunity.[45] American military culture did not encourage such outreach as an essential part of the mission of peacekeeping. The contracting firm of Brown & Root sought to make life on base self-sufficient. In this, the Army differed from other national armies in Bosnia.

By 2000, force protection had become a non-issue, taboo to discuss.[46] There was therefore little reflection of one's own behavior, even among American generals. Strange behavior can result from non-reflection. One such area pertained to travel methods of senior American commanding officers when they arrived by helicopter at MND-SW or MND-SE. Usually, they traveled with a huge security detail that reflexively fanned out on the landing site as if securing unknown terrain. Such behavior is both humorous and insulting to a foreign MND commander, humorous because it appears so inappropriate for the situation, insulting because it suggests other national contingents lack secure bases. Such behavior smacks of exaggerated self-importance and unnecessary individual protection.[47] In professionalism, both big and little things matter.

It didn't take much for Americans to raise their force protection levels. Some reaction bordered on the absurd. When the US bombed Afghanistan in 1998, for example, MND-N immediately went a high alert status. All military personnel had to wear full combat gear at all times. In one instance, officers and soldiers were required to watch movies in a theater on base dressed in Kevlar helmets and flak jackets.[48] World War II veterans shook their heads in disbelief when I shared this story with them.

The US military assigned a greater priority to the appearance of physical force protection when compared with other national contingents. Over the first six years of deployment, the American senior command in MND-N consistently maintained a higher level of force protection than in the other two sectors. A case study of Bosnia thus provides an excellent opportunity for employing the comparative method. Such comparison is essential if the US military institution is to conduct serious reflection of its own behavior. *Know thyself*, and know thy enemy.

A Different Philosophy

Other Western armies possess a philosophical approach to peace operations very different from that of the US Army. The comparative method shows that the US Army has not embraced peacekeeping as one of its *raisons d'etre*. The military establishment therefore suffers a bit from a weak and ambiguous tradition for peacekeeping. Its senior Army leadership has tended to embrace peace missions rather reluctantly and has drawn too much attention to its harmful effect on combat readiness.

Other Western armies possess a different peacekeeping philosophy and place great importance on the gathering of human intelligence by the regular forces. They talk more of "social patrolling," a concept that seemed more appropriate to Bosnia than force protection. To be effective in their mission, according to this philosophy, peacekeepers need to foster an ambiance of normalcy as much as possible. Dress and the manner of patrolling play a critical role in the pursuit of this goal. As early as the IFOR period, European armies began to adopt some combination of a soft cap, no flak jackets, and the weapons slung over the shoulder on patrols. In theory, this approach would appear less menacing and foster approachability. Soldiers could stop and have a coffee as a means for initiating dialogue with locals. Bosnia possesses "a café culture." Patrol commanders needed to exploit this gathering place for the exchange of ideas and information, taking time to sit with the locals and talk. A relaxed posture on patrol, again in theory, enhances force protection rather than detracts from it. Soldiers become more approachable and therefore better able to gather intelligence from locals. Through an interface with the local population, peacekeepers gain a sense of purpose.[49]

American special forces and counterintelligence operatives accept the above philosophy. But the US Army's senior leadership has resisted its application to regular forces and instead prefers to emphasize the combat nature of patrolling in peacekeeping. Indeed, advocates of the US style of force protection maintained that in war-torn Bosnia, it did not prevent contact with the people or stop the flow information.[50] Though patrol commanders conducted intelligence gathering, the US Army placed greater reliance on technology and on special units, such as special forces and counterintelligence, that worked semi-independently outside the normal command structure. This reliance on specialized units resulted in some uneven patrolling methods by conventional forces. As noted by one reporter, "some patrols did talk to the Bosnians. Some of the patrols did not. Some of the patrols had been restricted by their immediate commanders from doing such a thing."[51] Campbell saw a similar inconsistency when he learned that not all of his commanders were willing to demonstrate flexibility in force protection when offered the opportunity. This disparity reflects a weak peacekeeping tradition.

It is difficult to determine if either the European or American approaches are more effective in creating a secure environment for civilian reformers. Much certainly depends on the disposition of the local population and historical circumstances. Captain Jet Hayes, American liaison to the NORDIC Battle Group in Doboj, noted that regular patrols in his sector provided similar information as that gathered by special forces or counterintelligence units.[52] The difference in philosophy, however, is markedly clear. The European-Canadian method involves regular soldiers in intelligence gathering much more. Patrols can be more meaningful for individual soldiers if they have more responsibility and have more social contact with people. Situational awareness can only be enhanced with greater engagement, so goes the argument.

The Canadian army reflects the European philosophy regarding peace operations. Canadian peace operations in Drvar, a center of Croatian extremism, stand as a good example. In 1996, still under IFOR, Captain Ian Hope, the company commander in charge of the Drvar sector, initially adopted a high force protection posture but changed it rather quickly. He assessed that full body armor only aggravated relations with the local Croats. So Hope lowered the force protection within two to three weeks of his tour on his own authority. His soldiers did not wear helmets or flak jackets when on foot patrols, and they began emphasizing talking with people on the streets.[53] British practice was similar to that of the Canadians. In his Kermit Roosevelt Lecture Series to the student body at the US Army Command and General Staff College, General Sir Rupert Smith noted that a platoon commander in the British army had the authority to adjust force protection for his patrol. American officers in the audience expressed surprise and dismay at this state of affairs.[54] Such flexibility and decentralization down to platoon level were generally nonexistent in MND-N, the American sector, among conventional units.

The French example in Gacko helps illustrate a different philosophy in using the regular army in peace operations. Gacko is both a town and region located in MND-SE within the Republika Srpska. Before the war, the Gacko region numbered 10,844 inhabitants, of whom 62.4 percent were Serb and 35.3 percent were Bosniac. Serbs cleansed the region of non-Serbs, so that the population became almost exclusively Serb. The town subsequently had 8,000 Serbs and only 30 Bosniacs. Radical Serbs controlled the town; but Bosniacs did have three seats on the 12-member town council. In August 1999, the first Muslims returned to the county; SFOR had expected 600 but only 80 arrived. In January 2000, the French army decided to locate an infantry platoon in town and selected a house with one bathroom on a busy street just opposite a school. Soldiers rotated every seven days, while the company commander stayed for six months. The aim was both to better monitor conditions in Gacko and demonstrate a commitment to stability and security by means of a lasting, visible, and neighborly presence. The American division refused to expose its regular troops to such a situation.

In September 2000, Captain Michel Magne commanded the French platoon in Gacko. He never had expected to find himself in such a mission when he joined the army. His two main missions were to protect the Muslim refugees and to patrol the border with Montenegro. Approximately 80 percent of his company had seen service in Bosnia before. Magne stressed to his men that they needed to maintain two attitudes: friendly in the town but on guard when on patrol. Patrolling the border with Montenegro was a pure combat mission, providing a nice change of pace for himself and his soldiers. Interfacing with the population carried great importance. Soldiers played volleyball with the local children, for example. They were allowed to frequent a restaurant, but in groups of four with at least one soldier armed. Despite living among the people, Magne saw little progress. Gacko was a hard nut to crack. The region had the lowest rate of voluntary return of weapons in the division sector during OPERATION Harvest. Serb extremists controlled the town. Local Serb police visited Muslim returnees only when they knew an international official would inspect the area. Despite the difficulties of working in an area controlled by radicals, Magne remained committed to the French tradition for peacekeeping.[55]

Despite the emphasis on social instead of combat patrolling, commanders from other national contingents expressed concern about their soldiers becoming complacent. Soldiers need to be vigilant, for violence can occur at any moment. The transition from social patrolling to mortal combat is quick and not easy. In Doboj, for example, the Danes still used Leopard tanks in 2000 on select patrols to reinforce the message of deterrence, both to themselves and for the Bosnians.[56] Other Western armies carry the memories of losing soldiers to combat in Bosnia during UNPROFOR days. They stress to their soldiers that complacency can kill. Soldiers must always remember that they are soldiers, and Bosnia needs their professional soldiering for the maintenance of peace and security.

But what was the actual threat to American forces to warrant maintaining a high force protection level? The US Army generally assessed a low probability of major combat. Shortly before entry of Task Force *Eagle*, Colonel Greg Fontenot, commander of the 1st Armored

Brigade, concluded, based on his own reconnaissance of Bosnia, that all sides were exhausted and posed little threat to US troops.[57] Brigadier General Stanley Cherrie, assistant division commander in the 1st Armored Division, admitted that the division initially assessed mines or the odd sniper as the greatest threats.[58] Initially, it was quite prudent to err on the side of caution and enter Bosnia ready for combat, especially since there was serious concern about the possibility of a terrorist act. But rather quickly, it became apparent that the threat to IFOR was minimal. And history bears witness to this. From December 1995 to September 2002, not one American soldier in Bosnia was killed in combat from enemy fire.

Despite the lack of combat fatalities of a seven-year period, the US Army put forward many arguments to justify its higher-level force protection policy. None, however, silenced the growing number of sceptics. One argument stated that an American soldier carries more political value than a soldier from any other country. Therefore, the threat to American forces is always greater, by definition, than that to other national contingents. Still, an army must adjust its tactics to the threat, otherwise American soldiers would never remove their full battle rattle, and over time they did so in Bosnia.

There is a common view in the Army that the public is highly sensitive to casualties and would therefore quickly lose heart once some American soldiers were killed. But national commitment to military deployments is partly a function of the importance of the mission. Some Americans echoed the suspect argument that American generals care about their soldiers more than generals in other armies. Force protection, as has been argued in this chapter, has historically been driven as much by political and cultural as by professional considerations. Finally, some Americans have argued that their sector posed the greatest threat to SFOR. Hot spots included Brcko, Srebrenica, and Han Pijasek. Other MNDs, however, have their own troubled areas as well. MND-SW, for example, had responsibility for the towns of Mostar and Foca. MND-SE, for its part, included Prijedor and Drvar. Overall, no fully satisfying argument has been made to justify the US Army's history of force protection in Bosnia.

A handful of American officers interviewed for this study attest to the efficacy of having a lower force protection posture when attempting to engage the population while conducting patrols. One officer, for example, noticed a very different response from locals depending on his dress. In full battle rattle, the American intelligence officer found that adults and kids ignored his movement through the neighborhood. Several days later, a similar tour in the same neighborhood, but this time with a soft cap, resulted in kids stopping their soccer game and waving to him.[59] The second experience was more conducive to restoring normalcy in a traumatized society as well as gathering information.

Conclusion

By limiting social life to military camps with the excuse of force protection, the senior leadership denied its officers and soldiers a strong sense of purpose. By adhering to a combat mind-set for patrolling with its concomitant attire and behavior, the US Army unnecessarily erected barriers between itself and the local population, although locals learned to adjust to their new masters. Despite its shortcoming, the US Army admirably performed its mission of creating a secure environment for civil reforms.

The US Army's conduct of peace support operations indicates more about American military culture than anything else. In comparison with other Western armies in Bosnia, the US Army generally exhibited a cautious, risk-averse, more rigid, and less flexible mind-set among its regular forces. Military wisdom says that armed forces should train as they expect to fight. In this way, an army undergoes training that is intended to relate directly to combat. Might not the same hold true for peacekeeping? Practice peacekeeping in ways that develop the appropriate combat skills and mind-set. Army doctrine for conventional warfare stresses flexibility, audacity, and initiative. Yet the practice of peacekeeping in Bosnia reflected opposite tendencies. There is always the danger that this military culture in peacekeeping will carry over into conventional war. The warrior ethos does demand moral courage and risk taking, even in peace operations, and habits learned in one area can easily transfer into another area of military activity.

Notes

1. William Langewiesche, "Peace is Hell," *The Atlantic Monthly* (October 2001), 79.

2. Richard R. Caniglia, "US and British Approaches to Force Protection," *Military Review* (July-August 2001), 73.

3. Stanley F. Cherrie, "Task Force *Eagle*," *Military Review* (July-August 1997), 65-66.

4. Carl Bildt, *Peace Journey, The Struggle for Peace in Bosnia* (London: Wiedenfeld and Nicolson, 1998), 262.

5. James Gow, *Triumph of the Lack of Will: International Diplomacy and the Yugoslav War* (New York: Columbia University Press, 1997), 292.

6. Bildt, *Peace Journey*, 270.

7. Ibid., 172.

8. Colonel Ed Kane, interview with Robert Baumann, George Gawrych, and Walter Kretchik, 2 April 2000, Tuzla, Bosnia.

9. Larry K. Wentz, "Summary," in *Lessons from Bosnia: The IFOR Experience*, edited by Larry K. Wentz (Washington, DC: Command and Control Research Program, 1998), 412.

10. Colonel Greg Fontenot, US Army, Retired, interview with Robert Baumann and George Gawrych, 17 November 2000, Fort Leavenworth, KS.

11. The concept comes from an informal discussion with Major Joseph W. Ryan, Combat Studies Institute, US Army Command and General Staff College, Fort Leavenworth, KS.

12. Major Fred Drummond, interview with Robert Baumann and George Gawrych, 24 April 2000, Fort Leavenworth, KS.

13. Colonel James Greer, discussion with Dr. George Gawrych, 15 November 2001, Fort Leavenworth, KS.

14. Captain Greg Sharpe, interview with Robert Baumann and George Gawrych, 24 October 2000, Fort Leavenworth, KS

15. Greer discussion, 15 November 2001.

16. Walter Kretchik, "Force Protection Disparities," *Military Review* (July-August 1997), 73.

17. Major Michael Kasales, interview with Robert Baumann and George Gawrych, 18 January 2001, Fort Leavenworth, KS.

18. Fontenot interview.

19. Larry K. Wentz, "Intelligence Operations," in *Lessons from Bosnia: The IFOR Experience*, edited by Larry K. Wentz (Washington, DC: Command and Control Research Program, 1998), 57.

20. Cherrie, "Task Force *Eagle*," 72.

21. Lieutenant Colonel Walter Kretchik, US Army, Retired, discussion with George Gawrych, 19 August 2001, Leavenworth, KS. Kretchik was present at the meeting.

22. Cherrie, "Task Force *Eagle*," 65.

23. Richard Swain, *"Lucky War": Third Army in Desert Storm* (Fort Leavenworth, KS: US Army Command and General Staff College Press, 1994), 336-37.

24. Langewiesche, "Peace is Hell," 72.

25. Colonel Chris Baggott, interview with Robert Baumann, George Gawrych, and Walter Kretchik, 2 April 2000, Tuzla, Bosnia.

26. Several unnamed political advisers, interviews with Robert Baumann and George Gawrych.

27. Major James Dugan, informal discussion with George Gawrych, 17 July 2003, Fort Leavenworth, KS.

28. Bildt, *Peace Journey*, 109.

29. Wesley Clark, *Waging Modern War: Bosnia, Kosovo, and the Future of Combat* (New York: Public Affairs, 2001), 91.

30. Dana Priest, *The Mission: Waging War and Keeping Peace with America's Military* (New York: W.W. Norton & Company, 2003), 46.

31. United States General Accounting Office, *Bosnia Peace Operation: Mission, Structure, and Transition Strategy of NATO's Stabilization Force* (Washington, DC: GAO/NSAID, October 1988), 6.

32. *Task Force 1-41 Infantry in Bosnia-Herzegovina: Operation Joint Guard, April – October 1997* (Fort Riley, KS: 1998), 23-24.

33. Brigadier General Robert Wood, interview with Robert Baumann and George Gawrych, 17 March 2000, Fort Leavenworth, KS.

34. Lieutenant Colonel Walter Kretchik, casual discussion with George Gawrych, no recorded date, Fort Leavenworth, KS.

35. Major Joe Diminick, interview with George Gawrych, 3 May 2000, Fort Leavenworth, KS.

36. Greer discussion; Soller interview; Sharpe interview.

37. General Montgomery Meigs, interview with Robert Baumann and George Gawrych, 1 November 2000, Fort Leavenworth, KS.

38. Major General James Lowell Campbell, interview with Robert Baumann, 9 February 2001, Fort Drumm, NY.

39. Major General Robert Halverson, interview with Robert Baumann and George W. Gawrych, 25 January 2001, Austin, TX.

40. *Task Force 1-41 Infantry in Bosnia-Herzegovina*, 24.

41. Langewiesche, "Peace is Hell," 53.

42. Darrell Lewis, "Seeing the Sights of Sarajevo: MNR Tour Gets Troops Off Base and To Somewhere New," 18.

43. Ibid., 19.

44. Halverson interview.

45. Langewiesche, "Peace is Hell," 53.

46. Robert Baumann and George Gawrych, discussions with several political advisers (Polads). The Polad is a senior State Department official of general rank who acts as adviser to the commanders of SFOR and MND-N.

47. Robert Baumann, George Gawrych, and Walter Kretchik, discussions with senior and junior officers from other national contingents, September 2000, Bosnia.

48. Major Robert Timm, interview with Robert Baumann and George Gawrych, 11 January 2001, Fort Leavenworth, KS.

49. Lieutenant Colonel Marvin Makulevich, interview with Robert Baumann, George Gawrych, and Walter Kretchik, 16 September 2000; Lieutenant Colonel Sjir Hanssen, interview with George Gawrych, 17 September 2000, Banja Luka, Bosnia; Lieutenant Colonel Michael Griffiths, interview with Robert Baumann, George Gawrych, and Walter Kretchik, Mrkonjic Grad, Bosnia. Makulevich and Griffiths commanded the Canadian and British battle groups respectively. For written treatment of social patrolling, see A. P. Watson, "Social Patrolling: A Discussion of Humint Gathering at the Company Level," *Bulletin* 7 (March 2001), 5-9.

50. Fontenot interview.

51. Langewiesche, "Peace is Hell," 73. His observations have been confirmed in a number of interviews by the authors of this study.

52. Captain Jet Hayes, interview with George Gawrych, Doboj, Bosnia, 5 April 2000.

53. Major Ian Hope, interview with Robert Baumann, 18 August 1999, Fort Leavenworth, KS. The Canadians took a similar approach elsewhere, Captain Deren Coombs, phone conversation with George Gawrych, 3 October 2000.

54. General Sir Rupert Smith, Kermit Roosevelt Lecture, 24 September 2001, US Army Command and General Staff College, Fort Leavenworth, KS; student and faculty comments to George Gawrych, 24-27 September 2001, Fort Leavenworth, KS.

55. Captain Michael Magne, interview with Robert Baumann, George Gawrych, and Walter Kretchik, 20 September 2000, Gacko, Bosnia.

56. Danish officers, interviews with George Gawrych, Doboj, Bosnia, 5 April 2000.

57. Fontenot interview.

58. Brigadier General Stanley F. Cherrie, US Army, Retired, interview with Robert Baumann and George Gawrych, 26 October 2000, Fort Leavenworth, KS.

59. Interview with a dozen officers at the US Army and Command and General Staff College who served in Bosnia, Fort Leavenworth, KS, 1998-2001.

Chapter 6

Use of Force: The Brcko and Drvar Riots

George W. Gawrych

They [the Serb rioters] were deliberately trying to provoke us by calling us names (in English), making obscene gestures to my women soldiers, using racial name calling to provoke any kind of response out of the soldiers. The soldiers showed a tremendous amount of restraint—nobody made any faces, said anything back to the crowd, or even moved when apples, bell peppers or small rocks were lobbed. . . . Sergeant First Class Garcia got hit in the groin. . . . We saw 3 Molotov Cocktails being prepared. We were concerned about the crowd throwing them. Because it was considered deadly force against us, "should we shoot them?" was the big question in our minds.

Second Lieutenant Anna Maria Ford, platoon leader
2nd Platoon, 1st MP Company
US Army, Brcko[1]

I drew, cocked my pistol and took aim towards the lead person in the crowd. They [the Croatian rioters] advanced to within six to seven meters of me. I then fired a warning shot into the soft ground at the leader's feet as I was not sure where the bullet would land if I fired it in the air. They stopped prior to the point of impact, drew slightly back, screamed and taunted me and then promptly sacked and set fire to the ITI warehouse next to the school.

Major Howard Coombs, company commander
Charles Company, 1st Battalion
Royal Canadian Regiment Battle Group, Drvar[2]

A riot presents a serious challenge to Western armies. Use of deadly force against civilians must occur as a last resort, in self-defense. Training for conventional warfare, however, fails to prepare officers and soldiers to employ restraint when confronted with verbal and physical abuse. Both the US and Canadian armies underwent special training for including the rules of engagement (ROE), but neither was prepared for a major riot. On the other side of the ledger, those opposed to the NATO mandate resorted to civil protest in an attempt to stop or arrest reforms. The adversary thus developed the riot into an organized display of "reasonably" controlled violence. Bosnian police were expected to handle minor disturbances, but local police were not readily inclined to confront fellow citizens. In the five years of US and Canadian peacekeeping involvement in Bosnia, two major riots each caught peacekeepers ill prepared for the challenge. This chapter examines these two incidents: Brcko and Drvar.

The Brcko Riot: Background

Competition between two rival political leaders in Republika Srpska formed the background to the Brcko riot of 28 August 1997. In July 1996, Carl Bildt, the High Representative, brokered a deal to have Radovan Karadzic, an indicted war criminal, step down as president of the Republika Srpska. Biljana Plavsic, Karadzic's protégé and vice president since 1992, became the acting president until the national elections held in September 1996. She won the election for the office of president in the Republika Srpska with 59 percent of the vote. Karadzic, however, continued to hold the reins of power from Pale and tried to relegate Plavsic to obscurity in Banja Luka. Refusing to be a puppet, Plavsic fought back, criticizing the Pale leadership as corrupt. More important, she agreed to cooperate with NATO in implementing the Dayton Accords.

A fierce competition between the Plavsic and Karadzic camps flared with the approach of municipal elections scheduled for 13 and 14 September 1997. At the end of June 1997, Plavsic returned from meetings in London only to be arrested in Belgrade. Slobodan Milosevic then had her shipped to the Bosnian border, where Serb hard-liners intended to whisk her off to Pale. Fortunately for her and the international community, SFOR foiled the kidnapping attempt at the border crossing. Escaping Pale's clutches, Plavsic now stepped up her attack on Karadzic and his cronies. In July, she dissolved parliament and moved slowly to wrest control of the entity's police force away from Karadzic's control. NATO was determined to help Plavsic in her endeavor.

On 10 July 1997, General Wesley Clark assumed his double-hatted position of the Supreme Allied Commander, Europe, and the Commander in Chief, US European Command. In late July, General Eric Shinseki became the commanding general of SFOR. With the encouragement of NATO Secretary General Javier Solana, Clark set out to provide active support to assist the civilian authorities in implementing the Dayton

Accords. Determined to support Plavsic in her struggle with Karadzic and Krajisnki, he ordered Shinseki to aggressively pursue the restructuring of the police forces and to gain control of the Interior Ministry's Special Police (MUP).[3] Encouraged by this new SFOR determination, Plavsic moved on her own initiative to seize control of the police station in the town of Banja Luka on 17 August and appoint her supporter as the new chief of police. She also agreed to the restructuring of the Republika Srpska's entire police force and even called for the removal of the interior minister, Dragan Kijac, a strong supporter of Karadzic.[4] These moves portended ill for Karadzic in Pale.

In late August, Shinseki ordered Major General David Grange, the commander of Multinational Division North (MND-N), to help police loyal to Plavsic gain control of the police station in Brcko.[5] Moreover, Grange would assist the International Police Task Force (IPTF) officers in their effort to inspect the Interior Ministry building in Bijeljina. Serb hard-liners got wind of the operation several days in advance and prepared an appropriate response. Later, in early September after the Brcko riot, Milosevic would embarrass Clark in a meeting held in Belgrade. The Serb president produced a copy of Clark's letter to Shinseki ordering SFOR to "split the Serbs."[6]

Lieutenant Colonel James Greer, commander of the 1st Battalion, 77th Armor Regiment, received the mission for the two towns of Brcko and Bijeljina. Scheduled to conduct his operation on the morning of 28 August, Greer designated Bijeljina as his main effort. Before the war, Bijeljina had 37,200 inhabitants, the majority of whom were Bosniacs. Ethnic cleansing had created a city of Serbs, with only a handful of Muslims left. The region was hard-core Serb. The city hosted the Interior Ministry of the Republika Srpska. Dragan Kijac, the interior minister, was the most powerful member of the cabinet and a strong supporter of Karadzic.[7]

Anticipating possible opposition, Greer personally deployed with an M1 tank company, two mechanized infantry companies, and an engineer company to Bijeljina. His force ringed the outskirts of the city with checkpoints to prevent the entry of any busloads of demonstrators. Greer took a small force with him as a possible escort for the IPTF monitors who would inspect the interior ministry building. He also dispatched a tank company of M1s and an engineer unit to Janja, home to the RS's special police brigade under the command of Goran Saric. This brigade belonged to the MUP. As part of its arsenal, the MUP possessed rocket-launched grenades, antitank guns, tanks, and antiaircraft guns. In sending a force to Janja, Greer prevented the special police from coming to

Bijeljina. From Brcko, Greer dispatched a mechanized infantry company, reinforced by a mechanized infantry platoon and an MP platoon.[8] Finally, a task force seized the radio tower west of Ugljevik to prevent the hard-liners from using the airwaves for mobilizing people.[9]

To its debit, the US Army had decided against becoming involved in civil disturbances. American troops lacked shields and batons as standard gear in Bosnia and instead decided that responsibility for civil disturbances lay with the police. Bosnian police forces, however, were, for the most part, disinclined to engage angry crowds out of sympathy or fear. In fact, on 28 August 1997, local police forces were the target of inspections, and therefore many officers welcomed crowds demonstrating on their behalf. The US Army had thus willed away the problem, leaving Greer with a force ill equipped and ill trained for confronting well-organized and well-coordinated civil disturbances.[10]

Serb hard-liners had prepared for civil disturbances to oppose the moves in Bijeljina and Brcko. In Bijeljina, a number of Serbs had camped out around the interior ministry building. There, the town's air raid sirens went off at 0430. Within a half-hour or so, a crowd began forming in anticipation of the IPTF inspection. At 0800, Greer dispatched a company of infantry in Bradleys to secure the interior ministry building for the IPTF. The crowd turned back the Americans. At this point, Greer decided to accompany the IPTF officers. As the group walked toward the structure, 500 or so demonstrators moved forward to engage the party. They had set up barricades, using trucks to prevent vehicles from traveling on the road. When confronted by the large crowd, Greer decided to abort the operation and withdrew from the scene. He later returned to the area and tried to negotiate his way through, but he failed to achieve a breakthrough. By noon, it was clear that the IPTF would have to try an inspection another day.[11]

At this point, Greer decided to drive to Brcko to assess personally the riot, already in progress. Arriving at the city after over an hour of driving, Greer suddenly found his road blocked by angry demonstrators. Rather than negotiate through the maze of streets to link up with his units, he returned to Camp McGovern to monitor events in Brcko. Grange was already there.[12] To gain some direct observations of tactical situation on the ground, Granger and Greer flew over the riot areas in helicopters.

Meanwhile, Brcko had turned into MND-N's biggest headache, so much so that the entire day's events have become known in history as the Brcko Riot. The city of Brcko was located in the Posavina Corridor, an area of strategic importance linking western and eastern Republika Srpska. So contentious was the city and corridor to all three factions that

152

the negotiators at Dayton avoided reaching any final decision on Brcko and instead left it for arbitration with a decision due in a year's time. Before the war, the population of the Brcko *opcina* (county) stood at 87,627, including 38,617 Muslims; 22,252 Croats; 18,128 Serbs; and 5,731 Yugoslavs. The city itself numbered 41,406 inhabitants. Among these were 2,894 Croats; 22,994 Muslims; 8,253 Serbs; and 5,211 Yugoslavs. In the war, the Serbs had cleansed the town of its Bosniac and Croat populations.

Captain Kevin D. Hendricks was responsible for the Posavina Corridor and the town of Brcko. His mission for 28 August was vague. He was to ensure that policemen loyal to Plavsic secured control of the police station during the midnight shift by deploying a blocking force around the building. Oddly enough, Hendricks' superiors failed to provide him with the identity of the loyal police officer in charge of the operation.[13] The company, for its part, experienced some confusion about the mission. Many thought there was a hostage situation. As noted by one sergeant, "the circumstances surrounding much of the mission were vague and we were told on a need to know basis."[14]

For the operation, Hendricks commanded Delta Company of the 2nd Battalion, 2nd Infantry Regiment, reinforced by two military police platoons, a mechanized infantry platoon from the 1st Battalion, 18th Infantry Regiment, and a fourth platoon commanded by Lieutenant Greg Sharpe from Camp Colt as the quick-reaction force. The first platoon of Alpha Company from the 1st Battalion under Lieutenant Schumacher guarded the Brcko Bridge connecting Croatia with Bosnia over the Sava River. Hendricks always had to keep a platoon on the bridge. A squad of military police each established a checkpoint on the western and eastern entrances into Brcko. Three Bradleys with four military policemen each guarded the three bridges in the western part of the city. Lieutenant Anna Ford, with a squad of military police, established a blocking position on an intersection just west of the police station. A squad of infantry from Delta Company did the same for an intersection just east of the police station. The second platoon under Lieutenant Bill White kept watch over the regional police station, a weapons storage site, and the special police post. Hendricks took a platoon and two squads from another platoon to secure the Brcko police station.[15]

The Brcko Riot: 28 August 1997

By 0330 on 28 August, all the American units deployed to their assigned positions in Brcko. Hendricks then entered the police station, where he met with the Serb officer in charge. Unsure this individual's loyalty, the young company commander carried on a casual discussion, hoping to obtain some hint of the police officer's identity. After 15 minutes or so, Hendricks, unable to establish communications with higher headquarters, decided to depart and visit the regional police station. There, he found the chief of the local special police, local IPTF head, and an unknown US Army officer. After killing more time in conversation, Hendricks decided to return to the city station.[16]

Then at 0420, the city's sirens went off. Suddenly, hundreds of demonstrators emerged from surrounding buildings, swelling the crowd to what seemed like 1,000. Many appeared quite drunk. The American force numbered approximately 80 soldiers. The crowd quickly closed in on the Americans, separating squads from each other. With such disadvantageous odds, Hendricks quickly decided on an orderly withdrawal of all units to the Brcko Bridge. It took his troops some 20 minutes to move across the street and regroup facing the police station.

To help Ford with her military police detachment at the intersection west of the police station, Hendricks had already dispatched a first sergeant with a squad. There the Americans were outnumbered 20 to 200. The Serbs were pelting the Americans with all sorts of objects, including bricks as noted in the quote at the beginning of this chapter. Unfortunately, Ford had turned off the motors of her five Humvees, and one developed vapor lock. Starting it required opening the hood and pouring water on the starter. As she opened the hood and began pouring water on the starter, an object hit the back of her head. When the Humvee started, the driver backed it out hastily and hit the vehicle behind, locking bumpers. After disengaging the two vehicles, Ford ordered a retreat in the five Humvees. She managed to extricate her force to the Brcko Bridge.[17]

The squad guarding the intersection east of the police station faced overwhelming odds as well. Eight or nine soldiers in two Humvees faced about 100 rioters. Two soldiers were hurt. One American was cut on the head by a 2-by-4 with a nail in it. A second soldier suffered a concussion, as well as nose and eye damage. Fortunately, the entire squad managed to drive off to safety, join White's platoon, and then head straight for a hospital with the injured.[18]

With all his forces together or accounted for, Hendricks commanded an orderly retreat. Soldiers had to keep their line firmly tight. The rioters closed in on the Americans and began pushing, shoving, and hitting the soldiers. Hendricks ordered his men to "butt stroke liberally" but also encouraged them to be cautious about shooting anyone. He felt the Serbs were looking for a martyr. Buoyed by their commander's order, the

Photo 15. Bosnian Serb rioters challenged US military postion in Brcko

American soldiers fought back with fists and weapons. As his men pulled back, Hendricks could see numbers of Serbs lying on the ground injured by Americans fighting in self-defense. Fortunately for the Americans, many Serbs were quite drunk and thus possessed "beer muscles." The platoon had not been in mortal danger, but no one knew that for certain and the situation could have easily deteriorated. Fortunately, Hendricks was able to get his men back to the Brcko Bridge in one piece.[19]

By dawn, the crowd of over 1,000 began fanning out to confront other SFOR units in the city. Unlike in Bijeljina, the day would see much violence in Brcko. This was due in large measure to MND-N's refusal to abandon the Brcko Bridge. Hendricks had to make his stand there and not withdraw from harm's way as Greer could in Bijeljina. Several days after the riot, however, Grange would gain approval to remove the checkpoint on the Brcko Bridge, a move that the Serb hard-liners hailed as a victory. Militarily, the decision made sense; politically, it appeared as a setback for NATO.[20]

Having lost control of parts of the town, SFOR now scrambled to evacuate all international personnel in the city. White had to return to the city several times to remove joint commission observers, some 40 IPTF officers, and the mysterious Army officer at the regional police headquarters. The Americans were able to use a helicopter provided by Grange, the MND-N commander, to direct a relief force through various streets to avoid crowds so that they could reach the IPTF office and rescue approximately 20 civilians there. The American soldiers engaged

155

in shoving matches and even fought with demonstrators.[21] Grange used his own helicopter to crash the antenna of the local Serb radio station that was inciting people to violence.[22]

At the Brcko Bridge, Hendricks took command of his forces for the remainder of the day. He employed ROE in a graduated response, and the rioters never got inside the defense perimeter in front of the bridge. After ordering his men to chamber their rounds, he had them take ammunition out behind the line when a lull occurred. Loading and unloading the weapons gave soldiers a sense that they were responding to heightened tensions when they occurred and not just fixed in one position. Troops rotated through Croatia on the other side of the bridge to gain some rest during the standoff. Several times soldiers fired warning shots from their Bradleys. For their part, the rioters, whenever possible, threw back the American tear gas canisters. One Molotov cocktail caused a fire on an M113 vehicle.[23]

Around 0600, a very tense situation occurred when the crowd commandeered a fuel truck from a Muslim driver and a Serb drove it right up to the bridge. The rioters had earlier blown up a truck. Observing the approach of the fuel truck, Hendricks immediately grabbed his interpreter and a Serb policeman and marched to the truck. He put his pistol to the mouth of the driver and ordered him to drive the vehicle away or face certain death. The Serb quickly complied, much to the relief of the Americans.[24]

Hendricks spent the entire day at the Brcko Bridge, isolated from other troops. Sharpe had arrived with his quick-reaction force, but the mob had already interjected itself between him and the bridge. Separated by 200 to 300 meters, Hendricks ordered Sharpe to pull back and establish a checkpoint and prevent traffic from reaching the bridge. During some 17 hours of tension and confrontation, the crowd went through typical phases of confrontation followed by partying. Women came, went, and returned, serving food and liquor to help empower the crowd for more displays of violence. At times, Sharpe thought that he was witnessing a social event.[25]

Riots in Bosnia tended to fit a pattern with set tactics and strategy. There was a leader who orchestrated the organized event. Meanwhile, instigators relied on cell phones to coordinate action, for example to reposition the crowd. A camera crew stood on hand, looking to film an incident, preferably one offering a martyr for the cause. To augment local riots, buses brought outsiders to swell the ranks. Women and children, armed with rocks, bricks, and other projectiles, positioned themselves in front, while men and crowd instigators stood behind them. Speakers played patriotic music very loudly to stir the crowd into action and then toned down the decibel level when it was time to relax. Rioters understood NATO's ROE and therefore knew how to push the right buttons and then withdraw.[26] The Bosnians had developed the organized riots into somewhat of a science.

In response to the troubles in Brcko and Bijeljina, Grange gave Greer use of a cavalry squadron and a company of tankers riding in Humvees. Grange remained in support but let Greer handle the situation.[27] By 2000 that evening, a calm descended on Brcko. Krajisnik came to the city to congratulate the rioters on their noble effort and urged them to return to their homes.[28] Order came to Brcko the next day.

Throughout the ordeal, American officers and soldiers had maintained their composure and showed amazing restraint. Five soldiers received Purple Hearts for wounds received. No American soldier wounded a demonstrator with a firearm. While standing their ground, they understood that firing into the crowd would have potentially created a strategic incident. Hendricks had been indoctrinated and had trained his troops to avoid creating martyrs. Some fellow officers later criticized him for not firing into the crowd in self-defense, which according to the ROE would have been perfectly justifiable in his situation. According to Hendricks, this was not so easy. Often it was unclear who threw an object. Moreover, firing into a crowd at close range might have incited the rioters even more, an escalation that could have proved more dangerous to his soldiers. The Serbs had film crews on hand just to record such an occurrence.[29]

Looking back, Hendricks felt that he had helped prepare his company for the riot. On his own initiative, he had his company conduct mock drills of soldiers engaging angry rioters. Soldiers rotated between both roles. He also implemented boxing, wrestling, and shoving matches designed to prepare his soldiers for direct physical contact. Such training proved sagacious.[30]

But it was not easy to show restraint when facing bodily harm from a group of rioters. One staff sergeant noted the emotions running through him. His checkpoint in Celopek clashed with 120 demonstrators en route to help the Serb rioters in the north.

In Desert Storm, your enemy was far away and you never really 'felt' the combat. Here, it was definitely in your face. I was a little scared, mostly worried about my soldiers' safety, but I was also pissed and wanted to kill them. Once they advanced, I butt stroked one of the guys who instigated the crowd action. Once he saw blood, he took off. I remember SGT Bellis getting water and juice poured on him and others throwing punches. Almost immediately, we locked and loaded and the crowd backed off. At one point, I could feel a car bumper pressing against my knees and the crowd pushing it, but I wasn't moving. Just kept thinking I wanted to win, to show force and show that we were in control.[31]

Soldiers had to dismiss "natural" impulses and react in a professional manner despite the physical and verbal abuses.

The Brcko Riot taught the US Army that it had to be prepared to engage civil disturbances. After the incidents in Bijeljina and Brcko, for example, Grange ordered batons and shields from the US to distribute to his troops in MND-N in the event of similar disturbances. Task Force *Eagle* also implemented a new training program with emphasis on the use of nonlethal weapons such as foam batons, pellets, foam grenades, and dye markers. Soldiers gained confidence in dealing with future civil disturbances.[32] The US Army was now at least better equipped to confront a riot.

The Drvar Riot: Background

With the transfer of command from IFOR on 20 December 1996, SFOR faced increased pressure for helping implement civil aspects of the GFAP. One major issue was repatriation. GFAP awarded the right of return to their homes to "all refugees and displaced persons." Restoring Bosnia's prewar demographic diversity, it was thought, would help defeat the attempt by the extremists to create ethnically pure areas.

NATO received the task of creating a secure environment for returning refugees. This proved a formidable undertaking. Most abandoned or destroyed homes were in areas occupied by the ethnic group that had forced the exodus in the first place, and members of the other ethnic group already lived in the area. It was highly questionable how successful NATO could be in turning back the clock to prewar ethnic and religious population distributions. The year 1998 was proclaimed to be the year of the return of refugees, and Drvar turned into the international community's showcase.

The city and region of Drvar in western Herzegovina fell under MND-SW. Drvar was the most heavily Serb-populated area of prewar Bosnia. Serbs constituted 97 percent of the population of 17,000.[33] The town of Drvar had 9,000 inhabitants, with the remainder living in the numerous villages in the surrounding Drvar-Glamoc valley. Drvar had escaped the ravages of ethnic atrocities until the very end of the civil war. In August 1995, the Bosnian Croat Home Defense (HVO) seized the town in conjunction with OPERATION Storm conducted by Croatia. Expecting ethnic cleansing, Drvar's prewar Serb population, with the exception of approximately 120 individuals, fled the city and the region. Some 6,000 displaced Croats occupied the vacated homes and apartments in the town, along with 250 Bosnian Croatian Army troops and their families. Drvar was thus transformed into a Croat town and region virtually overnight.

The hard-line HDZ gained control of the local political system and economy and ran the area much like a mafia organization. Drago Tokmakcija, the deputy mayor and president of the local HDZ, held real political and economic power, much like a Mafioso. He had strong ties to the military and controlled the police. FINVEST, a commercial firm based in Croatia, began investing heavily in lumber, panel boards, and construction, offering livelihood to 500 workers. The company restricted hiring to Croats, refusing to hire any returning Serbs.[34] Only outside intervention could reverse the Croatization of Drvar.

The Canadians received control of this sector and assigned a rifle company to the area. The international community was determined to force the issue of repatriation. In May 1997, Serbs began returning in small numbers to the outlying region, raising fears among the Croat community. Initially, local Croats dissuaded the first returnees from remaining in the district by setting fire to their homes. But aggressive Canadian patrolling helped ensure a steady flow of Serbs into the Drvar region.

Architects of the Dayton Accords designed elections to serve as a major instrument for reversing the gains made by ethnic cleansers. Specifically, Annex 3 allowed displaced persons and refugees to vote in their prewar municipality even though they resided elsewhere. This arrangement permitted displaced Drvar Serbs to vote in the local election of 13 and 14 September 1997 and elect a Serb, Mile Marcetta, as mayor in a virtually homogeneous Croatian city. Serbs now dominated the town's executive council and began to fill positions in the civil administration. The local police force, however, remained exclusively in Croat hands.

Local Croats, all recent settlers, feared the Serbianization of the town and region. They felt that it was only a matter of time before they would be displaced. Canadian troops had to ensure the Serb mayor's safety whenever he came into town to conduct business. Marcetta lived in Banja Luka, so it was a strange arrangement. Political authority lay in the hands of Serb outsiders, while real power resided with Croat locals.

Drvar turned into a test case of the returnee problem. More Serbs were returning to Drvar than any other place in Bosnia with the exception of Sarajevo. General Clark visited Drvar and urged the Canadians to adopt a "hammer" approach whenever necessary. The Office of High Representative was determined to push hard the return of refugees and displaced persons.[35] On 23 February 1998, Lieutenant General Sir Hew Pike, deputy commander of operations at SFOR headquarters in Sarajevo, underscored that "the International Community will not tolerate anything less than a Serb led Canton, with Drvar a Serb town."[36] Nongovernment Organizations were just as determined to succeed in this endeavor. By April 1998, approximately 1,600 Serbs and 6,000 Croats lived in the town of Drvar; moreover, 450 Croatian soldiers were stationed there as well. The international community became obsessed with helping the Serbs to the culpable neglect of the Croats, fueling resentment and fears among the Croatian community.[37]

Suddenly, the Canadians found themselves engaged in what they considered a counterinsurgency but one without direct combat between the conventional force and irregular forces. Between February and the riot of 24 April 1998, an arson campaign conducted by local Croats resulted in the burning of approximately 50 Serb homes and properties. Some evenings witnessed two to three house burnings.

The Canadians could not be everywhere. Major Howard Coombs commanded Charles Company of the 1st Battalion, The Royal Canadian Regiment Battle Group, a force of 120 Canadian infantry soldiers reinforced with about 80 soldiers from other branches. Normally, Coombs was able to put 12 to 18 soldiers on patrols per shift. Each patrol required a minimum of six soldiers in an armored vehicle. This force structure allowed for four soldiers to conduct a dismounted foot patrol while two watched the vehicle. With only a reinforced company, the Canadians could deploy at best three to four patrols on a shift. Lieutenant Colonel P.J. Devlin, the Canadian battle group commander, periodically provided an additional rifle company to patrol the countryside so that Coombs could concentrate his troops on the city of Drvar. From Coombs' point of view, civilian authorities in Banja Luka understood the security risk but still kept pushing for more Serb returnees nevertheless. Coombs expressed concern several times to his superiors that the rate of returnees was moving too fast for his small force to provide at least the semblance of adequate security.[38]

Tensions escalated a notch after the announcement that the Croatian (HVO) 1st Guard Brigade troops and their families would be removed from Drvar. On 9 April 1998, Easter weekend, 150 Serbs moved into a downtown apartment complex, the former barracks for the Croatian brigade, amid a ceremony and press conference. The international media painted the event as a NATO success. Local Croats, however, tended to regard the announcement as a Croatian defeat and a Serb victory. The local Croats were determined to fight back. "Local Croat thugs began to taunt [Canadian] soldiers and to use their vehicles aggressively against foot patrols."[39]

On 16 April, unknown assailants murdered a Serb couple, Vojislav Tminic (age 62) and his wife Mileva (age 59) and set fire to their house. Shortly after 0100, a Canadian patrol happened to arrive on the scene and discovered the bodies before the fire had engulfed the structure. Soldiers pulled the couple from the house. Local police investigators arrived at about 0237 and left the bodies outside for 14 hours. When word reached Sarajevo of what had happened, the double murder suddenly became an incident of strategic import. The Office of the High Representative reacted swiftly, if perhaps irrationally. Deputy High Representative Jacques Klein, a retired US Air Force general, arrived in Drvar by helicopter. At the crime scene, he promptly dismissed the deputy mayor and demanded the removal of the chief of police and the cantonal interior minister, all Croats. To Coombs, Klein had acted like a bull in a china shop.[40] Depending on one's perspective, his knee-jerk or decisive action obviously upset the Croat community, providing radicals with the excuse they needed to mobilize a civil disturbance. In eight days, mob violence would hit the streets of Drvar.

The Drvar Riot: 24 April 1998

The riot was no doubt a planned event. An unusual number of cars bearing plates from outside the area were seen in and around town the day of the riot. That morning, local business establishments and factories let out their workers for a demonstration. Schools closed as well so that students could participate with adults. There was a clear leader. The mob avoided looting but instead concentrated on burning. Finally, a Croatian film crew appeared with the apparent intent of looking for an incident to broadcast to the world.[41]

The Canadians were even less prepared for riot control than the Americans had been in Bijeljina and Brcko. Canadian national policy prohibited the army from engaging in putting down civil disturbances. Consequently, Canada failed to provide its soldiers with training and equipment for handling crowd disturbances. For example, the Canadian company in Drvar was without any tear gas, batons, or shields with which to engage a crowd in a nonlethal manner. Coombs thus lacked the nonlethal weapons necessary for a graduated response to dealing with civil disturbance. Ottawa had left its troops vulnerable to mob passions.

The Drvar Riot occurred 24 April 1998. [42] At 1130, Coombs, who was on patrol in a Humvee with two soldiers and an interpreter, received word of a small crowd of 30 to 40 persons gathering in the center of town. He immediately dispatched an armored vehicle for observation. At 1140, 10 minutes later, a crowd now 70 strong suddenly began pelting the municipal building with rocks, breaking windows. Then the demonstrators entered the building, wreaking damage inside. Finishing in a matter of minutes, they rushed across the street and severely damaged the local offices of the High Representative, the IPTF, UN High Commissioner for Refugees, and the Organization for Security and Co-operation in Europe.

At 1200, upon learning of the civil disturbance, Coombs ordered the implementation of OPERATION Medusa, the evacuation of all international personnel to Camp Drvar. Some UN officials were already fleeing on foot or in vehicles toward the Canadian compound. Fire trucks dispatched to the scene turned back after being pelted by rocks, bricks, and stones. Canadian soldiers on the scene intervened to help the firemen escape with their vehicles.

Photo 16. An angry crowd assembled during tense moments in Drvar

Coombs proceeded to the riot scene. His immediate goals were to extract international workers back to Camp Drvar and protect the Serb population. By now the crowd had grown to 500, including women and children. As he entered the town, Coombs ordered his company sergeant major, Derek Ingersoll, to cock his weapon and be prepared to fire warning shots. Just then, a Croatian policeman approached the jeep with news that the crowd had badly beaten up the Serb mayor. Coombs quickly proceeded to the site and managed to extract the official. The Serb mayor looked dead, no life in him. Ingersoll later received a British award for his heroism related to this incident. Coombs hurried to Camp Drvar with the injured mayor to organize a relief force. Fortunately for him, a bus had just arrived at the camp with some 20 soldiers returning from leave. He gathered a force of 32 soldiers to return to the center of town. Meanwhile, the Serb mayor unexpectedly began to show signs of life.

At 1245, Coombs arrived back at the riot scene and surveyed the situation. Around him cars, trucks, and buildings were ablaze. Seventeen Canadian soldiers under the command of Captain Brian Bedard had just evacuated the 100 to 150 Serb returnees in the apartment complex and transported them to a nearby school. Fifty-one Canadian soldiers confronted a crowd of 300 to 500 angry men, women, and children armed

Photo 17. Angry Croat rioters in Drvar set fire to buildings and vehicles

with baseball bats, knives, rocks, and other lethal objects. Some rocks proved "as big as cantaloupes."[43] Two Canadians had been hit in the face, one by a rock and the other by a brick. Bedard had already fired a warning shot to keep the rioters at a distance.

Coombs immediately proceeded to the school, where he assumed command. Though events happened rather quickly, for Coombs everything seemed to be in slow-motion. Some soldiers had instinctively drawn and fixed bayonets, but his sergeant major ordered them removed unless authorized by the commanding officer. With his additional troops, Coombs deployed the platoon to establish a defensible perimeter. Some 20 Canadians occupied the school building, manning the windows to prevent anyone from throwing gasoline into the structure. Some rioters tried to set the school's generator on fire with gasoline but two warning shots scared them away. Another 12 to 15 Canadians formed a very porous line, with soldiers standing approximately 10 to 15 feet apart. Approximately 12 soldiers blocked the area between the school and the warehouse. This troop deployment left Coombs with no reserve.

Coombs decided that he would not allow the Croat crowd to close on his troops. There were not enough Canadian troops to form a defensive line, shoulder-to-shoulder. Especially vulnerable were the Canadians standing 10 feet apart from each other. Moreover, Coombs feared for the lives of the Serbs. The brutal beating of the Serb mayor attested to the potential danger facing the Serb men, women, and children returnees. The Canadian major therefore designated all returnees under military

Photo 18. Canadian soldier establish a perimeter druing disorder in Drvar

protection and sanctioned ROE in their defense. Coombs ensured that every soldier understood to show restraint, to use proportional force, and, if necessary, to fire in self-defense.[44]

Fortunately for the Canadians, Coombs possessed a light helicopter that overflew the riot area. The helicopter proved ineffective when it made a low pass trying to push the crowd back. But the crew did provide valuable intelligence on the crowd's movement behind the front line. Coombs learned that some rioters were armed with AK-47s.

The helicopter warned Coombs that the crowd was shifting its mass toward a 15-foot passage separating the school from the warehouse. The major quickly moved to the area with his sergeant major. As the crowd closed in on his position, Coombs realized a warning shot in the air would have no effect. The crowd noise would have drowned the discharge. And only 8 to 10 meters separated the two groups. In the background, just behind the crowd, the Canadian major could see apartment buildings on fire, and a couple of cars had just exploded behind the rioters. The area looked like a war zone with the perpetrators of the destruction closing on a small group of Canadian soldiers and Serb returnees.

So Coombs quickly pulled his 9mm pistol and cocked it to his side in such a conspicuous manner that the crowd could see his movement. Then he pointed his 9mm revolver at the leader's chest. Suddenly, instead of shooting him, Coombs decided at the last second to fire a shot just in front of the leader's feet. At this point, the rioters were only 6 to 7 meters distance from him. As soon as the bullet hit the ground centimeters in front of him, the mob leader stopped his advance. Meanwhile, Coombs returned his pistol back to pointing directly at his opponent's chest. The crowd leader took a couple of steps backward while raising his hands into the air. The crowd suddenly stopped its advance too, and then the rioters proceeded to clap their hands. Coombs had won this important confrontation with the crowd. He, his troops, and the Serbs were safe from bodily harm for the moment, at that spot

Before deploying to Bosnia, Coombs made a very important decision. If his troops had to fire into a crowd of civilians, he would have to fire the first shot. It was too much to ask young 18- or 19-year-old soldiers to take such a step without the example of their commanding officer to lead them. Conventional military wisdom, however, argues for the officer ordering soldiers to fire so that the commander is free to assess the situation. Contrary to this institutional reasoning, Coombs had decided that it was both a moral and ethical question, and he needed to lead by example. He had his sergeant major right with him, and Ingersoll was trained to assume command. So Coombs believed firing a warning shot would not compromise the integrity of his command.[45] Perhaps his weapon discharge worked so effectively precisely because it was an army commander facing off with a mob leader.

Though suffering a setback, the angry Croats were determined not to admit defeat. After a bit more verbal taunting, the crowd turned back and proceeded to burn a warehouse next to the school. Despite this destruction, the soldiers of the 1st Canadian Battle Group had won the face-off. At 1400, Delta Company and a reconnaissance unit arrived from another camp of the Canadian battle group. Within an hour, the crowd had largely dispersed, although groups of 20 to 30 roamed the streets until evening.

As the crowd began to disperse away from the school, word reached Coombs that five international officials were trapped in their office. He immediately dispatched a section of six to seven soldiers under the command of Warrant Officer George Laidlaw, who accomplished his mission. He also ensured the complete evacuation of UN personnel in the apartments opposite the school. Laidlaw later received a Canadian award for bravery.

In its press conference several days later, SFOR headquarters admitted that the riot represented "a tragic reversal of the progress made in Bosnia since the end of the war." SFOR reiterated that its mandate was not to stop the initial incidents. That responsibility fell squarely on the shoulders of the civil authorities. SFOR's task was to prevent any escalation and limit the loss of life and property. The Drvar police, however, had fallen far short of their responsibilities. They had failed to respond to the riot and might have even been accomplices to the event. The SFOR briefer confessed to some mistakes having been made by the international community. The town's police force, for example, had been left completely in the hands of Croats. SFOR addressed this problem immediately by setting a 48-hour deadline for the appointment of a Serb as deputy chief of police and for the assigning of 15 Serbs to the police force. The presence of Serb policemen would help calm some fears among the Serbs living in the Drvar region. In the press conference, the official from the Office of the High Representative noted that the percentage of returnees in Drvar had been high compared with other localities, and that this had resulted in "a lot of incidents in Drvar" before the riot itself.[46] The Canadians had been right in urging a slowdown in the rate of returnees. On 28 April, just four days after the riot, officials of Canton Ten signed an agreement in Livno for creating a multiethnic police force.[47]

The Drvar Riot forced SFOR to reevaluate its military strategy and force structure. As a general rule, Western armies are disinclined to engage in handling civil unrest and are thus not trained or equipped to handle rioters. Aware that local police might prove inadequate to handle civil disturbances, the North Atlantic Council agreed to the creation of a force gendarmerie or paramilitary forces called the Multinational Security Unit (MSU). The Italian Carbinieri and Spanish Civil Guard would play a major role in training the new organization, some 800 strong. The MSU filled the gap between the regular army and the local police, serving as the first choice for handling civil disturbances or hostage situations should local authorities prove inadequate.

The damage had been done in Drvar, however. Of the 160 or so Serbs who had moved into the apartment complex near the school, only about 20 remained in town; the others left. The Office of the High Representative decided on a cooling off period and temporarily stopped pushing returnees to Drvar. Clearly, the riot might have been avoided with better coordination between the civilian and military authorities so that one side could avoid getting up on a high horse and pushing matters beyond the other's capabilities to support. For his part, Coombs, as part of a larger battle group strategy, devoted more time and energy to meeting with local officials, trying to draw the religious leadership into helping in the reconstruction of town life. But after the riot, "everything was on thin ice."[48]

Conclusion

The Brcko and Drvar riots together demonstrated that whether an army wears soft caps or Kevlar helmets on patrols has little to do with preventing a local population from rioting. SFOR was, and still is, an occupation army to many Bosnians, and radicals found its presence a threat to their interests. There was no magical formula for effective employment of force to ensure total compliance from the local political leadership and the population. A number of war criminals remained in parallel structures of power, determined to enhance their power and derail the Dayton Accords. These individuals were able to inflame the passions of the people by appealing to fears and mistrust generated by the civil war. Hard-liners learned how to mobilize rioters on order and how to control the civil disturbance. SFOR today still resembles an occupation army that ensures a NATO protectorate over the country.

The Brcko and Drvar riots placed soldiers at risk and put company commanders in the precarious position of making difficult decisions in riot control. In each case, the field commander thought through possible scenarios and made some wise preparations. Hendricks prepared his company with exercises designed to prepare soldiers for possible fighting matches with rioters. Coombs decided he would have to lead by example if shots had to be fired into a crowd. His action certainly averted serious harm and fatalities. Both men had given some serious thought to when they would have to resort to deadly force. This, their own military institution could not, in the final analysis, determine for them.

Amazingly, in Brcko and Drvar, American and Canadian soldiers performed in exemplary fashion, eschewing the use of deadly force against civilians, even against those who seemed intent on inflicting serious bodily harm. Each company commander sought a different goal, based, in large measure, on differing circumstances. Hendricks wanted to prevent the creation of a martyr for the Serb cause, something his leaders had indoctrinated in him. For him, the Brcko Bridge served as a defensible position and one that the senior commander expected held. Coombs, on the other hand, was determined to prevent the rioting Croats from overwhelming his soldiers and thus threatening them. He also had the Serb civilians under his protection and thus lacked an easy retreat route. Only last-second thinking on his part averted the use of lethal force. Each riot, by its occurrence, set back reforms, however temporarily. Both men testify to the imperative of armies having to be prepared for civil disturbances in peace enforcement and peacekeeping operations.

Notes

1. Second Lieutenant Anna Maria Ford, notes on Brcko Riot, provided to author by Captain Kevin Hendricks, commander, Delta Company, 2nd Battalion, 2nd Infantry Regiment. Henceforth cited as *Delta Company Notes*.

2. Major Howard G. Coombs, memorandum, Account of Warning Shot of 24 August 1998, 2 May 1999. Copy of memorandum provided by Coombs to author.

3. Wesley Clark, *Waging Modern War: Bosnia, Kosovo, and the Future of Combat* (New York: Public Affairs, 2001), 80-84.

4. SFOR Joint Press Conference, 18, 19, 20 August 1997.

5. Clark, *Waging Modern War*, 86.

6. Ibid., 92-93.

7. Colonel James K. Greer, interview with Robert Baumann and George Gawrych, 23 August 2001, Fort Leavenworth, KS.

8. Greer interview.

9. Major Daniel E. Soller, interview with Robert Baumann and George Gawrych, 28 August 2001, Fort Leavenworth, KS.

10. Greer interview.

11. Greer interview; Soller interview.

12. Greer, discussion, 15 November 2001.

13. Major Kevin D. Hendricks, interview with Robert Baumann and George Gawrych, 17 September 2001, Fort Leavenworth, KS.

14. Sergeant Nicholas Garner, rifle team leader, *Delta Company Notes*.

15. Hendricks interview.

16. Ibid.

17. Master Sergeant Mark Schult and Private First Class Todd Edwards," "Soldiers Fend Off Rioters," *Talon* Vol. 3, No. 36, 5 September 1997, <www. rrmtf.org/first_division/society/bridgehead/bhs97/riot.htm>; Hendricks interview; and *Delta Company Notes*.

18. Hendricks interview; *Delta Company Notes*.

19. Hendricks interview.

20. Clark, *Waging Modern War*: 87-88; Soller interview.

21. Soller interview.

22. Greer interview, 15 November 2001; Clark, *Waging Modern War*: 87.

23. Hendricks interview; *Delta Company Notes*.

24. Hendricks interview.

25. Captain Greg Sharpe, interview with Robert Baumann and George Gawrych, 24 October 2000, Fort Leavenworth, KS.

26. Greer interview.

27. Ibid.

28. Ibid.

29. Hendricks interview.

30. Major Kevin D. Hendrick, interview with George Gawrych, 29 April 2002, Fort Leavenworth, KS.

31. *Task Force 1-41 Infantry in Bosnia-Herzegovina: Operation Joint Guard, April – October 1997* (Fort Riley, KS: 1998), 33.

32. *Task Force 1-41 Infantry in Bosnia-Herzegovina*, 36.

33. For a published treatment of the riot, see United Nations Mission in Bosnia and Herzegovina, "Recent Violence Against Bosnian Serb Returnees in Drvar," July 1998, www.unmbih.org/news/hrrep/drvar.htm.

34. Lieutenant Colonel P. J. Devlin, commander of the Canadian Battle Group, to Colonel R. R. Romses, "SFOR Reaction to Civil Disturbance," letter dated 25 May 1998.

35. Major Howard Coombs, interview with Robert Baumann and George Gawrych, 12 October 2000, Fort Leavenworth, KS.

36. Lieutenant General Sir Hew Pike to Major Howard Coombs, 23 February 1998. Copy provided to George Gawrych by Coombs.

37. Lieutenant Colonel William Sinnott, Master Sergeant Michael Hall, and Lance Corporal Lynne Blanke, interview with, 5 October 1998, High Commissioner Residence, Sarajevo. All three Americans worked in the Civil Military Cooperation element during the Drvar Riot. This evaluation was made with the benefit of hindsight.

38. Major Howard Coombs, Canadian Army, interviews with Robert Baumann and George Gawrych, 12 and 19 October 2000, Fort Leavenworth, KS.

39. Devlin to Romses, letter.

40. Howard Coombs, interview, 12 October 2000.

41. Lieutenant Colonel William Sinnott, Master Sergeant Michael Hall, and Lance Corporal Lynne Blanke, US Marines, interview with retired US Navy Captain James Orzech, 5 October 1998, High Commissioner Residence, Sarajevo. All three Americans worked in the Civil Military Cooperation element during the Drvar Riot.

42. General material on the Drvar Riot is based on Howard Coombs, interview, 19 October 2000; Howard Coombs, discussions with George Gawrych, 15 and 16 November 2001; Sinnott, et al., interview; Devlin to Romses, "SFOR Reaction to Civil Disturbance."

43. Sinnott, et al., interview.

44. Coombs, interview, 19 October 2000.

45. Coombs, discussions, 15 and 16 November 2000.

46. SFOR, Joint Press Conference, 27 April 1998. http://www.nato.int/sfor/trans/1998/t980427a.htm.

47. United Nations Mission in Bosnia and Herzegovina, "Recent Violence Against Bosnian Serb Returnees in Drvar," July 1998, www.unmbih.org/news/hrrep/drvar.htm.

48. Coombs, interview, 19 October 2000.

Chapter 7
IFOR, SFOR, and Civil Implementation

Robert F. Baumann

After one year, the Clinton administration proclaimed the IFOR mission a success. However, rather than marking the close of international peacekeeping and peace enforcement in Bosnia, 1997 ushered in a new phase of operations referred to as the Stabilization Force or SFOR. To those who had assumed from the beginning that the one-year IFOR mandate was unrealistically brief, the renaming of the mission provided political cover for the indefinite extension of US and NATO involvement in the Balkans.

Not long after the transition from IFOR to SFOR, the focus of military effort began to shift toward the civil agenda of Dayton. This implied greater involvement in supporting such objectives as refugee returns, creating a political climate in which nonextremist political groups could flourish, and building confidence in the future of an ethnically integrated Bosnia. To some degree, SFOR could advance these aims through the conduct of normal military operations such as patrolling towns and roads, escorting refugees, and deterring resistance through displays of strength. At the same time, however, the role of less traditional military operations such as public information and PSYOP (psychological operations) campaigns, as well as civil affairs, assumed increasing importance. This also called for a more nuanced tone depending less on the implied threat of force to ensure cooperation and move on to constructive engagement of the faction leaders.[1]

Information Operations

Many participants in the Bosnian peacekeeping mission concluded by the end of their tours that the main battle to implement the terms of the General Framework Agreement for Peace (GFAP) was being waged in the information realm. Compelling evidence to this effect was the effort made by hard-line faction representatives to dominate public perceptions and inflame fears and animosities. If successful in this endeavor, they could mobilize enough of the population to resist the civil implementation of the terms of Dayton and paralyze the international will to oppose them in a scenario not vastly different from that which vitiated the moral authority of UNPROFOR. Furthermore, opponents of the normalization of Bosnian society enjoyed significant advantages in the competition to shape the public mind. First, they were veterans of the propaganda and disinformation campaigns that attended the brutal civil war in Bosnia. Consequently, the information battlefield had already been molded to their liking. Naturally, the brutality and atrocities of the war—for which they bore heavy responsibility—provided deeply felt memories and antagonisms which they could and did exploit to arouse violent passions at every opportunity. The extremists had elaborate networks of contacts and a wide variety of established official and unofficial outlets for their messages. In addition, they had already driven most competing voices from the field through intimidation or worse. This reality was not lost on the leaders of IFOR and SFOR.

Reduced to its simplest terms, the IFOR-SFOR information strategy was twofold. First, the information warriors had to overcome or neutralize the advantages of the opponents of Dayton. Second, they had to bring to bear their own technologies and professional training to maximize a critical edge in their favor—Bosnians of all ethnic groups were on the whole terribly war weary. Thus, it was incumbent on the information specialists to energize the long-suppressed hopes of the population for security, normalcy and a better life.

Broadly speaking, the information campaign embraced two linked approaches: public information and PSYOP. The Joint Information Bureau assumed the role of coordinating agency for authorized news and messages emanating from both PSYOP and public affairs. In addition, it supported public information efforts of the State Department and other organizations such as the Organization for Security and Cooperation in Europe (OSCE) and World Bank. From a US doctrinal perspective, public information embraced all dealings with the media, whether international or local, and disseminated a clear, authoritative, and factual picture of IFOR-SFOR activities as widely as possible. In turn, PSYOP, separate and distinct at least in American doctrine, entailed an active effort to promote positive perceptions of the IFOR-SFOR mission in Bosnia and to influence public behavior in ways favorable to the Dayton process. Despite the fact that PSYOP consciously aims to influence chosen audiences, it, like public affairs, must be based on factual information. It therefore is distinguished in doctrinal terms from enemy propaganda, which is free to distort the truth or "invent" it altogether.

A classic instance of propaganda and distortion, at which all three former warring factions had exhibited unrelenting skill, was the performance of Bosnian Serb General Ratko Mladic as he orchestrated

MULTI-ETHNIC CULTURE

Harmony of the differences

On the way to a United Europe

Figure 4. The SFOR information campaign remains relatively optimistic about ethnic conflict

the massacre of the inhabitants of the Srebrenica safe area. There in 1995, following the capture of the Dutch military compound at Poticari, Mladic acted the part of a beneficent and compassionate conqueror for Serbian print and television reporters. Warm and gregarious, he had his soldiers dispense bread, water, and even candy to terrified Muslim

Figure 5. The SFOR information campaign linked crucial issues such as the right to travel and the conduct of democratic elections.

refugees while offering fervent assurances that no one had any cause to be fearful.[2] Though ghastly, it was a propaganda triumph, at least in the short term, for a man who would soon be reviled as a war criminal. Though apprehensive, the international community stayed its hand and did not immediately retaliate for the fall of Srebrenica. Overall, the record suggests that Mladic possessed a far superior understanding of the behavior of the international community than it had of him.

In contrast, lacking a deep appreciation of the Balkan cultural landscape, IFOR's early attempts to mold public perceptions were tentative and slightly wide of the mark. One example of PSYOP was the early attempt to employ quotations of the former Yugoslav leader Broz Tito to invoke a spirit of unity and tolerance associated with his nearly four decades in power. In contrast to crude propaganda, the purpose was not to deceive; the statements were faithfully reported and their intent was transparent. Neither, however, did the symbolic use of Tito reflect the purpose of public information to inform.[3] Tito's views were well known to anyone who cared. Rather, the purpose was to affect the social climate in a way that would make it more conducive to the fulfillment of the Dayton agenda.

Whether or not SFOR achieved its intended effect is problematic since Tito's memory resonated favorably primarily among elements of the populace who were already positively disposed toward Dayton.

174

Some other historical figures employed in early PSYOP were a good deal more curious and, from a Balkan historical perspective, obscure. In 1997 leaflets featured pro-democracy quotations from such persons as Thomas Jefferson, John Locke, Plato, and even Immanuel Kant.[4] The messages were laudable even if in the eyes of the local populace–not steeped in the traditions of classical and enlightenment democratic political philosophy—the moral authority of the individuals quoted was at best doubtful.

Beginning under IFOR, PSYOP struggled to find its way in an unfamiliar, ambiguous and delicately nuanced environment. Indeed, early failures alerted IFOR to the need to re-examine prior assumptions. Among the first challenges facing Commander IFOR (COMIFOR) Admiral Leighton Smith, was to convince Serbs living in the suburbs of Sarajevo not to flee into the newly created Republika Srpska following the consolidation of the federation territorial control. Serb hard-liners in Pale had other ideas, however. Early in 1996, large numbers of young thugs infiltrated Sarajevo to herd their fellow Serbs out by force if necessary. To expedite the process, they issued warnings, then carried out intimidation and beatings and occasionally resorted to arson.

Serious civil disturbances attended the official transfer of jurisdiction over five Sarajevo suburbs such as Grbavica, which had remained under Bosnian Serb control at the end of the civil war. The change of authority was in full compliance with the Dayton mandate, but if legal control of designated real estate was relatively easy to establish, jurisdiction over the populace was another matter altogether. In the weeks preceding implementation of the new internal boundaries of Bosnia, radical Serb nationalists resolved to compel a withdrawal of Serb residents. One apparent aim was to prevent the restoration of a cosmopolitan civil society that characterized life in Sarajevo before the war. An even more pragmatic objective, perhaps, was to relocate displaced Serbs to strategic locales in the Republika Serbska formerly inhabited by pockets of Muslim or occasionally Croat victims of ethnic cleansing. By so doing, RS authorities had in mind to prevent minority refugee returns.

Street violence and burning buildings inflicted by Serbs upon Serbs not only seemed to take IFOR by surprise, but provoked what many observers felt was a tepid and dilatory response from peacekeepers deployed to Sarajevo. This perception constituted a major public relations defeat. Typical of the public reaction was that of a spokesperson for the United Nations High Commission for Refugees (UNHCR), who exclaimed, "We're seeing a multiethnic Bosnia being flushed down the toilet." John Pomfret, a correspondent for the *Washington Post*, reported that French and Italian soldiers on patrol in the streets of Grbavica were reluctant to get out of their vehicles. A disgusted American UN employee commented derisively, "NATO is only concerned with protecting NATO."[5] No less disconcerting was the evident disinterest on the part of local Muslim officials in attempting to stem the outflow. In fact, in the wake of departing Serb mobs, Muslim looters entered the shattered neighborhood unimpeded by federation police.[6]

To the bitter consternation of observers such as Richard Holbrooke and Robert Gelbard, then assistant secretary of state for International Narcotic and Law Enforcement, neither IFOR nor the International Police Task Force (IPTF) personnel intervened despite their ample presence in the Bosnian capital. In fact, as reported by Holbrooke, General Michael Walker refused to intercede even upon the personal urging of Michael Steiner, the Deputy High Representative. Finally, under direct pressure from Secretary of State Warren Christopher and Secretary of Defense William Perry, Admiral Smith directed IFOR to act.[7] The result was a simple case of "too little, too late." Somewhat belatedly, Italian soldiers arrested a dozen Bosnian Serb thugs on 17 March, just two days prior to the transfer of authority. The action was inconsequential in the great scheme of events. That same day flames raged across Grbavica, destroying a market, a restaurant, and even a UNHCR warehouse.[8] The subsequent exodus of Serbs from the capital region was a major blow to the Dayton policy and a barrage of criticism followed.

PSYOP took its share of the blame. For weeks it had proclaimed widely that Dayton would guarantee the rights of all citizens of Bosnia and urged Serb residents to remain. The effort was to no avail, however. Still, General Walker was a believer in PSYOP, chaired meetings of the Information Coordination Group on a daily basis, and actively shaped the IFOR information campaign.[9] Fortunately, other PSYOP campaigns of 1996 proved more effective. Notable among them was the mine awareness campaign, highlighted by the production of messages in a special edition of a Superman comic book published by DC Comics. Other publications targeting a youthful audience followed under SFOR, including *MRCKO* and *Mostovi*. These glossy periodicals appeared in both the Latin and Cyrillic alphabets, interspersing messages about nonviolence and tolerance amid discussion of popular themes.

Perhaps the grandest and most challenging endeavor was to operate through the electronic media in Bosnia. For PSYOP personnel, Bosnia represented a new and more complex environment than those of other recent deployments. According to US Army Major Steve Larsen, PSYOP methods by 1996 had been adapted to work primarily in third world countries without extensive electronic media outlets. Bosnia, for all its troubles, was well developed in terms of television and radio transmissions. This meant that the usual techniques such as the manufacture of relatively simple handbills or even basic radio messages (such as those employed in Haiti in 1994) were not likely to be effective. The essence of the problem was not merely to disseminate SFOR messages, but to get people to listen. In competition with recent Western-produced television programs—"Deep Space Nine" and so forth—that now penetrated the Bosnian market, the old stuff simply would not do. Unfortunately, due in large part to a lack of familiarity with the Bosnian media environment, the 6th PSYOP Battalion from Fort Bragg had brought along its own relatively outdated equipment. Furthermore, the television systems they did have were designed for US production and incompatible with local technology. In any case, standard VHS tapes were well below the quality standard for recording in the former Yugoslavia.[10]

Within a short time, IFOR hired a civilian professional, Karen Holman, formerly of the BBC, to handle production. Although she was accustomed to working with more proficient technicians than the Army could supply, television production rapidly showed improvement. Once armed with more or less state-of-the-art technology, IFOR PSYOP dealt with a variety of messages aimed at carefully chosen audiences. One large concern was the mine threat, particularly in light of the regular incidence of deaths among Sarajevo children. Based on its audience analysis, Radio IFOR showered local youths with mine awareness messages during the preschool hours of the early morning. To ensure that the selected audience was tuned in, it emphasized contemporary rock and rap music during that time slot in its programming. To reinforce the theme, civil affairs officers passed hand bills and other printed material at local schools. Mine awareness slogans even appeared on specially made soccer balls distributed to local kids at playgrounds.[11]

While IFOR PSYOP had a national focus, it also devoted much of its effort to the Sarajevo locality. At the same time, each MND included an embedded PSYOP company to work at the tactical level. Unfortunately, at least in the experience of MND-N, the US division had comparatively little prior experience with PSYOP and therefore knew little either of its capabilities or limits.[12] This inevitably slowed the delivery of printed PSYOP messages. Initially IFOR, and then SFOR, dealt with a relatively small number of media outlets. Of course, in the former state run media system of Yugoslavia, few stations were required since there was little latitude for dissenting opinion. Moreover, in the early days of IFOR and SFOR, most media outlets in the RS were implacably hostile. One response was the employment of the EC-130E *Commando Solo* airborne broadcast system. Capable of transmission on AM, FM, high frequency and television bands, *Commando Solo* not only offered SFOR a means to disseminate its message but also provided the capability to override the signals of strident Bosnian Serb broadcasts.[13]

In late September 1997, with the expressed approval of the High Representative and the North Atlantic Council, SFOR exercised the authority of its mandate to seize five Bosnian Serb television transmission stations. This step occurred in response to the unremitting anti-Dayton tone of hard-line broadcasters who gave their allegiance to Karadzic. Moreover, it became necessary despite the agreement of Momcilo Krajisnik, the Serbian member of the BiH Joint Presidency and chairman of the board of directors of Serb Radio and Television (SRT), that SRT would "refrain from inflammatory reporting against SFOR and International Organizations supporting the Dayton Peace Agreement."[14] Particularly disturbing to the international community were false and

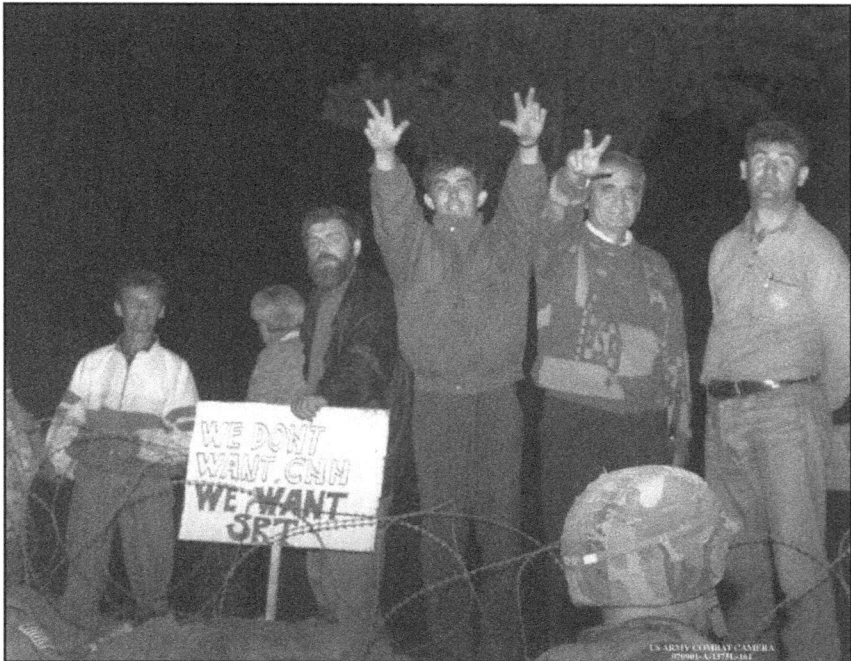

Photo 19. Bosnian Serbs protest SFOR attempts to gain control over Republike Srpske Television

provocative allegations that SFOR employed low-intensity nuclear weapons, images comparing SFOR soldiers to Nazis, and references to Bosnia's Muslim President, Alija Izetbegovic, as a "Muslim murderer." Within a year, SFOR returned four of the five stations to local control with the understanding that they provide more balanced coverage, include special programming on the peace-building process in Bosnia, and comply with periodic inspections. When in October, unidentified saboteurs succeeded, at least temporarily, in disabling transmitters in the eastern RS, SFOR was able to respond by using its *Commando Solo* aircraft to explain the interruption of service and counter hard-liner propaganda claims that SFOR itself was at fault.[15]

US Army Major John Venhaus, who managed radio and television operations in Bosnia as a PSYOP officer in 1998, found that the pool of television stations in particular swelled during his tenure as local media

Photo 20. Serb protestors gather to challenge SFOR
seizure of a television station

entrepreneurs discovered that telecasts could make money. Indeed, in the space of six months from January through June 1998, Venhaus noted that the number of television outlets grew from 34 to 41. In fact, SFOR contributed mightily to the process by paying attractive rates for broadcast time even though the terms of Dayton granted it the right to air time on demand. Again, during the first half of 1998, SFOR spent 2.5 million DM for broadcast time, primarily on television.[16]

Of course, air time was meaningless without messages. In addition to endlessly polishing SFOR's image, broadcasts focused on pivotal events. Arrests of persons indicted for war crimes (or PIFWCs–pronounced pifwiks) commanded priority attention from SFOR, at least in the public relations arena. Of foremost concern was the prevention of violence, which experience painfully proved often followed high-profile arrests by SFOR personnel. Thus, it was imperative to get facts before the public as quickly as possible. Failure to do so created a window of opportunity for extremist elements to spread claims of arbitrary detention and mistreatment.[17] To preclude such disinformation, SFOR emphasized the grounds for arrest as spelled out in indictments from the Hague as well as the humane terms of confinement and the right of the accused to a fair trial.

Given the secrecy surrounding plans to capture indicted war criminals, the information campaign to explain and justify events was necessarily reactive. A quick response demanded speedy investigation and scripting of a message. Moreover, if violence ensued, a more thorough treatment of public issues was called for. Fortunately, many events such as organized refugee returns or commemorative rallies such as the annual Women of Srebrenica assembly occurred on a relatively predictable basis. Under these circumstances, SFOR PSYOP planners could prepare the environment in advance. The proactive dissemination of key messages made it possible on many occasions to head off trouble before it could occur. In addition to the purchase of time through local media outlets, SFOR operated its own Radio Mir (*mir* being the word for peace in the local languages) out of Sarajevo, Tuzla, Brcko, and Dvornik. The latter station, situated in MND-SW, had previously been based in Banja Luka and the Mrkonicgrad. One favored television outlet in Sarajevo was a station called Studio 99 that catered to a young audience with music videos and typically did not charge to air SFOR messages. Better still, its new programming was independent and enjoyed a reasonably high degree of credibility with its viewers.[18]

Still, complications were a routine aspect of doing business. When the Women of Srebrenica scheduled their rally in 1997, two years after the infamous massacre, their planned route of march ran directly into

Serb-dominated territory across the Inter-Entity Boundary Line (IEBL) in the RS, thereby creating the likely possibility of violence. Adding to the tension, on 10July, just one day before the anniversary of the infamous massacre, SFOR soldiers carried out a raid in the volatile municipality of Prijedor to seize two indicted Serbian war criminals, killing one of them in a shootout. The Serbian Democratic Party immediately launched a media assault on SFOR.[19] Consequently, SFOR confronted a dilemma. To permit the march to proceed as its organizers hoped was bound to inflame tensions and possibly destabilize the whole environment in the eastern reaches of MND-N. However, not to allow the march would undermine the democratic principle of free assembly that the civil implementation agenda of Dayton was pledged to support. In its effort to balance civil liberties against the risk of public disorder, the SFOR PSYOP campaign consistently supported the right of assembly and expression, while adding the reminder that no one had the right to resort to violence in support of or in opposition to a given point of view. Striking this moderate stance as a matter of practical policy on the ground was a complex matter. Caught in this delicate situation, US and Russian soldiers working together in MND-N let the march go forward, but resort to simple subterfuge prevented the marchers from reaching the mass grave site, where an angry mob of Serbs had gathered to meet them. One key act in this scenario was the simulated temporary breakdown of a Russian armored vehicle so as to block the movement of buses along a key access route. Yet, the rally itself went forward at an alternative venue and, as reported by SFOR media, the principle of free expression was preserved.[20]

On one occasion in 1998, Venhaus discovered that the force protection policy at Eagle Base in Tuzla impeded a timely response. In this instance, Venhaus, along with Major Sue Lambert, was visiting Tuzla when the news of both an arrest and a mob reaction reached him. The incident occurred in MND-SW, which meant no TF *Eagle* forces were sent in response. To proceed to the scene, Venhaus and Lambert needed to muster the requisite four vehicles with additional personnel and a crew-served weapon before they were allowed to leave the American compound. Normally, either assembling the requisite armed caravan or gaining an exemption was a slow process that took 6 to 8 hours. Luckily, a group of Dutch military police who happened to be at Eagle Base agreed to form a hasty escort to the divisional border. Paradoxically, Venhaus and Lambert were able to abandon their escort when they entered MND-SW, the zone in which the episode of violence was actually occurring.[21] Ironically, in other words, the closer they got to the site of the disorder, the less force protection they required.

Photo 20. IFOR marked the first combined military operations with Russian units since World War II

Broadly speaking, Venhaus was concerned that the American approach to force protection constrained the effective execution of PSYOP. To illustrate his point, he drew a contrast with the British approach in MND-SW. There British and Canadian soldiers actively engaged the populace on a daily basis, stopping in cafes, holding casual conversations in the street, and making themselves seem both familiar and accessible figures. Among their routine tasks was the distribution of the local SFOR-produced publication called *Mostovi*, or bridges. In contrast, attempts to undertake a similar project in MND-N never got off the ground because the TF *Eagle* command concluded that the manpower requirements associated with US force protection standards would make it impractical.[22]

Only during SFOR 6, when the 10th Mountain Division under the command of Major General James Campbell assumed the role of Task Force *Eagle* in Tuzla, did force protection begin to make significant accommodation to the needs of PSYOP and other staff functions. In the first place, until then (and even afterward to a slightly lesser degree), force protection demands consumed up to 50 percent of the division's combat power at any given time. With gentle encouragement from Lieutenant General Montgomery Meigs, then commander of SFOR, the 10th began to relax the rules slightly. According to the SFOR 6 After-Action Report, "The decision was eminently sensible; it made us more accessible to the public, allowed us to increase our presence in the AOR, increased the staff's ability to go to subordinate units, and relieved our soldiers of an unnecessary personal burden."[23]

Despite episodic complications, SFOR managed to dominate the news agenda from time to time. In 1998, one of SACEUR Commander General Wesley Clark's priorities was to convince the population of Bosnia that the reduction of the SFOR strength in that republic was not to be construed as a sign of slackening resolve or military weakness. As a public demonstration of this point, NATO staged a strategic reserve deployment exercise, a multinational endeavor including a US Marine expeditionary unit and the flow of converging forces into Bosnia. The combined display of air, land, and sea power constituted a powerful deterrent to any persons inclined to underestimate international resolve in support of the SFOR mission. Of course, SFOR could not guarantee that the local media, especially hostile outlets, would transmit its message and therefore was prepared on this occasion to exercise its authority established by Dayton to compel dissemination of its message and accompanying video images. In fact, compulsion was generally unnecessary. As Venhaus put it, "The news was for sale in Bosnia." The generous allotment of SFOR funds with which to buy time on the air normally guaranteed access. Despite the obvious advantages of this situation, Venhaus found this reality a bit disquieting for its subtly anti-democratic implication that the truth was the property of the highest bidder.[24] Overall, however, SFOR realized the impossibility of achieving both stability and democracy overnight in a land that recently had experienced neither.

Under the terms of Dayton, SFOR enjoyed the right to seize hostile media outlets in Bosnia and did so as in 1997 at Udrigovo.[25] Similarly, the OHR enjoyed the prerogative to fire duly elected or appointed public officials if they were deemed an obstruction to progress in Bosnia. Though clearly at odds with classic Western democratic practices, such action did not lack practical justification. In light of Bosnia's recent past, which demonstrated how demagogic politicians could exploit their freedom of expression to inflame hatreds and ignite civil war, such curbs dampened the risks of street violence. Moreover, they were perceived to operate in the interests of the safety of international peacekeepers, aid workers, and UN personnel. Still, it was difficult to dismiss perceptions that freedoms in Bosnia were being abridged.

Meanwhile, SFOR information operations drew criticism on other grounds as well. Some observers were skeptical of the logic both of centralized control of PSYOP from Sarajevo and the utility of the artificial doctrinal barrier separating PSYOP and public affairs. According to the SFOR 6 After Action Report compiled by the 10th Mountain Division for OPERATION Joint Forge, "Throughout the SFOR 6 rotation, there was no comprehensive SFOR Info Ops concept for BiH.... As a result, it is almost impossible to 'nest' an MND Info Ops concept with SFOR's. Additionally, lack of an overall strategy has two immediate results: a tendency to over-react to short-range objectives coupled with a passive approach to most other events." To give greater clarity to its own efforts, SFOR 6 sought to coordinate its work more closely with agencies such as the OCE and UNHCR, which in any case had the lead on tasks such as elections and refugee returns. The 10th Mountain Division further made a conscientious effort to arm its soldiers on patrols with "talking points" based more on cutting-edge issues at the local level rather than on fairly broad, abstract themes promulgated from SFOR headquarters.[26] The SFOR 6 After-Action Report further maintained that products emanating from the Combined/Joint Psychological Operations Task Force (CJPOTF) in Sarajevo occasionally reflected a lack of sensitivity for local conditions out in the division areas of operations. For example, a poster disseminated by SFOR depicting two churches and a mosque representing the three major faiths in Bosnia side by side over a Bosnian flag contradicted other general guidance to avoid religion as a topic. In this case, the SFOR theme proved susceptible to manipulation. Local Serbs began printing an adapted version of the poster showing a much-enlarged mosque, thereby implying that SFOR was giving preferential treatment to the Bosniac Muslims.[27]

Of course, each of the factions in Bosnia played the information game. Although Serb nationalists took second place to none when it came to galvanizing opinion among their own population, they were clumsy in the public relations with SFOR and the international community. According to Major Paul Schmidt, the Bosniacs postured publicly in a manner bound to earn sympathy. Bosniac leaders typically echoed the SFOR party line of tolerance and understanding, even if their deeds did not always match their words. In contrast, Serb spokespersons seldom struck a conciliatory note.[28] US Army Major Rob Timm, who served as an LNO to the Russian Brigade, concurred with Schmidt that Bosniac resettlement efforts tended to focus inordinately on strategically sensitive areas such as Brcko and the Posavina Corridor. Given the sensitivity of these locations, Bosnian Serbs commonly overreacted to such initiatives and appeared to be the instigators of violence.[29]

The SFOR 6 After-Action Report also expressed concern that the doctrinal distinction between PSYOP and public affairs was not as clear in the context of peace operations and required careful delineation. The AAR concluded: "Co-mingling of PA and PSYOP assets, bearing in mind the PSYOP mission to overtly co-opt and influence various population target sets, will significantly degrade PA's ability to maintain its 'just the facts' persona.... If operational necessity required PSYOP to actually conduct missions other than truth projection, and if prior to that time PA and PSYOP were co-mingled, then the PA mission would quickly fail and be viewed by the populace as a propaganda machine."[30]

Public Affairs

From the near fiasco at the Sava River in December 1996 to the turmoil of the war in Kosovo in the spring of 1999, IFOR and SFOR were deeply concerned about international press coverage of the mission in Bosnia. According to Major Perry Rearick, who served as a public affairs officer in Sarajevo, the most effective means of getting favorable coverage was to have reporters embedded in units in the field.[31] Given the opportunity to interact freely with ordinary soldiers and junior officers in the course of doing their jobs, most journalists came to respect both the quality of the force and the nature of the mission.

Colonel Lee Hockman, who served as chief of public information for SFOR in 1998 and 1999, found that two themes dominated public affairs efforts during his tenure: the nature of the SFOR mandate and the apprehension of war criminals. The former was simple enough but required endless repetition: "SFOR is there to provide a safe and secure environment so that the international community can go about the process of civil implementation of Dayton."[32]

The latter issue came up only intermittently but was always the object of great controversy. The problem began with SFOR's ambiguous mandate regarding war criminals. Strictly speaking, SFOR's mission as spelled out in the GFAP did not specifically include the location and capture of war criminals, generally referred to as PIFWCs. In other words, they were not to operate as a police or detective agency; nor would they actively seek opportunities to apprehend war criminals. However, SFOR was authorized to seize and arrest PIFWCs when they came upon them in the normal course of business. In point of fact, most SFOR personnel wanted little or no part in the hunt for war criminals. Certainly, this feeling resonated widely at the Pentagon, where memories of manhunts were generally bad. During OPERATION Urgent Fury in Panama, US personnel had conducted a long, trying and well-publicized search for president Manuel Noriega. Worse still was the experience in Somalia when US Army Task Force *Ranger* attempted to capture the rogue clan leader Mohamed Farrah Aideed in Mogadishu. This ill-fated episode ended in a fierce firefight resulting in hundreds of Somali and 18 American dead. The final consequence in Somalia was a reversal of US policy and the withdrawal of American forces. The lesson taken to heart by most military observers was that hunts for renegade faction leaders tend to be difficult, ineffective, costly, and dangerous. Thus, the last thing the Army wanted to tackle was the roundup of large numbers of war criminals in the politically explosive environment of Bosnia.

The US joint chiefs withheld their approval of the GFAP until the language was purged of any implicit requirement to capture war criminals. When questioned about the matter later, Task Force *Eagle* Commander William Nash reflected, "The war crimes thing ... was one of those things we hoped would go away."[33] To be sure, the Americans were not the only ones to practice PIFWC avoidance. Widespread suspicion attended French involvement in Bosnia as well. Some critics related this to a general reluctance to punish the Serbs, while others attributed the passive French posture to a quiet deal to secure the release of a captured French pilot in 1995.[34]

However, the international outcry for justice that brought UN, IFOR, and SFOR peacekeepers to Bosnia in the first place generated considerable pressure to capture those responsible for mass atrocities during the civil war. During IFOR, the press repeatedly hounded the allied command over the perceived failure to move against the murderers of Bosnia's civil war. Scrutiny spiked especially following reported close encounters with Mladic. For example, following the highly public confrontation with the

Serb 65th Protection Regiment related to a planned weapons inspection at Mt. Zep in August 1996, journalists attempted to corner General John Sylvester into acknowledging that IFOR personnel had come face to face with Mladic and done nothing. As one challenged, "Here is one of the world's most wanted war criminals at your disposal ...and you drop the ball. Why?" Without conceding that Mladic had actually been present, Sylvester argued that even if Mladic had been there, a 24-man inspection team would have been in no position to seize an unwilling general from "two to three hundred armed men who have sworn to protect this guy..." In other words, stumbling upon a person indicted for war crimes did not mean that IFOR must take him whatever the cost.[35] IFOR and subsequently SFOR were not going to pursue high-profile fugitives at the risk of numerous casualties.

Louise Arbor, the prosecutor for the International Criminal Tribunal for Yugoslavia at the Hague, objected strenuously to what she regarded as SFOR's passivity with regard to the goal of arresting PIFWCs. Hockman himself noted that SFOR only nabbed one PIFWC during his half-year tenure in Sarajevo.[36] Although IFOR/SFOR were not specifically held to account for catching war criminals, the signatories of Dayton had pledged their countries to the effort. Given that the local police in Bosnia were hardly likely to take up the challenge, it was inevitable that IFOR/ SFOR would play a role. SFOR did pick up mostly mid-level criminals at a modest rate from 1997, when the British made the first arrest, but suspicions remained that it was doing as little as it could manage.[37]

Yet, in fairness to SFOR, arrests of criminals are not normally the business of armies—especially armies of democratic countries. US law, for example, contains extensive prohibitions against involvement in domestic law enforcement. The historic reason is that the framers of the constitution considered militaries to be easily subject to misuse by would-be tyrants. Hence, in American tradition, the role of the Army on the whole has been to focus on foreign threats, although it has occasionally been called upon to support the preservation of domestic order. In any case, the import of this legacy for American soldiers is that they are not trained as conventional city policemen and do not welcome the assumption of law enforcement responsibilities. Indeed, the only reason that soldiers are deemed more equipped for such tasks than diplomats or government bureaucrats, for instance, is simply that armies possess and know how to use powerful tools of coercion. However, the US and other armies are structured on the whole to engage in combat and destroy heavily armed foes with an implicit understanding that collateral damage and casualties occur. Police officers, in most countries at least, though able in the employment of light weapons, are taught to work surgically and patiently root out individual miscreants without any endangerment to the general public. US Army military police, though trained to operate up and down the spectrum of violence, are principally employed in such functions as crowd handling, providing security, manning check points, or conducting search and seizure missions. In these roles, they have proved themselves effective in peacekeeping missions in Haiti and elsewhere. They are not, however, organized for general community policing. To be sure, some countries, such as France and Spain, possess national police organizations—the Gendarmerie and Carbinieri—more adept at such functions, but they were not committed to the mission in Bosnia until the late 1990s.

In the meantime, Colonel Hockman made it his goal to hold the public relations initiative as much as possible. One means of accomplishing this aim was to get COMSFOR Lieutenant General Meigs on Bosnian television with regularity. Recognizing the importance of the information mission, Meigs was ever ready to do his part. Indeed, Meigs was willing to enter the spotlight more perhaps than any commander since Major General Rose during UNPROFOR. This, incidentally, reflected a more proactive media approach than Meigs himself had employed when serving as the commander of Task Force *Eagle*.[38] Meigs was also more willing than most of his counterparts to assume the "prudent risk" that accompanied a proactive public profile. According to Major Rearick, who served as a public affairs officer in Sarajevo, the bolder tone began when General Wesley Clark replaced General George Joulwan as Supreme Allied Commander Europe in 1997. Indeed, owing in part to his own direct knowledge of the Dayton negotiations, Clark directed SFOR to assert its prerogative to shut down several hostile and defiant Bosnian news outlets. Whereas critics among all factions viewed these actions as arbitrary and undemocratic, Clark was simply striking a blow against what he considered an asymmetric threat. At the COMSFOR level as well, approaches often came down to the personality of a given commander. Rearick observed that although General William Crouch did many interviews while COMSFOR, his successor, General Eric Shinseki did few.[39]

In any case, as the chief of public information, Hockman was pleased with Meigs' approach. The nationalist Serb media, in contrast, were far less cooperative. Indeed, according to Hockman, "The biggest challenge– getting COMSFOR on Serb television was a big challenge."[40] The most resistant outlet was Serb national television, which remained under great pressure from nationalist hard-liners not to cooperate with SFOR. In fact, Hockman was never successful in getting air time for the COMSFOR on Serb national television but did succeed in gaining access to a smaller station in the Republika Srpska.

In addition to contrary factions, events often took a hand in dominating the news agenda. Within 1 hour following an attack on several US Army special forces soldiers in 1999, during which one of them shot and killed a Serb, Belgrade media described the incident as an unprovoked murder. Hockman realized the urgent need to issue a statement to the press but had to get the facts first. That required an additional 2 1/2 hours. Once he had what he believed to be "ground truth," Hockman made it his first priority to get word directly to the Associated Press, Reuters, United Press International, and the French Press Agency. Despite this quick response, Meigs expressed frustration that SFOR's enemies had gained an early edge in the information battle. Of course, as Hockman explained, "Well sir, I have particular criteria—I have to tell the truth. They don't."[41]

Hockman thus put his finger squarely on a seemingly insoluble dilemma. How could SFOR assemble information that was both timely *and* accurate? Based on a methodological template tested under IFOR, SFOR relied on what it termed "single source reporting," according to which accounts of breaking events were to be transmitted directly from the field to the TF *Eagle* battle captain at headquarters. From there the division public affairs officer would write a news summary for approval by the Joint Information Bureau. Of course, even under the best of circumstances, this system entailed a modest delay in the release of information and depended on the accuracy of accounts from the field.[42]

As the aftermath of the Brcko Riot of 28 August 1997 revealed, sometimes the system came up just a bit short on both counts. That morning, even as events in Brcko were taking place, an SFOR major in public information had the unenviable task of dealing with a group of news-hungry reporters whose information from the scene surpassed his own. When challenged to comment on reports from various wire services that American soldiers were under assault by a throng of angry Serb civilians, the major could only reply that no confirmation had yet come from the field and that available reports remained sketchy. Spokesmen for the OHR and the IPTF participating in the press conference had little to add. Next a persistent journalist from the BBC insisted that corroboration had already been provided by another source within SFOR. Worse still, the word was out that the Americans had withdrawn under a barrage of sticks and stones.[43] This incident suggested that the major not only was behind the curve of events but appeared to have been kept in the dark by his own organization. In reality, the reasons for the major's predicament may have been both numerous and unavoidable. Perhaps it was even attributable to simple bad luck. Whatever the case, the consequences were twofold. First, the episode cast the SFOR public information command in a poor light and could only encourage eager journalists to rely on competing sources of news. Second, it ensured that the SFOR account of the Brcko incident—entailing not only the facts of *what* occurred but *why* certain decisions were made—would trail behind the impressions left by other accounts, whether accurate or not.

The point is not to suggest that SFOR's public information priority of accuracy over haste was wrong. Indeed, it was almost certainly sensible considering the greater damage that might have been done as a result of the dissemination of erroneous reports. The question remains, however, as to whether SFOR as a whole or TF *Eagle* did all that it could to facilitate the rapid flow of information. Should greater assets have been committed to the collection of information from the field? Does single source reporting operate primarily in the interest of accuracy or is its primary function that of information regulator?

The press conference also left the spokespersons for SFOR, the OHR, and the IPTF wriggling on the hook of the delicate question of neutrality. In short, had SFOR soldiers intruded themselves into the dispute between police forces loyal to Plavsic and those devoted to Karadzic? All three spokespersons insisted that the international community had not become an active player in the political struggle, but rather was acting only in support of the requirements of Dayton and the BiH constitution. When pressed, however, Duncan Bullivant, speaking on behalf of the Office of the High Representative, conceded that although Plavsic possessed no clear legal authority to remove local police officials, the intransigent attacks of Karadzic's hard-line Pale faction on the Dayton process and human rights imperatives necessitated presidential action. As Bullivant finally put it, "The rule of law is not the point of debate, it's the president doing the right thing at the right time."[44]

In the end, SFOR suffered still another political setback over public perceptions in the aftermath of the Brcko riot. The decision of TF *Eagle* commander Major General David Grange to pull the US platoon off the Brcko Bridge was widely construed as a retreat. Yet, as reported by SACEUR General Clark, who personally approved the decision, a tactically sound choice conveyed the wrong impression. Clark resolved to avoid such misleading appearances in the future.[45]

Ambiguity was the ever-present companion of the Dayton process. In the absence of effective institutions and the requirement for ad hoc arrangements at every turn, the role of personality assumed special significance. According to Lieutenant General Meigs, the ability to establish a personal working rapport with a wide variety of individuals was indispensable.[46] As a matter of necessity, COMSFOR bet heavily on his credibility not only in the information fight but occasionally within the coalition itself. The value of this currency may have proved critical in dealing with the largest crisis of 1999, the outbreak of the air war over Kosovo and the response of the Russian Airborne Brigade. As conflict over Kosovo loomed as a result of the ethnic cleansing unleashed by Belgrade's forces, the Russian commander advised SFOR in advance that he was likely to receive an order to cross the Drina and seize the airport in Pristina. This act of trust may have helped prevent a spasmodic reaction during a most delicate situation. Most important, "the Russian commander signaled it [this action] did not convey an intent of Russia to pull out of SFOR."[47]

Ultimately, most of the brigade remained in Bosnia, a fact vital to the continuing integrity of the coalition at a time when relations between NATO and Russia were terribly strained. Furthermore, developments in Kosovo were of utmost significance to Bosnia lest the wounds of civil war so recently closed should open again. Thus, the essence of the SFOR message to the populace was that the war in Kosovo had nothing to do with Bosnia.[48] SFOR would not be involved in any way but would remain on the job in Bosnia. The object of this line was not merely to calm the populace but to head off possible Serb attacks against SFOR personnel. In sum, as strange as it sounded, SFOR troops belonging to the same NATO states that were conducting war in the adjoining region of Kosovo were to be regarded as neutral, uninvolved observers in Bosnia.

Perhaps under these circumstances, the local Bosnian press, generally uninitiated in the ways of their eagerly questioning Western counterparts, served SFOR particularly well. Speaking of the local reporters, Hockman reflected, "They come to the press conference, they sit, they take what you say, they don't ask probing questions, they don't press you for information, so they're very malleable and easy to deal with."[49] Luckily, at the time most Western correspondents turned their attention away from Bosnia toward the suddenly more compelling unfolding drama to the south in the Yugoslav province of Kosovo.

Civil Affairs

During IFOR and the first year of SFOR, the role of civil affairs in the military mission remained nebulous. For the first 45 days, IFOR concentrated on assembling its focus in Bosnia and implementing the objectives of Dayton's military annex. During this time, the Office of the High Representative was not fully operational and therefore was not yet pressing civil implementation.[50] This also contributed to initial confusion. Many IFOR officers apparently presumed that the OHR would operate as a parallel headquarters for civil implementation. At the same time, lacking even a common NATO doctrine, the different national contingents had yet to arrive at a shared definition of civil affairs operations. However, with the theater calm by D+120 and military objectives largely fulfilled, the ARRC and HQ IFOR looked to press ahead with civil progress. By this time, the IPTF was running and providing the ARRC with invaluable information on local affairs.[51]

In addition to an SFOR civil-military cooperation (CIMIC) element in Sarajevo, each MND organized its own CIMIC in conformity with prevailing national norms and command relations. MND-N, a US command embracing component forces from Scandinavia and Poland (the NORDPOL Brigade), Turkey, and Russia, established a CIMIC on the Task Force *Eagle* compound in Tuzla, where American CA officers supported not only US units down to battalion level, but NORDPOL and the Russians as well. The Turkish Brigade conducted civil affairs on its own through its G5 staff section. Meanwhile, in MND-SW, the British formed a civil affairs team to coordinate within the division and keep CIMIC activities in view of the command. Finally, in MND-SE, the CIMIC effort operated through the military police elements (Gendarmes, Guardia Civil, and Condottieri) as well as logistics, medical, and communications units.[52]

Under Commander SFOR General William Crouch, IFOR and SFOR focused on implementation of the military annex of Dayton, largely in conformity with the view in Washington. In fact, when certain nongovernment organizations (NGOs) sent delegations to Heidelberg to brief the staff at HQ LANDCENT, military personnel neither availed themselves of the opportunity to learn more nor promptly reciprocated by conducting return visits.[53] Despite the sluggish start, this approach began to broaden as it became apparent that SFOR would not come to an end in 1997. The new sense of direction owed much both to a change in personalities and a clear understanding that the SFOR mission would not end until civil objectives of the GFAP were met. Thus, as summarized in a report prepared for the US Congress by the US General Accounting Office in 1998, "In mid-1997, SFOR intensified its support for the civilian aspects of the Dayton Agreement..."[54]

To be sure, the various national contingents did not entirely neglect civil affairs during the first year of the mission. In fact, some, such as the British, treated it as an important aspect of their effort virtually from the start. This was in large measure a function of their range of past experience in peacekeeping operations in Northern Ireland. There they discovered that soldiers cannot afford to apply themselves exclusively to traditional military tasks but must interact with the community in positive ways that both assist the population and cast the force in a favorable light. Of course, the lengthy record of British activity in Belfast also demonstrated that even this might not bring complete success. Still, the British retained a deep-seated faith in the validity of their approach. The British also enjoyed an additional advantage in terms of the interagency dimension of their experience. The British Department for International Development came to Bosnia prepared to allocate funds for worthwhile projects. This support included a modest allowance for each battle group to undertake simple projects such as purchasing soccer balls for local schools and so forth. The Canadians enjoyed a similar relationship with the Canadian International Development Agency. In the main, however, civil affairs projects undertaken by the British and Canadians in MND-SW did not fit into any overarching plan from SFOR. Rather, they were low level or tactical in significance. The French, in turn, took a distinctive approach of their own, beginning with a project to rebuild the telecommunications infrastructure of the RS.

In contrast, the Americans at first lacked a systematic, integrated approach to civil affairs although there had been a dedicated contingent in Bosnia. In general, CA in MND-N labored under restrictive force protection requirements that to some degree impeded the mission. First, by situating its CIMIC within its highly secure compound, MND-N made direct access by representatives of international organizations (IOs) and NGOs far more difficult than in the other division areas, which conducted CA operations from within local communities. At the end of the first year, an IFOR-directed study concluded that relations with the UNHCR, OHR, IPTF, and other organizations were "much closer" in MND-SW and MND-SE.[55] To be sure, the overall SFOR relationship with civilian organizations in Bosnia sometimes left much to be desired. A basic problem was to define and systematize the roles of liaison officers to nonmilitary organizations. Moreover, no central figure or cell monitored interaction to avoid redundancy or contradiction when civilians dealt with more than one military unit or headquarters.

Thus, when US Army Lieutenant Colonel Dana Eyre arrived in May 1997 as part of a composite CA unit out of the 351st Civil Affairs Command, he was surprised by the prevailing state of CA in Bosnia. Equally startling was the lack of any coordinated handover of the mission. Indeed, while Eyre was training prior to deployment, the link to CA personnel in theater was, in his words, "beyond weak—it was nonexistent."[56]

Questions remained about CIMIC integration into SFOR 6 in 1999. The 10th Mountain Division found, according to its AAR, "The relationship between the MND G5's and the CJ9 in Sarajevo is weak at best." Meanwhile, Major General Campbell tightened staff linkages within Task Force *Eagle* by bringing the G5 into the division operations center. Staffed by personnel from the CIMIC battalion, the G5 proved to be an outstanding source of information on the work of the international community and the progress of civil implementation of Dayton goals.[57]

Still, if the military had difficulty with integration, it was not alone. At the very least, military institutional culture recognizes a broad requirement for unity of effort and command. Therefore, it was able in most instances to establish communications links to forge more unified plans and operations. In contrast, international aid organizations tend to function in a highly decentralized fashion, and their employees and volunteers are fully accustomed to this mode of operation. Each organization has a comparatively narrow focus and works in relative isolation. Individually, unlike their military counterparts, civilian aid workers do not belong to a highly disciplined culture in which individual operatives are required to subordinate themselves completely to the will of a command hierarchy. In many cases this may be advantageous, especially when the individual initiative of just a few persons can make a difference. Sometimes, however, a spirit of self-reliance ossifies into a single-minded pursuit of narrow agendas. To some SFOR observers, the vision of many NGO operatives did not reach beyond today and tomorrow.[58] More seriously, NGOs often fail to collaborate because they are competing against one another for funding. Under IFOR no less than 300 registered NGOs were active in Bosnia.[59] Not all came prepared to work directly with military peacekeepers. For example, according to the Task Force *Eagle* After-Action Review, during election planning in 1996, timely information from the Organization for Cooperation and Security in Europe (OSCE) was not forthcoming, and its members often did not attend meetings.[60] Consequently, persuasion and informal leadership are of paramount significance in directing international aid efforts toward a common purpose. To forge a greater degree of cooperation, international organizations in Bosnia formed the International Council of Volunteer Organizations, which met monthly under the chairmanship of Mike Young of the United States. Unfortunately, in the estimate of Lieutenant Commander Hans Ligtenbarg, a Dutch officer who served on the SFOR staff as liaison to NGOs in 2001, the council itself does not function effectively.[61] Similarly, according to one Canadian assessment, "Although it was clearly not an SFOR responsibility the only effective coordination that took place was when SFOR took the lead."[62]

Civil affairs officers could occasionally assist in bringing them together, but some NGO and IO personnel preferred to keep SFOR soldiers at arm's length, tending to view the international military mission as an occupation force that had no further constructive role to play.[63] Another basic clash in operational cultures stemmed from the classified nature of military planning. On occasion, SFOR could not share plans that depended on effective linkages with NGOs or private volunteer organizations. Under such circumstances, it is understandable that some civilian humanitarian workers did not readily view themselves as operating in partnership with SFOR. This further eliminated any possibility of joint rehearsals of anticipated operations. Conversely, information provided to SFOR by civilian agencies sometimes did not receive appropriate attention from SFOR staffers because it did not come through familiar military channels.[64]

Certainly, breaking down barriers between the two groups was more difficult by virtue of the rapid turnover among the military contingents. Hence, there was little opportunity to build continuity in terms of working relationships, and SFOR personnel necessarily at times adopted a six-month perspective on the situation in Bosnia. In their perception, civilian agencies too often came to them with requests for support beyond the authorized scope of their mandate to fulfill. In contrast, by virtue of their presence in the communities, many NGO personnel possessed exceptional knowledge of the social and political dynamics of Bosnian society. Yet, senior commanders seldom expressly sought out this knowledge.[65] To be sure, civilians employed by IOs in Bosnia often lacked familiarity with military terminology, staff procedures, or chains of command, a condition that hindered communication and made it more dependent on the establishment of personal rapport. Additional confusion flowed from the fact that SFOR, IPTF, UNHCR, OSCE, and the OHR did not observe the same operational boundaries. Thus, in any given situation, it might be necessary to secure cooperation from multiple representatives of the same organization. Sadly, this problem was identified in operational assessments throughout SFOR's presence from 1996 to 2001.[66]

Of course, SFOR encompassed not a single military culture, but many. Each national military contingent possessed its own doctrine, terminology, organizational structure, and outlook based on different experience. (The shared experience of NATO armies mitigated this problem to a degree but not in every way.) Specifically, these differences were on display in terms of approaches to force protection or civil affairs. The US Army was widely perceived to be obsessive about the former and cautious about the latter. Such peculiarities, normally based on sound organizational logic reflecting both habit and national concerns, also had a bearing on interaction with NGOs in the field.

According to a study conducted by Dr. Susan Archer in March-April 2000, IO and NGO personnel expressed frustration with the multiple vehicle and armed personnel requirements for US troops moving about the theater to attend meetings or otherwise work with non-military personnel. The effect of US force-protection policy was to create both a psychological distance and real practical obstacles—such as the need to organize a small caravan to move from point to point in MND-N—to achieving the mission. Archer concluded, "[US military] Training needs more emphasis on cultural expectations and social interactions, negotiation and conflict management at a number of levels of intensity/hostility." Indeed, one civil affairs major suggested that the concentration of vehicles, weapons, and personnel at civilian meeting sites actually created an increased threat.[67] A separate study commissioned by IFOR in 1996 reached the same broad conclusion: "Procedures were regarded as excessive and hampered CIMIC operations in particular, in that it made them less accessible to the population; meetings were missed when four vehicles were not available; the ability to respond in a timely fashion to rapidly emerging situations or needs was reduced." The report further contended, in light of the extravagant self-imposed requirements, that the US Army should have provided CIMIC with the vehicles to function.[68]

Meanwhile, US units preparing to deploy continued to focus training on worst-case scenarios for potential combat in a hostile environment. According to Major Walt Piatt, who served as a battalion S3 in Bosnia with the 10th Mountain Division, the reality he actually encountered was quite different from the one he trained for. On the job in Bosnia, he found himself most concerned with supporting refugee returns and coordinating with NGO personnel. Remarkably, despite the limited training focus on such activities, Piatt felt that a cooperative relationship with many NGOs prevailed in the US sector. Moreover, the 10th made a concerted effort to understand and support the NGO agendas. They even took to heart advice to appear as nonthreatening as possible, and platoon leaders in particular gave great attention to meeting the public while on patrol. In turn, 10th units received ample help. For example, members of the IPTF came and taught classes on their role in Bosnia.[69]

Reflecting yet another source of cultural dissonance, some NGOs and IOs refused to admit armed military personnel into their offices. Of course, NGO and IO personnel were themselves multinational, and therefore culturally diverse, and many were ideologically committed to nonviolence. Fortunately, mission training for American soldiers bound for Bosnia increasingly incorporated scenarios involving working with NGO and IO operatives.

In fact, beginning in 1997 American civil affairs officers, as well as special forces (who were never subject to the force-protection standard while in the field) and intelligence personnel, appreciated their relative freedom from many of the force-protection restrictions. This exemption from the uniform requirement for body armor and helmets at all times was based on a frank recognition by the command that a less forbidding appearance was essential for soldiers whose missions relied on direct communication with the populace.[70]

Many other national SFOR contingents in Bosnia assumed that the art of communication was so important to successful peacekeeping that, unless a specific threat condition compelled them to don their battle gear, it was best to adopt a less combat-ready posture. In particular, British, Canadian, French, and German soldiers became involved in civil affairs aspects of the mission on a routine basis. In so doing, they assumed that they were in no way compromising their "force protection." Ordinary soldiers routinely contributed their labor to civil projects. In fact, a belief prevailed among these contingents that closer contact with the populace was itself invaluable to mission accomplishment and subscribed to the view expressed in an official German briefing that civil affairs was a direct contributor to force protection.[71] In the same spirit, the French maintained platoon houses of ordinary infantrymen in residential neighborhoods, where they routinely interacted with locals in all kinds of informal ways. In contrast, especially in the beginning, US conventional soldiers kept direct contact with the population to a minimum.

Photo 22. French soldiers bring gifts to a grammar school in MND SE

Under the best of circumstances, the standard six-month rotation period for most SFOR personnel complicated communication with the public simply by guaranteeing a certain level of discontinuity. Meanwhile, international aid organizations were performing their principal function in areas such as Bosnia and normally kept their personnel in place for years instead of months. Consequently, they were often better able to determine when they were accomplishing something, at least on a local level. They could measure their work in terms of funds spent, quantities of food distributed, or schools repaired. For Army civil affairs, the measurement of progress was more problematic, particularly since its role consisted extensively of coordination and building liaisons between providers of services and worthy recipients rather than direct action. To be sure, especially under IFOR, military engineers repaired a number of bridges and roads in Bosnia and conducted demining training, but these tasks were undertaken for military as much as societal reasons.

In the meantime, in some fundamental ways, Bosnian society itself proved resistant to progress. Ligtenbarg believed, for example, that much of the population was disposed toward a "welfare psychology," an expectation that others would simply help them while they stood by. In this respect, the Dutch officer cited USAID for special praise for stressing the principle of self-help. Furthermore, he said, "When they take on a project, they do it right," taking into account the larger picture and factors such as project sustainability. The absence of such "systemic thinking," he believed, was one of the problems hampering refugee returns. For example, villages that had tractors and livestock before the war presently had none. Under such circumstances, people would be unlikely to return even if the environment were relatively secure. The failure to achieve project integration was a direct reflection of the inability or unwillingness of NGOs to work together.[72]

A host of converging factors contributed to sharpen the focus on the civil affairs mission in 1997. Personalities changed at the highest levels. Madeleine Albright replaced Warren Christopher as secretary of state and General Wesley Clark took over as SACEUR. In turn, General Eric Shinseki replaced General William Crouch, who construed the mandate more narrowly, as COMSFOR. Collectively they brought a more activist philosophy to a situation in Bosnia that itself had become increasingly stable. In turn, the civil affairs component in Bosnia formed a Combined Joint Civil Military Task Force (CJCMTF) under Brigadier General William Altschuler, who was determined to define the CA mission. Yet another development was the arrival of a German contingent in Bosnia, marking the first foreign deployment of German soldiers since World War II. Driven in large measure by a need to prepare the way for the return of Bosnian refugees temporarily in Germany, German participation simply added to the impetus for support of civil implementation of the Dayton Accords.

Thus, the first key task of the CJCMTF was integrative, that is to integrate civil affairs into the larger SFOR mission and to mold the multinational CA presence into a cohesive organization. Second, there was a need to draft an overall campaign plan for CA in Bosnia. Third, the CJCMTF had to find ways to measure the progress of the mission, with particular emphasis on tasks such as housing construction and refugee returns. The new approach did not produce an overnight transformation of CA goals and methods but did gradually help SFOR focus on key aspects of the mission.

As with public affairs and PSYOP, the media played an integral part in the civil affairs mission. Particularly troublesome in this arena was the persistent and insidious activity of Serb radio and television, most notably RSTV, which steadily saturated the airwaves with anti-SFOR messages. Thus, in 1997, Deputy High Representative Jacques Klein became so infuriated with unceasing efforts to undermine Dayton that he pushed an initiative to seize the microwave repeating tower on which RSTV depended. More proactive than his boss, Karl Westendorp, Klein found a kindred spirit in General Clark, whose willingness to assume greater risks would have a powerful impact on SFOR.

Of course, as is often the case, the solution to one problem only revealed new ones. Suddenly in control of the television tower, SFOR had to forge a plan to use it. Concern was immediate that simply to deny the population their customary television entertainment would hardly endear SFOR to already skeptical Serbs. Unfortunately, RSTV had been in the habit of simply telecasting pirated programs from the West, a practice that SFOR correctly concluded it could not continue. Remarkably, the SFOR CIMIC had Donna Hinton of Universal Studios on its staff but nonetheless had failed at first to anticipate a use for her professional skills; nor had anyone given advance consideration to the problem of coordinating programming with the overall SFOR mission.[73]

Meanwhile, relations with the Serbs caught the attention of SFOR in still another way. Opinion sampling had consistently shown that the Serbs perceived SFOR to be entirely one-sided in its activities, and upon serious reflection, SFOR civil affairs officers and others concluded that they and the international community overall had inadvertently done much to justify this perspective.[74] To a great extent, this problem stemmed from the widespread tendency to reward cooperation with Dayton policies and withhold assistance in return for noncooperation. Given the persistent activities of Serb hard-liners, the consequences were inevitable. Providing services for the Serbs often struck aid workers as a diversion of resources away from where they were needed most. In practice, this meant that Bosnian Muslims, and to a lesser degree Croats, benefited from SFOR's presence, while Serbs did not. Thus, for example, Serbs could hardly fail to notice the active flow of aid to Muslim-dominated Gorazde, which in fairness had justifiably been an object of international interest.[75] In the eyes of many, especially in the NGO and IO community, such a result was perfectly reasonable. Still, the recognition dawned slowly that more had to be done to reach out to the Serbs in the hope that they, too, might be induced to accept Dayton.

Lieutenant Commander Ligtenbarg agreed that there was substance to the Serb perception that only Bosniacs received help from the international community and furthermore that it posed an impediment to acceptance of the Dayton process. He noted, for example, how after a visit to a needy Serbian school in the RS, he sought money from international organizations but found funds were scarce because donors would only provide support for multiethnic educational institutions. While acknowledging the virtue of the goal to encourage the establishment of multiethnic schools as part of building a more tolerant society, Ligtenbarg also reflected, "These kids also need a future."[76] At the very least, this experience reflected that engagement with the Serbs remained a problem even early in 2001. It further illustrated a continuing operational disconnect between SFOR and many IOs and NGOs.

Despite a gradually widening concern that the Serbs were being treated as the "odd man out" in Bosnia, the fact of Serb intransigence with regard to the civil implementation of the Dayton Accords was inescapable. In Serb-dominated areas, the international goal to construct a democratic, tolerant civil society in Bosnia depended on progress in a number of discrete areas. Most important among them were the return of victims of "ethnic cleansing" to their former domiciles, the construction of a functioning police and judiciary, the conduct of free elections, and support for free and responsible media. In addition, many viewed economic revival as an implicit precondition to broad success.

Well-planned Bosnian Serb acts of resistance to Dayton occurred with regularity and assumed many forms—from attacks on returning refugees, to the destruction of residences, to orchestrated civil disturbances calculated to cast IFOR and SFOR in a negative light. This is not to say that Serbs were responsible for all of the obstruction of the Dayton process. In many places where the Serbs constituted a minority, and especially in hot spots such as Croatian-dominated Drvar, progress was slow, painful and occasionally accompanied by anti-Serb violence.

The most consistent flashpoint in Bosnia was the return of refugees to their former residences, especially in areas whose demographics had been drastically altered by "ethnic cleansing." Those who had perpetrated ethnic cleansing were not willing to sit by idly and watch the reversal of their efforts. Moreover, the dwellings of many refugees from any given community were frequently inhabited by other refugees of the now locally dominant ethnic group, who had in turn been driven from their original homes. Thus, the return of any group of refugees to their former homes typically entailed the displacement of others who had nowhere else to go in what amounted to a grand and tragic Balkans version of "musical chairs." Predictably, inflamed passions led to trouble.

Sabotage of minority resettlement plans took several common forms. The most subtle was the concealment or destruction of local property records so as to make it impossible for potential returnees to provide legal proof of ownership of their former dwellings. As the populace of a given locale rallied to prevent returns, public demonstrations and acts of intimidation typically occurred. Thugs might visit returnees at any time to issue a "final warning." Last, the most direct method, particularly if dwellings to be occupied by returning refugees were uninhabited, was simply to destroy or mine them. Such instances occurred throughout Bosnia and were not easily subject to SFOR control.

In one such case, officers in MND-N realized that rebuilding efforts by Muslims in the ZOS were encountering determined opposition. While by day in the winter of 1997 Muslims conducted repairs, by night Serbs slipped into the same area to carry out house demolitions. Consequently, in an effort to put a stop to this, MND-N organized a night watch in the ZOS to thwart or capture the perpetrators. According to Major Mike Slocum, then a US Army aviator, two Apache helicopters would hover from diverging viewing angles at a distance of about 2 kilometers from the observed area. They would thus always be sufficiently removed not to be heard but close enough to observe the area with night vision capability. Meanwhile, a patrol on the ground stood nearby to intercede when so directed. At one stretch, US forces maintained the watch for nine consecutive nights during which time they observed no one and no demolitions occurred. On the 10th day, when US forces suspended the mission to attend to safety and maintenance concerns, demolitions resumed. What was striking about this episode was that Serb observers had discerned what the Americans were doing and knew how to avoid being caught in the act.[77]

Of course, the joint responsibility of SFOR, the IPTF, and local police was to preserve security based upon an inherently defective division of roles. Unfortunately, local police bore sole responsibility for the investigation and arrest of persons responsible for acts of violence against returnees. All too often, they were unable or unwilling to perform these tasks. SFOR units were prepared to lend support to local police in the event of large-scale public disorders but not to substitute themselves for a functioning police force. The IPTF, in turn, also played an auxiliary role that consisted chiefly of advice and support. The problem of local law enforcement transcended training, however. The influence of ethnic politics, corruption, and criminal connections was pervasive and corrosive. The European Union had assumed the task of training local police departments but through 1997 provided an insufficient number of experts to do the job.[78] In some instances the failure to execute their responsibility under the law became so blatant that the high representative took it upon himself to fire local officials. Meanwhile, efforts to forge ethnically mixed police departments, another significant indicator of progress, proceeded at a glacial pace.

Joint Commission Observers

Among the least visible but nonetheless vital missions performed in Bosnia was that of the JCO teams, which were instituted by Major General Michael Rose in 1994. Initially consisting of British special operations personnel, the team gradually became Americanized with the infusion of US Army SF personnel, occasionally supplemented by Navy Seals, into Bosnia. Living in groups of about six to eight men, JCO teams typically occupied residences in important communities for the purpose of maximizing their access to the population and especially local leaders.[79] A "strategic asset for COMSFOR, their objective was to work with key local figures and report the "ground truth" back to the CJSOTF in Sarajevo at SFOR headquarters.

The American JCO mission got rolling in 1997 in relief of the British, who had built the JCO network several years earlier. Lieutenant General Meigs was anxious to saturate the MND-N sector with teams operating as his eyes and ears in the field. Because of the high priority of the mission, senior SF leadership personally selected members of the initial six teams.[80] Major John White, who had served as a civil affairs officer in Bosnia during UNPROFOR, commanded the advanced operational base in MND-N, during which time the number of JCO teams expanded to 14. The goal was to maximize the flow of information from the streets as well as to influence the behavior of the factions.[81] At least initially, the JCO teams did not coordinate particularly well with Task Force *Eagle*. A central component of the problem was the command and control arrangement that centralized authority over all teams at the combined joint special operations task force (CJSOTF) at SFOR headquarters in Sarajevo. This meant that division or battalion commanders could not control teams operating in their own areas of operations. This was particularly true during the period when JCO teams were British and clearly were not answerable to the US chain of command. The arrival of US Army SF soldiers as JCOs muddied this picture. Resultant confusion manifested itself in two ways. Sometimes local commanders believed they had authority over JCO teams when they did not. Conversely, local commanders often did not seek assistance from the JCOs that might readily have been given.[82]

An additional element of complexity at one time was simply the luck of the assignment process that put Major Darren Bender in the Special Operations Command and Control Element in Tuzla attached to the US division. At this particular moment in the winter of 1997, the US division was the 3rd ID, with whom Bender had previously served—unhappily. Still, there was more to the question than this inauspicious circumstance, although by Bender's own admission the relationship probably improved following his departure at the end of March.[83] Like most conventional units, 3rd ID had relatively little experience working directly with Army special forces.

As during the early phase of OPERATION Uphold Democracy in Haiti, friction born of profound differences in branch cultures and training manifested itself between SF and conventional troops. Unlike Haiti, however, the difference did not surface as a command-level issue. Most conspicuous, and therefore contentious at the soldier level, was the gap in force protection styles. Whereas US conventional forces through 1998 unfailingly wore kevlar helmets and body armor anytime they left Eagle Base (and for a time even while on Eagle Base), SF normally wore garden-variety BDU camouflage. This seeming trifle often surfaced as an issue because SF soldiers resented having to don the cumbersome battle gear during visits to Eagle Base. Indeed, the situation was richly ironic. Permitted to work without body armor and helmets in the field, SF personnel had to comply with Task Force *Eagle* force protection requirements to wear those very items upon entering the ostensible security of Eagle Base.[84]

SF branch culture tended to regard all the extra gear not only as unnecessary and uncomfortable, but as a genuine impediment to accomplishing the mission. Conversely, conventional troops sometimes viewed their SF counterparts as prima donnas who felt themselves above the rules. Of course, the nature of JCO business differed sharply from the standard patrolling and security tasks that constituted the focus of division activity. Because JCO tasks required daily intermingling with the local population, SF teams regarded anything that might create artificial distance between themselves and their neighbors as undermining progress. They moved in relatively unobtrusive small groups and often dined in local restaurants.[85] To further enhance trust, they asked questions openly, making no secret either of their purpose or the use to which information would be put.[86] For this reason, JCO teams initially wore civilian clothes but subsequently switched to generic camouflage BDUs without designation of rank.[87] Some, such as Bender, believed that even this concession to force protection concerns hampered mission effectiveness.[88] In any case, such issues seemed to some conventional soldiers to be petty and reflecting a superior attitude. More than a few officers at MND-N thought of the SF soldiers as "cowboys." Still, SF to some degree reveled in its independent image—notwithstanding efforts by its chain of command to emphasize a "one Army" approach.[89]

Other sources of difficulty between the JCOs and division were more practical. For example, when Bender arrived he found that the regular reports flowing from the JCO houses were detailed but often not coherently written. Though superbly trained in field craft and independent operations, many SF NCOs were not practiced writers and it showed. As a consequence, the rich information ore they were mining was devalued in transit to the division headquarters. Later in 1997, while he was commanding a JCO house of his own in Bijeljina, Bender found himself spending 2 to 3 hours daily as editor of the team situation reports. In fact, he often had to interview team members to make certain he fully understood the nuances that they had been unable to communicate.[90]

Like many of his SF counterparts, Bender was passionate about his work. Upon learning that he would lead a JCO team following his tour in the SOCCE, Bender wanted to be sure he knew what there was to know about his environment. Thus, prior to arriving in Bijeljina, he gathered all of the JCO after-action reports from the city and studied them carefully. In addition to time to prepare, he also enjoyed the luxury that about half of his team members from 3rd Battalion, 10th SF Group had previously served on JCO teams in Bosnia. Moreover, like all US military personnel deploying to Bosnia, SF soldiers went through obligatory training for a week at Grafenwoehr, Germany. Parts of the mandatory checklist, such as observing mine explosions were nothing new but the refresher on NBC training struck Bender as prudent and useful. Within his JCO house, Bender formed four two-man teams, each with a specific focus. The first, which he headed himself, zeroed in on the local Serb Army Corps headquarters as well as the headquarters of the so-called Special Police Brigade. Meanwhile, the second team concentrated on the Ministry of Defense and regular police in the Bijeljina area. The third team liaised with local political parties and their leaders, and the fourth team with members of aid organizations from the international community.[91] Major Paul Schmidt, who successively commanded JCO teams in Zvornik and Brcko, deployed his teams in a similar pattern. In Brcko, Schmidt assigned one pair each to focus on the respective minority Croat and Muslim populations, for example, and regularly passed information to Brcko Arbitrator Robert Farrand.[92]

The range and nature of JCO tasks made it abundantly clear why their experiences differed so much from those of conventional US soldiers in

Photo 23. Members of the French Battle Group in MND SE work
to clear unexploded ordnance near an uninhabited dwelling

theater and why SF depends inordinately on individuals who are both self-reliant and self-disciplined. Bender found, for instance, that much of his time involved meetings with army and special police commanders and that these meetings consistently entailed the liberal consumption of alcoholic beverages such as rakiya or sliivowitz. To be sure, this was very much in the line of duty. Staying in communication with key local figures, winning their trust and, to the extent possible, their cooperation depended in some measure on respect for their habits—among which was occasionally indulging their proclivity to get drunk by noon. If local commanders would not speak with him, Bender could not accomplish his mission. At the same time, of course, the consumption of alcohol, even in modest quantities, was forbidden for US troops at MND-N in accord with General Order #1.[93] This duty-related exemption became one of the small perquisites of the job, as was the authorization to travel about the country more freely.[94] Conversely, troops at Eagle Base who were not actively patrolling seldom ventured outside the compound under any circumstances. Certainly, they never socialized with Bosnian faction leaders. In any case, the trust gained by the JCO approach yielded advantages early and often. On one occasion in 1997, a JCO was able to head off a civil disturbance by proving to a Bosnian Serb military commander that a rumored Muslim mobilization was not in fact occurring.[95]

As liaison to General Saric and the Serbian Special Police Brigade, Bender had an extraordinary opportunity to monitor one of the crucial organizations in the Bijeljina area. With respect to the special police, SFOR had two interests. First, it was necessary that the organization cooperate insofar as possible with the Dayton agenda for Bosnia. Second, the organization itself needed a role that would keep it out of mischief. That meant at the very least keeping individual policemen employed, thereby giving them some stake in normalcy. SFOR arranged for some police training under the auspices of the IPTF but, for the most part, prohibited the sort of tactical training to which the brigade was accustomed.[96]

Of course, the broader mission of the JCO team in Bijeljina encompassed dealings with many of the community's figures and activities. On the whole, Bijeljina had endured relatively little destruction by the war in physical terms, although most of the Muslim population had been ethnically cleansed in the early stages of fighting. What particularly struck Bender was the rich social atmosphere of the community, despite the fact that perhaps two-thirds of the populace had resettled from other areas. During the evenings Bijeljina came alive with young people filling the cafes. Bender and his team managed to fit in. He even spent Christmas with one local family that turned out to be rather representative of the Bosnian dilemma.[97] Driven from its own home in Tuzla, the family resided in the house of a Muslim family that had escaped to Tuzla. Remarkably, the families kept in touch, perhaps offering a glimmer of hope for Bosnia's future.

Overall, JCO teams not only worked well with key elements in local communities, but also fed a wealth of information to the chain of command. The JCO mission, which came to an end in May 2001, called for the very kind of cross-cultural engagement for which SF personnel specially train. This is not to say that such a mission could never be undertaken by US personnel from other branches, although in fact it was not in Bosnia. What is noteworthy in this regard, however, is that some other armies—in particular the British, French, and Canadian armies—routinely expected that their ordinary infantrymen could effectively tackle some of the engagement-related tasks that in the US Army are reserved for SF. Canadian and British infantrymen as a matter of routine engaged in "social patrolling" during which they would relax in cafes or shop, all the while rubbing elbows with the locals. In this manner, they both disseminated the views of their command to the locals and were able to take the pulse of the communities where they worked. Similarly, the

French distributed small units into towns in MND-SE. These platoon-size elements occupied residences and interacted extensively with the neighbors. Informal fraternization took the form of volleyball games or sharing meals. The result was both a calming community presence and a wealth of insight.[98] Beyond that, like American SF, they were able to establish the kind of personal rapport that could provide a valuable conduit for information in the future.

Notes

1. Major Mark Solomon, interview with Dr. Robert Baumann, 27 October 2001, Fort Leavenworth, KS.

2. For a splendid account, see David Rohde, *Endgame, The Betrayal and Fall of Srebrenica: Europe's Worst Massacre since World War* II (New York: Farrar, Strauss, and Giroux, 1997), 187-91 and William Shawcross, *Deliver Us from Evil: Peacekeepers, Warlords and a World of Endless Conflict* (New York: Simon and Schuster, 2000), 164-65.

3. Not all nations participating in IFOR-SFOR shared the US doctrinal approach. However, because the commander of IFOR and SFOR was always a US general officer, American practice generally prevailed.

4. Thomas Adams, "Psychological Operations in Bosnia," *Military Review* (December-February 1999).

5. John Pomfret, *The Washington Post*, 18 March 1996.

6. Chris Hedges, "Bosnia's Checkerboard Partitions: Instability More Likely," *The New York Times*, 20 March 1996.

7. Richard Holbrooke, *To End a War* (New York: The Modern Library, 1999), 316.

8. Chris Hedges, "NATO Forces Have to Watch As a Sarajevo District Burns," *The New York Times*, 18 March 1996.

9. Major Steven Collins, "A War of Words: The Media Clash in Bosnia-Herzegovina and the Impact of U.S. Army PSYOP," unpublished manuscript, 8 June 1998, as cited in Stephen C. Larsen, "Conducting Psychological Operations in Sophisticated Media Environments" unpublished Master of Military Arts and Science thesis, US Army Command and General Staff College, 1996, 26-27.

10. Major Steve Larsen, interview with Major Don Phillips and Dr. Robert Baumann, Fort Leavenworth, KS, 18 February 1999.

11. Ibid.

12. Ibid.

13. Thomas Adams, "Psychological Operations in Bosnia," *Military Review* (December-February 1999).

14. Office of the High Representative press release, Sarajevo, 2 September 1997; Wesley K. Clark, *Waging Modern War* (New York: Public Affairs, 2001), 100-01. According to Clark's account, the proximate cause of the move was Serb editing of an interview of a representative of the ICTY so as to make it appear complimentary toward Karadzic. Clark, as SACEUR, felt it essential for SFOR credibility to enforce the terms of the media agreement. The high representative, Carlos Westendoerp, had urged just such a step. Some, however, such as COMSFOR General Eric Shinseki, were convinced that seizure of the TV towers constituted an overreaction. Unable to dissuade Clark, Shinseki asked for a written order to conduct the mission. Clark further asserts that this action set the stage for setbacks suffered by Bosnian Serb hard-liners in the local elections that followed.

15. Information Operations: "IO in a Peace Enforcement Environment," Center for Army Lessons Learned (CALL) Newsletter No. 99-2, January 1999, 16-17, 21.

16. Major John Venhaus, interview with Dr. Robert Baumann, Fort Leavenworth, KS, 15 February 2001.

17. Colonel Lee Hockman and Major Ian Hope, as interviewed by Dr. Robert Baumann in *Armed Peacekeepers in Bosnia: The Paradoxical Mission*, a documentary film, 2003. Also Hope interview with Dr. Robert Baumann, Fort Leavenworth, KS, 25 March 1998 and Hockman interview with Dr. Robert Baumann, Fort Leavenworth, KS, 21 September 1999.

18. Steve Larsen interview.

19. *Report of the High Representative for Implementation of the Bosnia Peace Agreement to the Secretary-General of the United Nations*, 16 October 1997, 10.

20. Major Greg Cook, interview with Dr. Robert Baumann, Fort Leavenworth, KS, March 2001.

21. Venhaus interview.

22. Ibid.

23. SFOR 6 After-Action Report, Operation *Joint Force* (circa 1999), 3-16.

24. Venhaus interview.

25. SFOR transcript, joint press conference, 2 September 1997; OHR SRT News Summaries, 28 August 1997.

26. SFOR 6 After-Action Report, Operation *Joint Forge*, 3-72/74.

27. Ibid., 3-77.

28. Major Paul Schmidt, interview with Dr. Robert Baumann, Fort Leavenworth, KS, 31 March 2003.

29. Ibid. and Major Rob Timm interview with Dr. Robert Baumann, Fort Leavenworth, KS, 11 January 2001.

30. SFOR 6 After-Action Report, 3-75/76.

31. Major Perry Rearick, interview with Dr. Robert Baumann, Fort Leavenworth, KS, 25 April 2001.

32. Colonel Lee Hockman, interview with Dr. Robert Baumann, Fort Leavenworth, KS, 21 September 1999.

33. Chuck Sudetic, "The Reluctant Gendarme," *The New Yorker*, April 2000, 93.

34. Ibid., 94.

35. IFOR AFSOUTH, transcript of press briefing, 14 August 1996.

36. Hockman interview.

37. Clark, 79-81. Clark noted that at about this time NATO Secretary General Javier Solana began pressing for a more active role by SFOR in support of civil authorities. Clark explains that this decision, combined with a more assertive posture concerning special police units, constituted a "significant departure" from past NATO practice.

38. Solomon interview.

39. Rearick interview.

40. Hockman interview.

41. Ibid.

42. *Operation Joint Endeavor Bosnia-Herzegovina: Taskforce Eagle Continuing Operations*, B/H CAAT 3/4 Initial Impressions Report (Fort Leavenworth, KS: March 1997), 13.

43. Transcript, joint press conference, SFOR, 28 August 1997.

44. Ibid.

45. Wesley Clark, *Waging Modern War* (New York: Public Affairs, 2000), 87-88.

46. Lieutenant General Montgomery Meigs, interview with Dr. Robert Baumann and Dr. George Gawrych, Fort Leavenworth, KS, 1 November 2000.

47. Hockman interview.

48. Ibid.

49. Ibid.

50. IFOR Final Analysis Report, CIMIC Operations, (undated, circa January 1997), 1-5-1.

51. IFOR Final Analysis Report, 1-5-9.

52. Ibid., 1-5-12,13.

53. Memorandum for Commander, SFOR: HQ LANDCENT IFOR/SFOR After-Action Review (Draft), Chief CJ5, 28 July 1997, 19.

54. "Bosnia Peace Operation: Mission, Structure, and Transition Strategy of NATO's Stabilization Force" (Letter Report, 10/08/98, GAO/NSIAD-99-19), 6.

55. IFOR Final Analysis Report, 1-5-22, 23.

56. Lieutenant Colonel Dana Eyre, interview with Dr. Robert Baumann and Dr. George Gawrych, Fort Leavenworth, KS, 6 October 2000.

57. SFOR 6 After-Action Report, Operation *Joint Forge*, 3-62/63.

58. Solomon interview.

59. Lieutenant Colonel Dana Eyre, "Working with NGOs: What Every SOF Soldier Should Know*," Special Warfare*, spring 1998, 15.

60. Task Force *Eagle* After-Action Review, 1354. On the other hand, IFOR force protection requirements complicated the ability of military representatives to get out and attend meetings hosted by other organizations.

61. Lieutenant Commander Hans Ligtenbarg, Holland, SFOR CIMIC LNO to NGOs, HQ SFOR, interview with Dr. Robert Baumann, Camp Butmir, 16 July 2001.

62. Operation Palladium Lessons Learned, Canadian Army, 1997, Question Series 81-3.

63. Ligtenbarg interview.

64. Memorandum for Commander, SFOR: HQ LANDCENT IFOR/SFOR After-Action Review, 28 July 1997, 19-20.

65. Ligtenbarg interview.

66. Memorandum for Commander, SFOR: HQ LANDCENT IFOR/SFOR After-Action Review, 28 July 1997, 19; Eyre interview; Operation Paladium Lessons Learned, Question Series 81-4, 81-5.

67. Susan Archer, "Feedback Interviews from 49th ID at Camp Eagle Tuzla, 1-3

April, 2000," Bosnia Report, March-April, 2000, 1, 5.

68. IFOR Final Analysis Report, 3-4-17.

69. Major Walter Piatt, interview with Dr. Robert Baumann, 8 February 2001, Fort Drum, NY.

70. Major Yvette Hopkins, interview with Dr. Robert Baumann, Fort Leavenworth, KS, January 2000; also Hopkins as interviewed by Dr. Robert Baumann, Fort Leavenworth, KS, in *Armed Peacekeepers in Bosnia: The Paradoxical Mission*, a documentary film, 2003. Major Dan Larsen, interview with Dr. Robert Baumann, Fort Leavenworth, KS, 30 November 2000; Eyre interview. In fact, this observation was made by many interviewees.

71. German Civil Affairs Briefing, Camp Rajlovac, 22 September 2000.

72. Ligtenbarg interview.

73. Eyre interview.

74. Solomon interview; Ligtenbarg interview.

75. Eyre interview.

76. Ligtenbarg interview.

77. Major Mike Slocum, interview with Dr. Robert Baumann, 2 November 2001, Fort Leavenworth, KS.

78. Barbara Crossette, "UN Members Slow to Send Police," *The New York Times*, 21 March 1996; Lester Brune, *The State and Post Cold War Intervention: Bush and Clinton in Somalia, Haiti, and Bosnia 1992-1998* (Claremont, CA: Regina Books, 1998), 128.

79. Major Dan Larsen, A644 briefing, US Army Command and General Staff College, February 2002.

80. Lieutenant Colonel Roy Hawkins, interview with Dr. Robert Baumann, Fort Leavenworth, KS, 22 August 2000.

81. Major John White, interview with Dr. Robert Baumann, Fort Leavenworth, KS, 22 February 1999.

82. Hawkins interview; Major Richard Rhyne, interview with Dr. Robert Baumann, Fort Leavenworth, KS, 6 May 2004. One consideration in selecting this arrangement was the desire on the part of US Army special forces not to decentralize authority over its personnel. See Lieutenant Colonel Michael Finley, "Special Forces Integration with Multinational Division North in Bosnia-Herzegovina," unpublished AYSOF SAMS monograph 1997-98, 40-49.

83. Major Darren Bender, interview with Dr. Robert Baumann and Dr. George Gawrych, Fort Leavenworth, KS, 21 February 2001.

84. White interview, Hawkins interview.

85. For a published description, see Richard Newman, "Living with the Locals: A Very Public Mission," *US News and World Report*, 6 July 1998, 48-49.

86. Hawkins interview. Above all, the JCOs did not want to be publicly associated with military intelligence. In fact, the CJSOTF and the SOCCEs did not want JCOs to be viewed as an intelligence asset in the strict sense even by US or SFOR headquarters. They did not accept taskings through military intelligence channels but operated independently.

87. Hawkins interview. According to Hawkins, the concern with visible

manifestations of rank was that they might interfere with optimal relationships in the streets. All SF personnel, irrespective of rank, had to be able to interact effectively with the natives.

88. Bender interview.

89. This observation is based on the general tone imparted in a number of separate interviews both at MND-N and Fort Leavenworth. While it would be a mistake to make too much of such "culture classes" among convention soldiers and SF, this phenomenon was to some extent in evidence both in Somalia and Haiti as well.

90. Bender interview.

91. Ibid.

92. Schmidt interview.

93. Bender interview.

94. Hawkins interview. According to Hawkins, the preceding British teams took to the use of alcohol on duty a bit more naturally than their American counterparts. Of course, British soldiers were never subjected to US General Order Number One prohibiting alcohol consumption.

95. Newman, 49. In another instance reported to Newman by Robert Farrand, the American arbitrator in Brcko, information from JCOs proved crucial to overcoming political resistance to issuing identification cards to returning Muslim refugees.

96. Bender interview.

97. Ibid.

98. Lieutenant Tom Arsenault, "Community a Platoon House in a Theatre of Operations," *Infantry Journal* (Canada), April 2000, 6-8. Perhaps the presence of platoon houses in MND-SE helps explain why, according to Lieutenant Colonel Roy Hawkins, US JCO teams in the French sector attracted little interest from the French.

Conclusion

The Measures of Progress

Robert F. Baumann

Today's Bosnia and Herzegovina consists of three de facto mono-ethnic entities, three separate armies, three separate police forces, and a national government that exists mostly on paper and operates at the mercy of the entities.

(From "Is Dayton Failing:
Bosnia Four Years After The Peace Agreement"
by The International Crisis Group,
Balkans Report No. 80, 28 October 1999.)

At the dawn of the new millennium, following five years of international engagement in Bosnia, some observers were slowly coming around to the conclusion that the Dayton process was failing, indeed congenitally flawed. Such expressions of fundamental doubt were seldom heard previously. The reason for the striking shift stemmed from an important difference of perspective. Prior to Dayton, the focus of the international community was to bring peace to Bosnia and broker a balanced arrangement for democratic power sharing among the three warring factions within a unified state. The process of achieving initial aims was infinitely complicated. The international community understood that it could not impose a durable solution from outside but would have to seek agreement by the Bosnian faction leaders and other influential actors such as Slobodan Milosevic. Inevitably imperfect, the Dayton Accords served as a compromise that solved some issues of dispute but deferred the resolution of others on which no common position seemed possible. Unfortunately, the accords, perhaps the best deal that could have been achieved under the circumstances of the time, created a Byzantine political system of checks and balances, a virtual formula for paralysis in the hands of fiercely entrenched constituencies. Epitomizing the logical inconsistency of Dayton is the simultaneous recognition of two entities—the Federation and the Republika Srpska—but three nations, namely those of Bosnian Serbs, Croats, and Bosniacs. By 2000, one result of this apparent contradiction was the emergence of a "third entity movement" among Bosnian Croats, who constitute the minor partner in the Federation dominated by Moslem Bosniacs. Though making no less sense than creation of the Republika Srpska, the splitting off of a self-governing Croat entity within the Bosnian state would undermine Dayton and open the door to unforeseen and possibly destabilizing consequences. To be sure, despite the superficial calm throughout the country, Bosnia's foundation was shaky even by the most favorable appraisal. More to the point, few observers in 2001 believed that the uneasy peace would last more than a few months if SFOR abandoned Bosnia.[1]

Reduced to its essentials, the international agenda for progress in Bosnia from 1995 to 2000 focused on five broad tasks: establishing and maintaining general peace, engineering the return of refugees and internally displaced persons to their homes, facilitating elections, forging common governmental institutions, and assisting the reconstitution of the economic infrastructure. According to the plan, measurable and sustained progress toward those objectives would provide essential benchmarks for success and pave the way for a fully functional, independent Bosnian state. With a particular focus on the role of the military, this discussion examines the achievements of the international community to date and considers whether success, if it is properly understood in the first place, can be attained by the means chosen in Bosnia.

The military instrument of power, beginning with IFOR and continuing as SFOR, was the principal player in achieving the first task, integral to the second and third, and limited to a supporting role in the remaining two tasks. Indicative of the general course of progress, SFOR mission requirements shifted gradually over several years from conventional military tasks to support of the civil annexes of Dayton. To be sure, not all elements of SFOR's organization could effect this transition comfortably. For example, intelligence priorities were slow to adjust from normal military "targets" to support for the information and presence missions that by 2000 constituted the focal point of activity.[2]

By consensus assessment, IFOR fulfilled the objectives stated in the military annex of the Dayton Peace Accords before the close of 1996. The warring entity armed forces quickly ceased to be a dominant factor in Bosnian affairs although their activities remained subject to constant monitoring. Above all, they did not interfere with the general peace that IFOR and SFOR were charged to ensure. Some military planners and leaders wanted to construe their mandate narrowly so as to consider their mission virtually complete at this stage.[3] Among Americans serving in IFOR/SFOR, this view manifested itself as avoiding dreaded "mission creep." In the eyes of critics, it reflected "the fear of body bags."[4] Of course, approaches varied among each multinational division and indeed among the various national contingents. As noted in the preceding chapters, these differences reflected diverging national interests, perceptions of the problem in Bosnia, and distinct military cultures.

Whatever their differences, however, in terms of completion of the international mission in Bosnia, it soon was clear that fulfillment of the military annex of Dayton was but a first step in the eyes of the High Representative and the international community. Therefore, the collective effort of the OHR, assorted NGOs and IOs, and SFOR soon focused on reversing the results of ethnic cleansing and establishing an internationally recognized government by means of free and fair elections. Although these tasks lay well beyond SFOR's ability to fulfill on its own, they did constitute areas in which armed peacekeepers could make a substantive contribution. For instance, IFOR and SFOR supported the conduct of elections by providing security and logistic support.

The first statewide election in Bosnia under the auspices of the international community occurred on schedule in December 1996. IFOR and SFOR provided security in conjunction with the United Nations International Police Task Force (IPTF), as well as transportation and staff support to the OSCE, which could not manage the election solely on its own resources. For a first attempt, the election went well. There was little violence despite fears that some hard-liners might attempt to prevent voters from crossing the IEBL to cast their ballots. Fortunately, the IPTF received cooperation from local police in most instances. Predictably, however, coordination among the various agencies involved could have been smoother. Still, the experience provided lessons, such as the need to reach earlier decisions, that were applied to good effect in subsequent rounds of voting.[5] Unfortunately, the meaning of the event was problematic. Indeed, many would later argue that its very conduct had been an error.[6] The structure of the existing electoral system itself was a key piece of the problem. The political climate of Bosnia in the wake of warfare and widespread acts of genocide was hardly conducive to the spirit of accommodation essential to democracy. With the division of the electorate into mutually exclusive ethnic camps, the vote in each individual district ultimately resulted in a "winner takes all" scenario in which the defeated were left entirely out in the cold.[7]

The first municipal elections in Bosnia took place on 13-14 September 1997. Once again, calm and order prevailed. To be sure, political wrangling among the entities over procedures and participation proved troublesome but did not either delay the voting or significantly diminish the turnout. Following the event, the OHR arrived at a positive assessment: "As elections are the confirmation of the constitutional system envisaged in the Peace Agreement, future elections in Bosnia and Herzegovina will be of paramount importance for the implementation of the Peace Agreement."[8]

Meanwhile, at the highest level, the system of entities and nations brokered at Dayton, though intended to balance the influence of the three sides, actually confirmed the isolation of the Serbs, Croats, and Bosniacs into separate voting blocs by requiring the election of one member of each to the shared presidency. Policy logic translated into practice was equally flawed at the local level. Electoral laws permitted citizens to vote either in their place of current or former residence, a provision conducive both to confusion and abuse. Not surprisingly, the International Crisis Group concluded in 1999 that the rules written by the Provisional Election Commission (under the leadership of the OSCE) virtually invited gerrymandering that allowed ethnic groups to establish a political grip on areas where they had not been dominant prior to the war.[9] Even after the April 2000 elections, hard-line parties retained considerable influence and continued to oppose the further consolidation of the Bosnian state. Above all, they hindered "the unification of the command structures of the three armies, the implementation of a recent Constitutional Court decision on the constituent peoples [of BiH] and the creation of a single economic space in Bosnia."[10]

Even in 1996 the inherent instability of the political formula was apparent, but the international community did not believe that it could retreat from its commitment to early elections. In reality, the reverence for elections as integral to the legitimacy of any international intervention was important to the mission. Other political imperatives played a role as well, such as the reluctance of the United States to indefinitely extend its troop commitment to Bosnia beyond IFOR. The quest for rapid results perhaps accorded with the goals of contributing states and international organizations but could only do so much to improve the situation in Bosnia. In a postwar environment where the very extremists who brought war and civil strife to Bosnia retained a tight grip on all levers of power, the election did little more than affirm a status quo judged wholly unacceptable by the world at large. Some subsequent electoral results proved more to the liking of the international community but fell far short of demonstrating that Bosnia had a functioning civil society. At heart, the question was whether Bosnia was to enjoy democracy in form or in substance. The latter, most concluded, would require far more preparation of societal conditions as a whole. Necessary steps included the capture of war criminals, the reigning in of extremist politicians and dismantling their monopolies over means of the dissemination of information, and resolving a host of complex problems of residency and voter registration.

Beginning in 1997, the OHR concluded that the situation required more active intervention by the international community. As the OHR acquired new prerogatives such as the authority to fire elected officials, some described Bosnia as a protectorate of the international community.[11] Given the presence of an OHR equipped with extensive powers to dictate compliance with the GFAP and the presence of SFOR military contingents to guarantee the peace, this conclusion had a degree of merit. Still, the power to change—or prevent change in—Bosnian society lay with the squabbling factions, who actually learned in time to exploit the very structure of Dayton to resist achievement of its stated goals.

If elections defined the political process prescribed by Dayton, reversing ethnic cleansing was the animating principle of international intervention. The Dayton Peace Accords established unequivocally the right of refugees and displaced persons "freely to return to their homes of origin."[12] Progress, however, proved painfully slow. By mid-1997, only about 300,000 Bosnians had found their way home, leaving as many as 900,000 displaced within their national borders and an equal number still living abroad.[13] Even these figures masked the full depth of the problem since over 90 percent of the returns were to areas where the refugees' own ethnic group predominated.[14] From the end of 1996, the OHR and the United Nations Human Rights Commission focused increasing attention on this problem. Attempted solutions had to take account of extraordinary obstacles. Particularly intractable were the intense animosities and profound sense of personal insecurity resulting from the brutal ethnic warfare in Bosnia and Herzegovina. Under such circumstances, to expect minorities to return to their former communities and live calmly side by side with people who only months earlier had been willing to drive them away forcibly or worse was just short of utopian.

SFOR support to minority returns began with a direct role in establishing and protecting freedom of movement. This entailed providing armed backup for international police monitors, who conducted their duties unarmed. In addition, SFOR patrols shut down illegal checkpoints established by the former warring factions across Bosnia. Beginning in the summer of 1997, SFOR patrolled neighborhoods as minority returnees inspected or repaired their former homes. Still, lending a more direct hand, such as logistic support, in assisting the OHR's Return and

Reconstruction Task Force or RRTF rested largely with the discretion of each national contingent. Although SFOR did not normally conduct demining operations except to clear main routes of movement or its own encampments, it did establish training centers for Bosnian deminers.

On a purely practical level, a housing shortage resulting from wholesale destruction compounded the effects of massive population displacement. Those driven from their homes, whatever their ethnicity, found whatever housing they could in their place of refuge. Not infrequently, they occupied dwellings belonging to members of another ethnic group who had themselves been forced to flee. Unfortunately, the early response of the international community to the housing crisis was inadequate. According to Carl Bildt, "By the end of 1996, all the money that had been allocated and cited in the media had barely managed to build a single house in Bosnia. There were explanations for this miserable state of affairs, but they bordered on the scandalous."[15] Generally, ethnic cleansing policies practiced in some measure by all sides tended to create areas that were overwhelmingly Serb, Bosniac, or Croatian. Hard-line nationalist political leaders frequently urged fugitives of a given ethnic group to settle in communities captured by their side in the war. This served both to concentrate their own ethnic population and consolidate their political grip on territory acquired during the war. Then, having gathered refugees of their own ethnic group in an area under hard-liner control, the politicians erected obstacles to prevent the new settlers from returning to their original homes. As a final barrier to resettlement, local hard-liners often insisted that no minority refugees should come in unless the very refugees that they themselves were not permitting to leave were returned to their homes. The result was paralysis.

Still, SFOR made headway. When the 10th Mountain Division arrived in 1998, it counted a significant increase in the number of "new" return sites. To further ascertain the level of progress, the division monitored the number of families returning with children, the arrival of construction materials to building sites, and the number of NGOs actually working on reconstruction projects in any given area. In short, the more secure environment established by SFOR seemed to be conducive to positive results. Still, the 10th regularly re-examined its measures of progress to avoid the possibility of self-delusion that all was going well.[16]

Even so, inextricable linkages between the objectives of the international community meant that progress in one area could only be sustained if commensurate gains were made elsewhere. Restoration of the demographic status quo ante demanded in turn a functioning legal system capable of fairly adjudicating property claims. Unfortunately, impartial justice was a scarce commodity in the postwar BiH. So, too, in many cases were property records, either as a result of destruction or deliberate withholding by noncompliant officials. Over and over again, local officials failed to honor bargains freely entered into with agencies such as the UNHCR. For example the "Open Cities Initiative" constituted the core of the UNHCR effort in 1998 to stimulate minority returns. The concept was that municipalities declaring their willingness to accept minority returnees would benefit from the focused channeling of assistance projects. In 1998, the UNHCR dedicated 80 percent of its Bosnia funds to this purpose.[17] Accordingly, the UNHCR selected eight municipalities, six in the Federation and two in the Republika Srpska. The results were extremely disappointing. Close scrutiny by the International Crisis Group detected not only that the rate of returns was far below projections but that so-called open cities were doing no better than other municipalities.[18] Even the municipality of Konjic in the Mostar region, considered the most favorable case, could not succeed in integrating eight Serb families during the first quarter of 1998. Many critics cited a lack of political will on the part of local authorities, but willful noncompliance might have been a more appropriate description. Especially distressing in this instance was the fact that the prospective Serb returnees faced not only obstruction by Konjic officials, but also from Serb officials in the Republika Srpska who wanted to prevent their departure, which of course would only lead the international community to invite the return of non-Serbs.[19] For 1998 as a whole, approximately 35,000-40,000 minority returns took place—a notable improvement over 1997—but made just a small dent in the problem. In 1999, to systematize administrative procedures for returns, the OHR mandated the establishment of housing offices in cantons and municipalities.[20] Perhaps for that reason, minority returns increased sharply in the first half of 1999.[21]

Often the most effective refugee return programs were self-organized efforts undertaken by displaced persons themselves. In such cases, groups of displaced persons formed political parties, aggressively lobbied, took part in elections in the municipalities to which they wished to return (as specifically provided for in the Dayton Peace Accords), coordinated with international NGOs, and arranged trips to conduct damage assessments and repairs of their former homes.

The city of Drvar, site of one of Bosnia's worst civil disorders under SFOR in April 1998, served as a perfect example of how such grassroots efforts worked and the risks that they ran in the process. The quest to return to Drvar began within months of the establishment of IFOR in 1996 under the leadership of the Drvar Association, headed by future mayor Mile Marceta. The Association actively engaged the Coalition for Return and other support organizations. Then, in the fall of 1997, the association took advantage of Dayton's absentee voting rules to capture a majority in the Drvar Municipal Council. The elected remained absentee office holders, however, as they were in no position to immediately assume their prescribed duties. Whatever the electoral outcome, Drvar remained hostile territory for Serbs, who once constituted the majority there. According to Major Ian Hope, who commanded a Canadian company in Drvar in 1997, the city at that time was regarded as an extremely difficult case.[22] Still, with minimal financial or practical assistance from international organizations, the association achieved its first returns to Drvar before the end of 1997. The number of Serbs resettled in Drvar reached 1,600 early in 1998. As the trickle of returnees to Drvar expanded, international organizations began to take notice and provided modest assistance. Unfortunately, local HDZ (the Croat hard-line nationalist party) leaders regarded the flow of returns as dangerous to their control of the city. In the meantime, they attempted to place Croatian refugees coming back from Germany in homes formerly owned by Serbs so as to block Serb returns. Conversely, the international community managed to secure the removal of a modest number of Croat Defense Council soldiers from apartments in Drvar to create space for an additional 160 Serb returnees early in 1998.[23]

On 15 April, conditions in Drvar abruptly took a turn for the worse when Croat extremists murdered an elderly Serb couple. Presuming the complicity of local Croatian officials whom he regarded as accountable for the security of Serb returnees, the High Representative fired the local police chief and suspended the mayor. The subsequent investigation of the deaths by Croatian police was a charade in the opinion of Canadian Major Howard Coombs.[24] Amid heightened tensions the infamous Drvar riot followed.

The response of the international community to the disturbance evoked controversy. In the first place, a vacuum continued for several weeks at the level of municipal government when Serb officials were driven out and no replacement was promptly named for the chief of police. Meanwhile, with encouragement from SFOR, the UNHCR temporarily suspended support for returns, thereby fostering the impression of a retreat in the face of violence. More serious in the eyes of critics was the fact that the international community, and the United Nations in particular, was unwilling to face either the gravity of the event or its implications. Instead of regarding the riot as a well-planned assault on the returnees, it treated the matter as a spontaneous eruption reflecting Croatian frustrations at the enormous difficulties facing Croatians seeking to return to the RS. As efforts to reform the Drvar police force sputtered, all forward momentum in Drvar seemed to have evaporated.[25]

Events in Drvar cast a sobering light on contradictions evident in the amalgam of approaches by various international organizations. Where reversing the effects of ethnic cleansing was concerned, guaranteeing the personal security of persons seeking to return to their homes in communities now dominated by a rival ethnic group posed virtually insurmountable difficulties. The only agency with the assets to address the problem in the near term was SFOR, which already was heavily committed to a host of missions and rightly feared the drastic broadening of its mandate that 24-hour policing would entail. The stretching of SFOR assets became more acute with force reduction and the commitment of NATO countries to a peacekeeping effort in Kosovo, known as KFOR, in 1999.

In light of these conditions, the approach of SFOR and the international agencies working in the BiH evoked frustration and criticism. One stern appraisal came from the International Crisis Group (ICG), an independent organization composed of experts from the international community. Specifically, in a report dated 1 May 1997, the ICG faulted the illogic of relying on local authorities, many of them former ethnic cleansers, to provide security for returnees. The assessment also took SFOR to task for a failure "to interpret its mandate in a more robust manner" caused by a "near phobia about mission creep" and an acute aversion to casualties.[26] The latter critique, widely echoed in NGO circles, held SFOR could assume greater responsibility for maintaining public security. Similar criticism followed in the wake of violence in Drvar.

SFOR spokespersons, in contrast, emphasized not only that their mandate did not extend to community policing, but also that they lacked the trained personnel and resources to undertake such a mission. In principle, the only international agency with even a limited responsibility for police functions was the UN-sponsored IPTF. Recruited from among police forces around the world, IPTF personnel acted as advisers and role models for the police in BiH. While their work was often laudatory, they were in no way a realistic substitute for a properly functioning domestic police force. They were neither armed nor thoroughly grounded in the languages and cultures of the BiH. Consequently, they were unable to serve as a true investigative agency. Indeed, because of the diversity of its makeup, IPTF lacked a unified operational culture of its own. Nevertheless, the IPTF served as an invaluable conduit for information by virtue of its role in communities in Bosnia, especially where the activities of local police were concerned. Moreover, when the IPTF did become directly involved in officially authorized duties, such as the inspections of police compounds, they could expect SFOR reinforcement. Nevertheless, the creation of professional police forces in the Western sense—apolitical, impartial and fundamentally honest—remained the only viable long-term solution, and by 2000 it was little more than a distant dream. Central to this process was the ethnic integration of police units, a goal occasionally achieved in form if not in substance. It was one thing to employ members of different ethnic groups together but quite another to get them to cooperate. Further, in the context of a corrupt and inefficient judiciary, it was but one part of a more deeply entrenched problem.

Once again, many in the international community hoped that SFOR could step into the breach created by a failing justice system to provide law enforcement. However, the expectation that SFOR could become an antiterrorist and neighborhood police force in addition to operating as the watchdog over the entity armed forces and special police units reflected a poor understanding of military organization and culture, and especially US military organization and culture. Trained, structured, and equipped for high-intensity combat, modern armies could not always adjust easily to missions that emphasize the restraint and almost superhuman patience often required for street-level peacekeeping. Even the Military Police Corps, though highly trained and well attuned to the handling of delicate, potentially escalating situations, could not begin to assume this burden. Its ranks were too few and it lacked personnel with specific linguistic and cultural tools to take on the job. Of course, some specialized units such as the Italian Carabinieri were brought in to provide investigative skill and muscle to the process of rooting out some of the worst of Bosnia's criminal class, but they, too, were overmatched by the sheer magnitude of the endeavor.

Still, SFOR did incrementally intensify its efforts in one crucial aspect of law enforcement, the pursuit of war criminals. Overall, SFOR showed little inclination to engage in manhunts during the early years of the mission. This was especially true for the Americans, whose recent peacekeeping experiences in Somalia and Haiti had in turn proved tragic and tiresome. The death of 18 Army Rangers in Mogadishu on 3-4 October 1993 had the indelible impact of touching a hot stove. Reluctantly sent to Africa, the Army's return was humiliatingly precipitous. For a generation of senior officers who endured the bitterness of the Vietnam War, there was a gnawing perception that they were being ordered to take on inappropriate missions and, when things went wrong, would be unceremoniously yanked. The special operations raid that went wrong in Somalia overshadowed two years of patient and effective work in a situation that hardly lent itself to successful intervention. Then, in OPERATION Uphold Democracy in Haiti in 1994, the Army's extreme caution and a preoccupation with force protection marked the conduct of operations in Port-au-Prince. One veteran observer referred to the prevailing psychology as "Vietmalia syndrome."[27]

However, by the new millennium, thinking on the matter began to evolve rapidly. Perhaps one cause was the advent of the Global War on Terror, launched by President George W. Bush in the wake of the attacks of 11 September 2001. Numerous commentators had already observed that as long as the most infamous criminals of the Bosnian civil war remained at large, reformist forces in Bosnia would have trouble mastering widespread grassroots support.

Certainly, by 2002 a shift in SFOR thinking seemed in evidence. As explained by Major General Kenneth Quinlan, former assistant chief of staff for Operations in 2002, war criminals constituted an integral part of a "parallel power structure" that thwarted broad progress. In Quinlan's words, "If this [Bosnia] is a garden where we're growing democracy, then what we need to do is plow the ground and pull the weeds out.... Some of these weeds are called PIFWCs." Enjoying greater operational latitude than in the past, SFOR became more aggressive. As Quinlan put it, "'safe and secure' is not getting it done!"[28]

One vitally important influence on the change in approach was the new High Representative, Paddy Ashdown, himself a former British Royal Marine. Frustrated with the slow pace of progress and aware of the international community's mounting impatience, Ashdown was prepared to ask more of SFOR even though its multinational divisions had shrunk to brigades. Fortunately, in SFOR Commander Lieutenant General John Sylvester, he found a willing partner. SFOR brought more of its intelligence resources to bear on the problem.

In October 2002, SFOR staged a raid on an aircraft facility in Bijeljina, which in addition to a variety of activities in violation of Dayton, had been secretly selling material to Iraq in violation of international agreements. Within the facility, intelligence officials found a number of computers, one of which Quinlan characterized as a "lodestone" leading to a series of related raids and apprehensions. In all, SFOR arrested six indicted war criminals from June 2002 to June 2003.[29] This compared favorably with the total of 23 PIFWC arrests, an average of just over three per year, during the first seven years of the IFOR/SFOR mission.[30]

Despite its cultural baggage, by 1997 the US Army was becoming reconciled to assisting in the implementation of the civilian annexes of the DPA. Task Force *Eagle* commanders from the start had direct dealings with area commanders and officials of the three entities but the range of issues increasingly transcended military affairs. As the international community grew more frustrated over its inability to advance the return of internally displaced persons and refugees, the various agencies looked ever more to SFOR to lend a hand. SFOR units routinely patrolled areas of resettlement and, in coordination with the UNHCR and other organs, met busloads of prospective returnees during home visitations to ensure their protection.

In dealing with the situation, SFOR had to be aware of the occasionally conflicting principles inherent in its mandate. The need for protection and the avoidance of violence was self-evident. To let the caravans go forward as planned virtually guaranteed hostilities that might further inflame Serb-Bosniac antagonisms. To call a halt to the event, on the other hand, would mean curbing the rights of free assembly and free movement asserted in the DPA. This represented a serious concern in view of ongoing criticisms that SFOR had yet to establish open movement across the IEBL. As stated in a 17 July 1997 report of the US General Accounting Office, "Bosnians of all three ethnic groups could not freely cross ethnic lines at will or remain behind to visit, work, or live without facing harassment, intimidation, or arrest by police of other ethnic groups.[31]

Still, SFOR planners were taking nothing for granted as the Women of Srebrenica planned their annual pilgrimage in 2000. In addition to maintaining a security presence, SFOR conducted an elaborate information campaign entailing bilateral meetings among key leaders as well as a media barrage to stress the importance of both tolerance of differing viewpoints and the preservation of basic civil order. Specifically, the information operations annex to the overall plan prepared by the US 49th Division headquarters emphasized impressing upon the Women of Srebrenica and other involved groups the need "to refrain from inflammatory or political rhetoric and statements designed to increase tensions among BiH citizens and to be tolerant of others who want to honor their war victims." Significantly, the annex took full account of likely contingencies, including the chance that the Women of Srebrenica buses might have to be diverted, and outlined "talking points" for explaining breaking events to the press. Careful coordination with the Office of the High Representative, the UNHCR, UNCA, and the IPTF kept all key international agencies "in the loop" as preparations progressed. Presence on the ground was entrusted primarily to the 3rd Battalion 3rd Cavalry Regiment, which moved efficiently and proactively to head off trouble.[32] Ultimately, preparation paid off. Despite legitimate fears of violence, the events associated with the fifth anniversary of the fall of Srebrenica passed without incident.

Whether such initiatives could alter the political, social, and economic climate in Bosnia remained to be seen. Despite years of peace, many young Bosnians had given up on their country's prospects. Major General James Campbell, commanding the 10th Mountain Division in Bosnia in 1999-2000, recalled a sobering encounter with a local high school assembly at which his attempt to strike a hopeful note ran smack into the demoralizing realities of Bosnian life. Trying to inspire his audience, Campbell told the students, "You are Bosnia's future." He added that any one of them might be the next mayor or chief of police. In reply, one student remarked skeptically, "You don't know anything about us" and proceeded to detail the depressing futility of economic and political life in her country.[33] The incident reminded Campbell how hope had worn thin in Bosnia, especially for the young.

Sadly, building an efficient government and revitalizing the economy are goals that do not lend themselves in any but the most indirect ways to military solutions. On the other hand, SFOR's absence would disastrously impair the prospects for advancement of these ends, both of which must be based on broad confidence in a secure future. Such faith, some believe, is not likely to arise until the foremost Bosnian Serbs indicted by the International Criminal Tribunal for Yugoslavia—Karadzic and Mladic in particular—are brought to justice. In the meantime, though in hiding, they wield subtle influence behind the scenes. Were they captured and taken to the Hague, moderate Serb politicians would be in a position to operate more freely and chart a new course. In the meantime, SFOR continues to adhere to a policy that keeps it out of the manhunt business. Yet, arrests have occurred, and Lord Robertson, chairman of the North Atlantic Council, warned in July 2001 that Karadzic and Mladic had nowhere left to hide. Whatever its limitations, SFOR's presence remains a crucial symbol of international commitment to an independent, democratic Bosnia.

Certainly the assorted international organizations in Bosnia, aside from Bosnians themselves, must play the most direct role in advancing civil development. This will not become easier. Indeed, the extent of the international commitment to Bosnia has recently been in decline and will almost certainly diminish further.[34] The reasons for this are twofold. First, there are other urgent cases such as Kosovo, and subsequently Afghanistan and Iraq, which have commanded increasing attention and resources. Second, the international community may well be experiencing a form of "donor fatigue" after a decade of involvement in the BiH.

Consequently, resources in the future must be carefully focused. Some observers now believe that any future solution in Bosnia will require modifications to the Dayton Accords. This will be particularly difficult from a political standpoint in light of the fact that Dayton has been treated as a sacred cow by the international community up to this point. Indeed, it has repeatedly been invoked to legitimize actions by the OHR and SFOR to shape the behavior of the three entities. As a result, there is legitimate cause for concern that a retreat from the terms of Dayton might destabilize Bosnia. Despite such objections, some key figures have concluded that necessary progress cannot occur within the terms of the GFAP. Lieutenant General Michael Dodson, COMSFOR in 2001, publicly described the Dayton terms as "a floor, not a ceiling."[35] The implication, subtly stated but evident to careful listeners, was that Dayton by itself is not a satisfactory blueprint for Bosnia's future.

In Major General Quinlan's estimation, the customary indicators of success that for years have served as the international community's benchmarks for progress may have meant little in the absence of a concerted assault on the "parallel power structure."[36] By focusing on data such as returnees, patrols, housing, elections, schools, and economic output—all highly relevant to be sure—the international community and SFOR may have been monitoring the symptoms while failing to confront the underlying disease. The nexus of violence, corruption, and nationalist politics that stunts development in Bosnia will not wither away on its own. Perhaps even continued arrests of war criminals as well as common criminals will prove insufficient to overcome the many ills that plague this fragile state.

In fairness, the Office of the High Representative, SFOR, and the numerous NGOs working in Bosnia have to date made great strides in reversing the effects of ethnic cleansing and civil war in Bosnia-Herzegovina. Sarajevo once again has a flicker of cosmopolitan vibrance and other glimmers of hope can be seen as well. Yet, there is room to question whether a truly stable state can ever emerge within the framework of the Dayton General Framework Agreement for Peace. Though clearly necessary, and probably the best deal that could be reached at the time, the political structure to which it gave birth ever more resembles a great albatross. Flaws in its design often abet the behavior of nationalists who oppose its implementation. The weakness of central structures, beginning with the presidency, at the very least ensure that future gains will come at a pace that will exhaust the patience of the international community. The very plan that laid out a path to success in time has become an impediment to fulfillment of some of its own stated objectives. This does not mean that Dayton is the core problem in Bosnia. Rather, it may be time for new, creative approaches that could necessitate a new agreement better tailored to changing circumstances. With the advent of more recent crises in Kosovo, Iraq, Africa, and elsewhere, the attention and resources of the international community are moving. The application of effort to salvage Bosnia must become more economical and focused to the greatest possible effect.

Notes

1. This conclusion is based upon approximately 200 interviews conducted by the authors of this study with military and civilian participants in the peace-building process in Bosnia.

2. Future SFOR Targeting Process, information brief to COMSFOR, 5 January 2000.

3. Lieutenant Colonel Bud Bowie, interview with Dr. Robert Baumann, Fort Leavenworth, KS, August 5, 1999.

4. "Is Dayton Failing?: Bosnia Four Years After the Peace Agreement," ICG (International Crisis Group) Balkans Report No. 80, 28 October 1999, 6.

5. Elections 1996 After-Action Review, briefing slides, United Nations International Police Task Force, Peter Fitzgerald, Police Commissioner.

6. See, for example, "Is Dayton Failing?: Bosnia Four Years After the Peace Agreement," 11. The authors also heard this view expressed by a number of observers on the ground in Bosnia.

7. For an excellent discussion of this dilemma, see a report titled "Doing Democracy a Disservice," International Crisis Group Balkans Report No. 42, 9 September 1998, 4-5.

8. Report of the High Representative for Implementation of the Bosnian Peace Agreement to the Secretary-General of the United Nations, 16 October 1997, 9.

9. "Is Dayton Failing?," 12.

10. "Bosnia's November Elections: Dayton Stumbles," ICG Balkans Report No. 104, 18 December 2000, 9.

11. Ibid., 5-6.

12. The General Framework Agreement for Peace in Bosnia and Herzegovina, Article II, Paragraph 5, Annex 4, signed 21 November 1995.

13. UNHCR, "Return and Reconstruction in Bosnia," Box 4.4, www.unhcr.ch/refworld/pub/state/97/box4_4.htm.

14. International Crisis Group, "Dayton: Two Years On, A Review of Progress in implementing the Dayton Peace Accords in Bosnia," ICG Bosnia Project, Report No. 27, 19 November 1997, 7. According to this report, by November 1997, only 1,200 Bosniacs had returned to the zone of separation on the Republika Srpska side of the border.

15. Carl Bildt, *Peace Journey: The Struggle for Peace in Bosnia* (London: Weidenfelt and Nicolson, 1998), 215.

16. Major Walter Piatt, interview with Dr. Robert Baumann, 8 February 2001, Fort Drum, NY.

17. International Crisis Group, "Minority Return or Mass Relocation?," ICG Bosnia Project, Report No. 33, 14 May 1998, ii.

18. Ibid., 15-18. In particular the ICG reported that project accountability was weak and that in any case open cities did not appear to be receiving greater aid.

19. Ibid., 18.

20. Brad Blitz, "USIP Special Report: An Overview of Refugee Returns and Minority Registration," 21 December 1999, 7.

21. International Crisis Group, "Bosnia's Refugee Logjam Breaks: Is the International Community Ready?," Balkans Report No. 95, 30 May 2000.

22. Major Ian Hope, interview with Dr. Robert Baumann, Fort Leavenworth, KS, 11 January 1999.

23. International Crisis Group, "Minority Return or Mass Relocation?," 25-26.

24. Major Howard Coombs, interview with Dr. Robert Baumann and Dr. George Gawrych, Fort Leavenworth, KS, 5, 19 October 2001.

25. International Crisis Group, "Minority Return or Mass Relocation?," 27-28.

26. International Crisis Group, "Going Nowhere Fast: Refugees and Internally Displaced Persons in Bosnia and Herzegovina," ICG Bosnia Report No. 23, 1 May 1997, iii, 9.

27. Richard Rinaldo, "Warfighting and Peace Ops: Do Real Soldiers Do MOOTW?," *Joint Forces Quarterly,* Winter 1996-97, 113.

28. Major General Kenneth Quinlan, interview with Dr. Robert Baumann, Joint Forces Staff College, Norfolk, VA, 7 November 2003.

29. Ibid.

30. SFOR Fact Sheet. Persons Indicted for War Crimes. NATO/SFOR Informer. At <http://www.nato.int/sfor/factsheet/warcrime/too1161.htm>. Accessed 18 February 2004.

31. United States General Accounting Office, "Bosnia Peace operation: Progress Toward Dayton Agreement's Goals–An Update," (Testimony, 07/17/97, GAO/T-NSIAD-97-216), 4.

32. Annex P (Information Operations) to IMPIN XXXX to OPORD XXXX, 49th Division Headquarters; Annex Q (Public Affairs) to IMPIN XXXX to OPORD XXXX, 49th Division Headquarters; Annex R (Psychological Operations) to IMPIN XXXX (Gallant Vigil) to OPORD XXXX; Briefing by Major Harlan Harris, 49th Division After-Action Review, January 2001, Austin, TX.

33. Major General James Campbell, interview with Dr. Robert Baumann, 9 February 2001, Fort Drum, NY.

34. Lieutenant Colonel D. E. Barr, "Update on Op Palladium Roto 6: Extract from End-Tour Report, September 2000," *The Bulletin*, The Army Lessons Learned Centre, Canada, Vol. 8, No. 1, April 2001, 17.

35. Press Conference with Lord Robertson and Lieutenant General Michael Dodson, Coalition Press Information Center, Sarajevo, Bosnia, July, 2001.

36. Quinlan interview.

GLOSSARY OF ACRONYMS

ACE	Allied Command Europe
AFSOUTH	Allied Forces Southern Europe
ARRC	Allied Rapid Reaction Corps
BiH	Republic of Bosnia and Herzegovina
BSA	Bosnian Serb Army
CA	Civil Affairs
CIMIC	Civil-Military Cooperation Center
CPIC	Coalition Press Information Center
CJCMTF	Combined Joint Civil Military Task Force
CJPOTF	Combined/Joint Psychological Operations Task Force
EC	European Community
EU	European Union
GFAP	General Framework Agreement for Peace
HDZ	Croatian Democratic Alliance
IFOR	Implementation Force
IEBL	Inter-Entity Boundary Line
ICRC	International Committee of the Red Cross
IO	Information Operations
IPTF	International Police Task Force
JNA	Yugoslav People's Army
JCO	Joint Commission Observer
JMC	Joint Military Commission
MND-N	Multinational Division North
MND-SE	Multinational Division Southeast
MND-SW	Multinational Division Southwest
MPRI	Military Professional Resources Incorporated
NAC	North Atlantic Council
NATO	North Atlantic Treaty Organization
NGO	Nongovernmental Organization
OHE	Office of the High Representative
OPLAN	Operations Plan
OSCE	Organization for Security and Cooperation in Europe
PSYOP	Psychological operations
RS	Serb Republic
RSRT	Republika Srpska Radio and Television
SACEUR	Supreme Allied Commander Europe
SF	Special Forces
SHAPE	Supreme Headquarters Allied Powers Europe
SFOR	Stabilization Force
UNHCR	United Nations High Commissioner for Refugees
UNPROFOR	United Nations Protection Force
USAREUR	United States Army Europe

INDEX

236

Powell, Colin, 38
Psychological Operations (PSYOP), 43, 103, 171, 186, 188

Raznjatovic, Zeljko, 25
Rearick, Perry,185
Republika Srpska (RS), 25-26, 28, 30, 39, 97, 110-113, 122-124, 138, 141, 150-
    152, 175, 178-179, 181, 189, 193, 199-200, 215-216, 221
Republika Srpska Radio and Television (RSRT), 199-200
Revolt of 1804, 6
Rhode, David, 48
Roman Catholicism, 2, 4
Roman Empire, 3
Rose, Sir Michael, 40, 42, 47-48, 189, 203
Russian Airborne Brigade, 191

Sarajevo, 3, 9, 19, 26-29, 39-40, 42-45, 47, 49, 51, 53-54, 63-66, 69-70, 79, 85,
    102, 108, 110, 121, 123, 125, 134, 175, 177, 180, 184-185, 187-188, 192,
    194, 203
Sava River, 3, 32, 37, 76, 81, 05, 153, 185
Schifferle, Peter, 71
Schmidt, Paul, 185, 203
Serb Radio and Television (SRT), 107, 178-179, 199
Serbian Democratic Party (SDS), 24, 40, 111, 122-123, 181
Seymour, Bill, 106, 108
Shalikashvili, John, 99, 105, 132
Sharp, Walter, 139
Sharpe, Greg, 126, 127, 153, 156
Shinseki, Eric, 150-151, 188, 199
Short, David, 110
Shultz, George, 38
Slocum, Mike, 100, 202
Smith, Leighton, 60, 66, 76, 107, 125, 128, 175-176
Smith, Rupert, 47, 67, 120, 125, 141
Solana, Javier, 110, 150
Southern European Task Force (SETAF), 61, 69, 71
Spaho, Mehmed, 11, 12
Srebrenica, 25, 28-30, 40, 45-46, 48-53, 66, 69, 119, 121, 143, 173-174, 180,
    226-227
Stabilization Force (SFOR), i, 16, 121, 123, 124-126, 131-134, 136-138, 141,
    143, 150-151, 155, 158-160, 166-167, 171-172, 174, 176-178, 203, 207,
    216-17, 219-28
Stalin, Joseph, 18-19
Steiner, Michael, 176
Sterling, Jack, 81
Supreme Allied Commander Europe (SACEUR), 60, 97, 121, 130, 132, 150,
    188, 190, 199

Supreme Headquarters Allied Powers Europe (SHAPE), 60
Swain, Richard, 130
Sylvester, John, 113, 187, 225

Task Force *Able Sentry*, 67
Task Force *Eagle,* 37, 74, 76-77, 80-81, 83, 95, 98, 103, 105, 114, 120, 125, 130, 142, 158, 183, 186, 188, 192, 194, 203-204, 226
Task Force **Ranger**, 186
Timm, Rob, 185
Tito, Jozef Broz, 2, 15-24, 74
Tudjman, Franjo, 22-23, 26, 29-32
Tuzla, 19, 25, 40, 45, 52, 65, 67, 72, 75, 79, 81, 111, 121, 130, 134, 138, 180-181, 183, 192, 204, 207

Ugljevik, 121, 151
United Nations, 37, 39, 44, 46, 48-49, 52
United Nations High Commissioner for Refugees (UNHCR), 42, 63, 111, 175, 176, 184, 193, 195
United Nations Human Rights Commission, 219
United Nations Protection Force (UNPROFOR), i, 24, 27, 37, 39-40, 42-54, 63-64, 67-70, 79, 85, 120, 125, 128, 142
United Nations Security Council, 27, 39, 46, 48, 59
United Nations Security Council Resolution 713, 63
United Nations Security Council Resolution 743, 39
United Nations Security Council Resolution 776, 39
United Nations Security Council Resolution 819, 45
United Nations Security Council Resolution 1031, 78, 120
United Nations Security Council Resolution 1088, 123
United Nations War Crimes Tribunal, 28
United States Army Europe (USAREUR), 61, 67, 69, 71-81, 86
United States European Command, (EUCOM) 61, 72-73, 75, 78-80, 85, 150
Ustashe, 14-17, 31

Vance, Cyrus, 44
Vance, Michaela, 138
Vance-Owen Peace Plan, 64, 67-68
Venhaus, John, 179-183
Vitez, 26-27
Vojvodina, 11, 13, 17, 21, 23, 25
Vuono, Carl, 28

Walker, Sir Michael, 60, 104-106, 108-110, 113, 124, 176
Warsaw Pact, 19, 22, 79
Weedy, Charleton, 109-110
Westendorp, Karl, 200
White, John, 203

White, Thomas, 138
Women of Srebrenica (WOS), 180, 226-227
World War II, 2, 12, 15-17, 19-20, 26, 31, 129, 139, 199
Wright, James, 61, 74

Young, Mike, 195
Yugoslav People's Army (JNA), 24

Zimmermann, Warren, 38, 48
Zone of Separation (ZOS), 76, 83, 96-97, 101, 102, 114, 120, 121, 126
Zubak, Kresimir, 123

Units

About the Authors

Robert F. Baumann is the Director of the Graduate Degree Program and Professor of History at the U.S. Army Command and General Staff College. He received a B.A. in Russian from Dartmouth College (1974), an M.A. in Russian and East European Studies from Yale University in 1976, and a Ph.D. in History from Yale University (1982). From 1979-1980 he was a graduate exchange student at Moscow University with grant support from the Fulbright-Hayes Program and the International Research and Exchanges Board. Baumann was subsequently a Research Associate at Leningrad State University during the summers of 1990 and 1991. In addition to over 20 scholarly articles and book chapters, Baumann is the author of *Russian-Soviet Unconventional Wars in the Caucasus, Central Asia, and Afghanistan* (Combat Studies Institute [CSI], 1993), as well as coauthor of *Invasion, Intervention, Intervasion: A Concise History of the U.S. Army in Operation Uphold Democracy* (CSI, 1998) and *My Clan Against the World: A History of US and Coalition Forces in Somalia 1992-1994* (CSI, 2004). A 1999 recipient of a research grant from the United States Institute of Peace in Washington, DC, Baumann is the writer-producer of a documentary film on the US and multinational peacekeeping mission in Bosnia. In addition to Russian military history, he has also written extensively on the history of the Bashkirs and taught briefly as a visiting professor of history at the Bashkir State University in Ufa, Russia in the fall of 1992.

George W. Gawrych received his PhD in late Ottoman history from the University of Michigan in May 1980. He joined the Combat Studies Institute in July 1984. During the 2002-2003 academic year, Gawrych was a visiting professor in the history department at West Point. In August 2003, he accepted a position as associate professor of Middle East History at Baylor University. In addition to a number of professional articles, Gawrych published *The Albatross of Decisive Victory: War and Policy between Egypt and Israel in the 1967 and 1973 Arab-Israeli Wars*.

Walter E. Kretchik is Assistant Professor, Department of History, Western Illinois University, where he specializes in US military history and foreign relations. He has taught at Bilkent University in Ankara, Turkey, and the Combat Studies Institute, US Army Command and General Staff College. A retired US Army lieutenant colonel, he served for six months in 1996 as the US Army Component Command Historian with USAREUR Forward in Taszar, Hungary, having responsibility for gathering the historical record for all US Army units in theater. He was awarded a Ph.D. in History from the University of Kansas in 2001 and is a resident graduate of the US Army Command and General Staff College and the School of Advanced Military Studies. His research interests include US Army doctrine, US military interventions, and foreign relations.

www.ingramcontent.com/pod-product-compliance
Lightning Source LLC
Chambersburg PA
CBHW081416090426
42738CB00017B/3388